Twayne's United States Authors Series

EDITOR OF THIS VOLUME

David J. Nordloh

Indiana University

The Popular American Novel 1865-1920

TUSAS 372

THE POPULAR AMERICAN NOVEL 1865—1920

By HERBERT F. SMITH

University of Victoria

TWAYNE PUBLISHERS

A DIVISION OF G. K. HALL & CO., BOSTON

Copyright © 1980 by G. K. Hall & Co.

Published in 1980 by Twayne Publishers,
A Division of G. K. Hall & Co.
All Rights Reserved

Printed on permanent/durable acid-free paper and bound
in the United States of America

First Printing

Library of Congress Cataloging in Publication Data

Smith, Herbert F   1933–
The Popular American Novel, 1865–1920.

Bibliography: p. 179–88
Includes Index.
1. American fiction—19th century—History and criticism.
2. American fiction—20th century—History and criticism.
3. Popular literature—United States.
I. Title.
PS377.S57   813′.03   79–25706
ISBN 0–8057–7310–X

To My Wife

Contents

About the Author

Preface

Acknowledgments

1. The Protestant Ethic   1

2. Drowning in Bathos: The Sentimental Novel   19

3. The Decline and Fall of New England   30

4. The Rise of the South   51

5. Social Satire in the Gilded Age   64

6. Exotics, Fantastics, and Cowboys   78

7. The Political Novel   96

8. Toward the Modern: Some Reluctant Innovators   119

   Notes and References   163

   Selected Bibliography   179

   Index   189

About the Author

Herbert F. Smith is currently Professor of English at the University of Victoria in British Columbia. In addition to authoring books on Richard Watson Gilder and John Muir for Twayne, he has edited *The Literary Criticism of James Russell Lowell* (Nebraska, 1969) and Washington Irving's *Bracebridge Hall* (Twayne 1978).

Professor Smith is a member of several editorial boards and has written articles on Thoreau, Melville, and John Barth. His dramatization of Melville's *The Confidence Man* was performed in Madison, Wisconsin in 1968. Among his non-academic interests are tennis and good wine.

Preface

To write a history of the American novel for the period 1865 to 1920 with an emphasis on the minor writers is not necessarily to write *Hamlet* without Hamlet, or to write a social or cultural history, or to poke fun at the literary fads of an earlier day. But inevitably these elements intervene. *Caveat lector.* Do not read this work without being versed in the works of Twain, Howells, James, Crane, Norris, Frederic, De Forest—to merely skim from the top of the list of novelists included in the Twayne U.S. Authors Series and thus relatively excluded from this work. Do not expect to find merely literary judgments here either. Social and cultural significance is necessarily a criterion for inclusion in a work like this; as a result, some hilariously inept journeymen writers are examined with a (usually) straight face. Nor can the writer of this study ignore the mass voice of popularity or the vagaries of idiosyncrasy. If the many thousands who were not reading Henry James's *The Ambassadors* were reading Elinor H. Porter's *Pollyanna*, we might enquire as to the reason. Similarly, we may pose the question whether the critical reception of mordant works by Frank Norris and Stephen Crane among the few might not be related to the response among the many to works like Fanny Burnett's *Little Lord Fauntleroy*.[1]

These are neither idle nor foolish concerns, and they are not concerns likely to be addressed in histories of the novel with a more usual format. A literary historian faced with the period 1865–1920 must choose between mass culture and elitism. His problem is in some ways an analogue of that faced by Hyacinth Robinson in *The Princess Casamassima*, whose unhappy end points out the seriousness of the dilemma.[2] This study is intended as at least a partial advocacy and sympathetic view of the mass culture. That is not to say that no standards are being upheld; but all standards are to come under scrutiny.

The intended result is a work that will supplement in several ways the serious student's inquiries into the literature written in America between 1865 and 1920. First, it will present and explain to him the larger context of the literature of the period, especially as that literature was shaped by popular taste and by national ideals. Second, it will introduce the reader to the various strategies used by the novelists of the period to circumvent, to recondition, or to subvert that popular taste. It is at precisely this interface between the pressure of the mass culture and the individuality of the artist that criticism should begin, particularly in the case of American literature and even more particularly in the case of the American novelist. No other literature, no other genre has been so critical of the tastes, morality, ethics of its own audience, most strikingly during this period of transition from romantic to realistic literature. Howells, Twain, and James are rebellious and subversive writers! Yet how many survivors of "survey courses" of American literature are really aware of what these major writers were rebelling against, what they were trying to subvert? This study has as its first objective a complete survey of the plains and prairies of late nineteenth-century, early twentieth-century fiction, if only so that the amplitude of Appalachian and Rocky Mountain novels may be fully appreciated.

But the metaphor can and should be carried further. The plains themselves have their hills and valleys, their rivers and oases, their Monadnocks. Many writers who lacked the genius of their great contemporaries could, nevertheless, frequently produce works that ought not to be forgotten completely. No novelist of this period, not Horatio Alger, not E.P. Roe—no, not even E.D.E.N. Southworth—was completely a philistine. Each has his strong points, each his moments of strength—of flight, however crippled, of the imagination. Discerning these moments and explaining them will be one of the pleasures of this book.

Thus the reader should be forewarned. This is an unbalanced book, which needs some study of the great writers of this period—the more the better—to offset its eccentricity. Its standards are not entirely esthetic; in the works it examines it seeks values different from those the literary historian and the inveterate novel reader seek. It could serve as a guide for the historian, the sociologist, the antiquarian. It examines some crannies of literature seldom observed, and many of those works that were, for whatever reasons, popular with their contemporaries. In short, it is intended as a study of the novel unlike any other that has ever been written. And, after having blown the dust off some hundreds of volumes in preparation for this work, the

Preface

author hopes only that he has done well enough that the project need never be tried again.

HERBERT F. SMITH

University of Victoria

Acknowledgments

I would like to acknowledge the help of sundry librarians at the University of Victoria, the University of Massachusetts-Amherst, the American Antiquarian Society, the Boston Public Library, and the Huntington Library. I would like to acknowledge no less the other kind of help from the Research and Travel Committee of the University of Victoria and the Social Sciences and Humanities Research Council of Canada. Then there were David Nordloh and Mim Baker—they also served—but are in no way responsible for the mistakes herein, only the good points.

CHAPTER 1

The Protestant Ethic

O NE of the curiosities of American literary history is the fact that not one of the major writers of nineteenth-century America was in tune with the dominant ethic of the time. All other national literatures had writers who were to some extent sympathetic with their country's ethic. Charles Dickens, William Makepeace Thackeray, George Eliot, Thomas Hardy portrayed most aspects of English life sympathetically, as did Flaubert and Balzac for the French and Tolstoy and Turgenev for the Russians. But Ralph Waldo Emerson and Henry David Thoreau imagined an ideal America far different from the one they inhabited; Mark Twain came to write more and more from *saeva indignatio*; and Henry James fled to England. In no case did a major American writer of this period attack only the hypocrisies and find value in the underlying ethic. Their contempt or distaste was with the ethic itself. And yet the Protestant ethic of the American heartland of the mid-nineteenth century passed virtually untouched from the Lyceum lectures of Emerson's day through the Chatauquas of the early twentieth century, identifying itself as an ideal in the face of the alternatives presented by writers as various as Emerson and Twain. Rock-solid, the Protestant ethic of America was based upon the triumvirate of values that support it still: success, reform, and piety.

It is, of course, not difficult to find writers of the period 1865–1920 to illustrate the three pillars of the Protestant ethic. But certain writers stand out even among the crowds of their contemporaries as "representative men," not, certainly in the sense that Emerson used that phrase, but rather standing almost as symbols instead of men, mocked by some cruel fate which denied them individuality, which made them caricatures of themselves. Horatio Alger is the chief of these, his very name representing to even the sub-literate a laughing-stock of the success-hungry young man. But Josiah Gilbert Holland

1

placed the emphasis on reform and was as associated in his contemporaries' minds with that third of the triumvirate as Alger was with success. The same is true for Edward P. Roe for the third pillar, piety. Each man had the other two qualities in profusion as well, but was nonetheless remarkably pure in his representative quality. Thus, by examining these three men in some detail we may discover versions of the principles by which the ethic of the period was transmitted through the popular literature.

I   *The Rationale of Success: Horatio Alger, Jr. (1832-1899)*

Horatio Alger's publisher, A.K. Loring, intended only a publisher's blurb when he described his most famous and most successful author as "the dominating figure of the new era. In his books he has captured the spirit of reborn America. The turmoil of the streets is in them. You can hear the rattle of pails on the farms. Above all, you can hear the cry of triumph of the oppressed over the oppressor. What Alger has done is to portray the soul—the ambitious soul—of the country!"[1] However, when allowance is made for Loring's own exuberance, the statement is not far from the verifiable truth of the nature of Alger's fiction and its effect upon his readership. Alone among the minor writers of his period, Alger's works are frequently required in survey courses of nineteenth-century literature and cultural history. Probably only Harriet Beecher Stowe's *Uncle Tom's Cabin* appears more frequently than *Ragged Dick* among texts required for their usefulness as cultural documents rather than for their literary value.[2] And while Loring's comment about the "cry of triumph of the oppressed over the oppressor" is fatuous in the extreme, a case could be made that the "turmoil of the streets" and the "rattle of the pails" are present in Alger's writings.

Alger's success is legendary. Author of more than one hundred books, many of which were kept constantly in print during his lifetime and some of which are still in print, he was the best-selling author of his time, perhaps of all time. Incredibly, every one of his books developed the same theme—how by the combination of *Luck and Pluck*, his hero, be he *Ragged Dick* or *Ben the Luggage Boy*, would, by being *Strong and Steady* and *Shifting for Himself*, be *Bound to Rise*, whether *From Canal Boy to President* or *From Farm Boy to Senator*, even though *The Odds Against Him* made his

Struggling Upward Rough and Ready and *Slow and Sure*.[3] It is fashionable to make fun of Horatio Alger, Jr., doubtless because it is so easy to do. It is not easy to explain how he could manage to achieve and to keep such an enormous audience without ever varying the monotony of his plot. Indeed, about the only way he can be explained is by taking seriously Loring's blurb. The problem divides neatly into two parts. First, how Alger managed to catch the "spirit of reborn America . . . the turmoil of the streets . . . the rattle of pails." Second, how he portrayed "the soul—the ambitious soul—of the country."

The first part is easy. Alger preceded the realistic movement in American literature with a kind of urban "veritism" that could make some of his novels pass functionally for city directories. If, as Mark Twain remarked, "the most valuable capital usable in the building of novels is personal experience," Alger was extraordinarily capable of converting that capital to use. More than any writer, Alger came at last to write only from what he knew, as, with his increasing fame, the world of "street-smart" newsboys, bootblacks, errand boys became his world. The other part of the world of his novels—the boarding houses, cheap restaurants, and popular amusements—had always been his world. As early as *Ragged Dick* (1868), his eighth novel and the one which made him famous, Alger had become a frequent visitor of the Newsboys' Lodging House on Fulton Street and a friend of the Children's Aid Society of New York, both of which organizations figure prominently in his works. His opportunities to observe the characters of the kinds of juveniles who were to populate his books almost exclusively were unique. Charles O'Connor, the superintendent of the Newsboy's Lodging House, came virtually to worship the ground Alger walked on, letting him write in his office, and talk, eat, and sleep in the same dormitory with the boys. Such free access was an experiential gold mine for Alger.

His own day-to-day existence in New York was the second great source for his realistic writing. The world of the mid-Manhattan boarding house, Fulton Street office, the Bowery, Taylor's Saloon at the corner of Franklin Street, Barnum's Museum—precisely located, earnestly described—was Alger's own world no less than Ragged Dick's or Mark the Match Boy's.[4] His descriptions of this world have authority because he lived in it. A bachelor, he lived in midtown boarding houses throughout his adult life; he attended the theater and Barnum's Museum; many of his friends worked in offices on Fulton Street. Thus Alger was uniquely fitted for the kind of fiction he wrote. Thoroughly acquainted with at least upper-middle class life in the city (the Alger canon reaches no higher), he needed his contacts with juvenile welfare facilities to fill him in on the seedier aspects.

Just as critics have not seriously attempted to account for Alger's success in terms of his ability to write realistic prose, neither have they been fair about his "rags to riches" formula. The ontology of the Protestant ethic demands a necessary cause-and-effect relationship between doing good, perfecting the self, and worldly success. It is not enough that one and two precede three; they must be clearly the cause of three. That is rarely so in Alger's writings; indeed, were it not for the necessity to read all of Alger's books to say so, I would insist it is never the case. Certainly, in all the works that I have read the element of luck bulks large indeed in the etiology of success, while the heroes seem to derive virtually complete satisfaction from their good works, and a Tennysonian complacency for their every step toward "self-reverence, self-knowledge, self-control."

These qualities are visible in Alger's most famous work, and one that might well stand at the head of our period as one of the shaping influences, *Ragged Dick* (1868). Dick is the archetypal Alger hero against which all the others should be measured. To begin with, he is more "real" than most. At the beginning of the novel he has vices—in profusion. He smokes; he swears; he gambles; he has extravagant tastes for theater and the like. But from the opening scene in the novel, in which, by innuendo, it is suggested that he might steal, he makes it clear that these sins, like his rags and dirt, are superficial, that at heart he is pure. "Oh, I'm a rough customer," he admits, "But I wouldn't steal. It's mean" (p. 40). The first virtues that he demonstrates are appropriate to him and to his circumstances. A clerk tries to diddle him out of $2, but he is too savvy to be taken in; con men abound in Alger's novels, and the greatest sin, by implication, is naïveté.[5]

The novel progresses without much regard to plot from these beginnings. Dick's "business" provides Alger with an opportunity to show off the boy's smart-aleck independence:

"How much?" asked a gentleman on his way to his office.
"Ten cents," said Dick, dropping his box, and sinking upon his knees on the sidewalk, flourishing his brush with the air of one skilled in his profession.

"Ten cents! Isn't that a little steep?"

"Well, you know 'taint all clear profit," said Dick, who had already set to work. "There's the blacking costs something, and I have to get a new brush pretty often."

"And you have a large rent, too," said the gentleman quizzically, with a glance at a large hole in Dick's coat.

"Yes, sir," said Dick, always ready to joke; "I have to pay such a big rent for my manshun up on Fifth Avenoo, that I can't afford to take less than ten cents a shine. . . ." (41–42)

Dick's flippancy is reflexive; he cannot possibly have understood the pun on "rent," but the aptness of his response ought to be judged in Alger's favor as a writer, particularly when one grants the efficiency and suggestiveness of that unobtrusive "who had already set to work." The writer who can throw away a clause like that is no amateur.

The novel really gets going when Dick, through a combination of plot-stretching coincidence and characteristic chutzpah, is chosen to be a guide to Manhattan for Frank Whitney, a young man of about his own age, but in considerably better circumstances. Reader, suspend your disbelief, for what follows is vintage Alger—a tour of Manhattan, complete with footnotes, from City Hall Park, Baxter Street, up Broadway to Union and Madison Squares, the Third Avenue and the Harlem line of horsecars, Central Park, and the Sixth Avenue cars back downtown. One can carp at this section of the novel as smelling of the lamp and the guidebook, but that is to miss the point. Dick and Frank *are* outsiders to the New York being described, Frank because he is a newcomer to the city, Dick because he is an economic outsider; but for that very reason their perceptions are fresh and interesting. Nor is the tour simply a guide to the places of Manhattan. As they proceed, they are witnesses to a "drop game" and a purse snatching which turns out to be a mistake. In both instances Dick behaves admirably, and the seeds of character which are later to bloom in his success are planted in the plot.

But, as I have mentioned earlier, Alger is anything but simplistic about the causes for that success. Frank and Mr. Whitney give Dick good advice about how to succeed, but Whitney admits that his own success came because he was "lucky enough to invent a machine" which brought him his fortune. So it is with Dick. He gives up some of his vices, takes up some new Protestant virtues, like a savings account, but Dame Fortune must intervene to provide the final peripety which leads to his success: he rescues a child from drowning and is rewarded with a job in which we are convinced he will rise quickly, since he has given over his youthful vices and taken up concomitant commercial virtues. Alger's message is quite clear: good and bad fortune happen to all, but what happens under the circumstance of each is a test of character. Different value systems will produce different results. Neither Norman Vincent Peale nor Jean-Paul Sartre would disagree.

This is not to forgive all the sins of Horatio Alger, Jr. However sympathetic one may be to Alger's pioneering realism and to his maligned ethic, he is impossible to read unless the reader forgives him countless vagaries of plot, extraordinary coincidences, and examples of unctuous editorializing. Reading Alger with pleasure will always be possible only for the very young and the professional historian. The general reader of our century has too many contemporaries to choose from who out-Alger Alger—and who include sex to boot. (There is no sex in any Alger work.) But Alger must be reckoned with as a force operating on the nineteenth century, probably the more so as his efforts were directed primarily at juveniles. Alger softened them up; Holland and Roe applied the *coup de grâce*; thus did the bourgeoisie perpetuate itself from the Lyceum to Chatauqua, in spite of Twain and James, Howells and Crane.

II   *The Exaltation of Reform: Josiah Gilbert Holland (1819–1881)*

Holland might stand as a prime example of an Alger hero. Born of a hard-working but improvident family and a victim of delicate health, Holland struggled unsuccessfully toward vocations varying from school teaching to medicine without success until, in 1850, he became associated with Samuel Bowles in the editing of the *Springfield Republican*. There his "luck and pluck" finally paid off. While Bowles wrote on matters of political significance, Holland concerned himself with reform of the customs and manners of his readers. His articles, collected under the title of *Timothy Titcomb's Letters to Young People, Single and Married* (1858), were incredibly successful, launching him on a career that was to make him Moralizer-in-Chief to the American public for the next twenty years. After *Timothy Titcomb's Letters* the vehicle became irrelevant. Whether he wrote in dramatic verse (*Bitter Sweet*, 1858), in homespun proverbs (*Gold*

Foil Hammered from Popular Proverbs, 1859), in political biography (*Life of Abraham Lincoln*, 1866), or in his three late novels (*Arthur Bonnicastle*, 1873, *Sevenoaks*, 1875, and *Nicholas Minturn*, 1877), the message was always the same.[6] Reform and regeneration in personal affairs, public affairs, and business were not only their own reward but led no less certainly to success and affluence. Conversely, meanness of any sort led inevitably to direct and condign punishment. One searches in vain for moral grayness of any sort in Holland's works. His villains are deep-dyed, his heroes simple, pure, and invariably successful, the remainder are ridiculed or punished as their foolishness or cowardice requires.

Of the three late novels, *Sevenoaks* (1875) is probably the best, and will certainly illustrate the Holland technique. Robert Belcher, the squire of Sevenoaks, a manufacturing town in which he owns the factory, is a perfected version of Dickens's Gradgrind. Not only is he vulgar and brutal in all aspects of his behavior, he manipulates and is manipulated by symbols in such a way that his character is mythicized at the same time that his daily villainies are presented in loving detail. He introduces himself to us (and later dwells upon himself admiringly) with a Richard III soliloquy combined with the witch of Snow White by speaking to that natural symbol of *superba*, his mirrored reflection. He is rapidly promoted from the unearned title of "*Colonel* Belcher" to the virtually noumenal "the General."[7] His pride leads him to blasphemy when he contemplates cynically the founding of a theological seminary to restore public confidence in himself:

"I tell you what it is, Toll, I believe I'm pining for a theological seminary. Ah, my heart! my heart! If I could only tell you, Toll, how it yearns for the American people! Can't you see, my boy, that the hope of the nation is in educated and devoted young men? Don't you see that we are going to the devil with our thirst for filthy lucre? Don't you understand how noble a thing it would be for one of fortune's favorites to found an institution with his wealth that would bear down his blessings to unborn millions? What if that institution should also bear his name? What if the name should be forever associated with that which is most hallowed in our national history? Wouldn't it pay?" (334)

Faustian, he finds the fires of lust burn ever less brightly unless replenished with more and more fuel. Asked by his handy confederate Toll why he must continue to stockjob and speculate when he is making money faster than he could spend it in his honest business, he cries from his pit, "but it's tame, tame, tame! I must have excitement. Theatres are played out, horses are played out, and suppers raise the devil with me. . . . It's like brandy; a man wants a larger dose every time" (350). Faustian, he talks of himself in the third person as "the General." Faustian, he discovers that at the very edge of the pit itself he might still turn his back on hell—but of course he cannot do so:

It was strange, even to him, at this point of his career, that he felt within himself no power to change his course. No one knew better than he, that there was money enough in Benedict's inventions for both inventor and manufacturer. No one knew better than he, that there was a prosperous course for himself inside the pale of equity and law, yet he found no motive to walk there. (378)

More than Faustian, Belshazzarian, he is destroyed at the end by, literally, handwriting on the wall illuminated by that source of all light, the sun. Thus, the critics of Holland who find Robert Belcher to be unrealistic might as well scout at the whale as a "montrous fable or hideous and intolerable allegory."[8] That is not to say that when Holland gets down to details he does not do a creditable job at making Belcher's villainies believable. His description of the stock-jobbing of the "Crooked Valley Railroad" is directly derived from his study of Belcher's prototype, James Fisk, Jr., and bears the hallmarks of some creditable research on Holland's part. Belcher's legalistic manipulations are well researched—and Holland's characterization of his amoral and high-priced lawyer, Cavendish, is simply stunning. No, the point of Belcher's character is simply the enormity of his crime, and for that purpose realism would be as inappropriate as the observation of the unities in a morality play.

Nor do the characters at the other end of the moral spectrum call forth Holland's realistic talents. It is as a matter of strategy, doubtless, that he splits his protagonist in two—one half a noble-savage type positively reeking of Natty Bumppo, the other a scion of society, good manners, and honesty at law. One can only say that Holland has read his Cooper well, particularly *The Pioneers*.[9] The best that can be said for Jim Fenton, Holland's version of a nature (excuse me, "natur") untouched by civilization, is that his mala-propisms out-Natty Natty, as in "Happy David" for "affadavit" (and I will not resist luring the unwary reader into the novel to see what he does with *mene mene tekel upharsin*). Holland's other protagonist, the lawyer Balfour, is presented simply as a virtually irresistible force for morality, law, and taste. Some of his character is summarized, but we see enough of his always honest but sharp legal tactics to identify him easily as The Superman as Lawyer.

But with the minor characters Holland is surprisingly subtle and effective. Oh, he has his Sam Yates, dehumanized by the effect of liquor to the point that he will do anything, including, as it happens self-contradictorily, drying out, in order to get it; and then, after he has dried out, he will promise to perform any villainy if Belcher will only put away his bottle of the Tempter, brandy. Little respect for logic or consistency has gone into his creation. Belcher's prime victim, Paul Benedict, is a more complex creation. He is driven insane by a combination of his own weakness, events, and Belcher's villainy. He is restored by Jim Fenton's kindness and "the influence of the subtle earth-currents" of nature at Jim's isolated hostelry, but his timidity remains striking through the book. His character owes something to Clifford Pynchon of *The House of the Seven Gables* by Nathaniel Hawthorne, but Holland obviously had some contacts with the insane, and developed his perceptions very humanly and well in his text.[10]

Other minor characters are sympathetically and almost subtly drawn, although their appearances in the book are too undeveloped to say much about them. Dr. Radcliffe touches the nerve of the physician more interested in pathology than eradication of disease. Miss Butterworth has just a hint of the provincial backbone that Mary E. Wilkins Freeman was to flesh over so well in sundry stories sharing the locale of Sevenoaks. The Reverend Snow seems real in his first gumptionless encounter with Belcher, chastened and still real in his sad wisdom after Belcher diddles the town for the last time. Belcher's servant Phipps presents a subtle face of the lackey in relation to a vulgar boss.

But there is one character in this novel who makes the reading all worthwhile, and that in spite of Holland's often apparent discomfort with her moral sophistries. Mrs. Helen Dillingham ranks with John DeForest's Mrs. Larue in her ability to stir passion in a man while holding to the forms of respectable social behavior, and with William Dean Howells's Alma Leighton in her ability to convert that passion into moral action. She is anything but a simple character, and

Holland's very efforts to clarify her murky moral role indicate his problems with his creation. On her first appearance in the novel, Holland uses a Jamesian subtlety to suggest her seductiveness. After dinner Belcher, smitten by her already, passes up cigars with the gentlemen to have coffee with the ladies. When Mrs. Dillingham sees her hostess, Mrs. Talbot, start toward them, she takes Belcher's arm:

"My dear Kate," said Mrs. Dillingham, "give me the privilege of showing Mr. Belcher some of your beautiful things."

"Oh, certainly," responded Mrs. Talbot, her face flushing, "and don't forget yourself, my child, among the rest."

Mrs. Dillingham pressed Mr. Belcher's arm, an action which said: "Oh, the jealous creature." (126)

Thus her first impression on the reader is as a homewrecker, a seductress who, within the bounds of propriety, is capable of alienating the affections of a married man. This impression is bolstered by her actions in decorating Belcher's house for him and is clinched by Mrs. Belcher's first reaction to her:

She [Sarah Belcher] saw that Mr. Belcher was fascinated by her, and that he felt that she had rendered him and the family a service for which great gratitude was due; but she saw that the object of his admiration was selfish—that she loved power, delighted in having things her own way, and, more than all, was determined to place the mistress of the house under obligations to her. (182)

Holland later explains her beginnings as a social temptress. She had married an older man, "had worried him out of his life, and he had gone and left her childless" (218). Now

her business was the manufacture of slaves—slaves to her personal charms and her imperious will. Each slave carried around his own secret, treated her with distant deference in society, spoke of her with respect, and congratulated himself on possessing her supreme favor. Not one of them had her heart, or her confidence. With a true woman's instinct, she knew that no man who would be untrue to his wife would be true to her. So she played with them as with puppies that might gambol around her, and fawn before her, but might not smutch her robes with their dirty feet, or get the opportunity to bite her hand (219-220).

All of this suggestive innuendo about her is in spite of her position in the main plot, where, as the sister of Paul Benedict, she reforms herself and becomes one of the most important instruments in his reestablishment—and, of course, in the downfall of Robert Belcher. But her great moment occurs when Belcher has the gall to present her with what to the twentieth-century ear is a most attractive, indecent proposal. The proposal itself is her punishment:

Humiliated, tormented, angry, Mrs. Dillingham sat before him, covering from his sight as well as she could the passion that raged within her. She knew that she had invited the insult. She was conscious that her treatment of him, from the first, though she had endeavored to change her relations with him without breaking his friendship, had nursed his base passion and his guilty purpose. She was undergoing a just punishment, and acknowledged to herself the fact. (369)

In this one instance Holland succeeded extraordinarily well in the creation of a complex character, a moral coquette who is hoist by her own seductiveness.

Other aspects of the novel help to account for its success: the details of Belcher's stockjobbing are fascinating; the account of his removal from Sevenoaks to New York is comparable in some ways to Howells's better job in *A Hazard of New Fortunes*,[11] but has the added piquancy of suggesting the different New Yorks as they appear to a married rake who enjoys "safe and half-reputable vice" on his occasional excursions there, but of course is seeking something quite different when he sets up house. But Holland more than compensates for his good effects with some incredible tortures to the reader's willing suspension of disbelief. There is, for example, his disposal of the Sevenoaks poorhouse after he is done with it. Having used it to introduce the villainy of Robert Belcher and the helplessness of Paul Benedict, and not wanting to leave it as a blot on humanity, Holland casually disposes of it, even at the cost of a complete contradiction of the character established for the residents of Sevenoaks. He has the administrator die of an apoplexy and the "Augean stables" of the establishment "cleansed by the Hercules of public opinion" (104).

These are all minor matters. Holland's readers knew what he was giving them, and neither subtleties of character, as in the case of Mrs. Dillingham, nor unexplained vagaries of plot, as in the case of the

Sevenoaks poorhouse, were central to their expectations. What they wanted and what he gave them was a moral tale in which a kind of ethical calculus was discernible and fiction fulfilled its proper role, which was simply to improve upon life—to reward piety properly and punish the sinful as they deserve—"to make the punishment fit the crime, the punishment fit the crime."

Almost certainly Robert Belcher is intended as a moral representation of James Fisk, Jr., created not to enhance the plot of the novel, but to rectify the inadequacies of life in human dealings. When Fisk died, Holland editorialized in *Scribner's Monthly* that

No man ever died a more natural death than James Fisk, Jr., excepting perhaps Judas Iscariot. . . . He was a bad man—bold and shameless and vulgar in his badness—with whom no gentleman could come in contact without a sense of degradation. . . . Let every man who wields a pen or has an audience with the public do what he can to counteract the poisonous effects of these lives on the young, by calling attention to the fact that these men have simply met the fate of eminent rascality. Honesty *is* the best policy. Virtue *does* pay. Purity *is* profitable. Truthfulness and trustworthiness *are* infinitely better than basely won gold. A good conscience *is* a choicer possession than power.[12]

Sevenoaks the novel and Robert Belcher the villain were created to improve on the life of Fisk. His sudden, violent death had a certain dignity to it; Belcher's ignominious flight and subsequent "career" as barman aboard a St. Lawrence steamer are more appropriate to his sins. More, Fisk was taken off at the peak of his powers; Belcher is allowed to ripen on the vine of criminality until a rather Platonic theory of meanness and criminality works itself out. As his moral coarseness increases, it causes a parallel coarseness in his intellect: "His mind was darkened and dulled by crime," (323) until his business speculations become, like his moral decisions, dulled and ineffectual. This is the negative side of the Holland theory of moral correspondence. The positive aspect is no less evident. Even Jim Fenton, uneducated, apparently obtuse, sharpens his social activity through moral fineness; Sam Yates's goodness expresses itself once the dulling effect of alcohol abuse is overcome, unwittingly, by Robert Belcher; the Balfours' social and personal success is an *a priori* result of their moral fineness. In essence, Holland has improved upon Emerson: instead of the laws of physics translating the laws of ethics, the laws of ethics translate business, social, and personal growth.

It is not at all difficult for a modern reader to understand Holland's popularity in his lifetime. *Sevenoaks* is still a pleasure to read, although it is true that some of the pleasure for the modern reader is in laughing at those same short sermons on ethics that Holland's contemporaries undoubtedly enjoyed for different reasons. Holland was unquestionably, as Walt Whitman said of him, "a man of his time, not possessed of the slightest forereach.... The style of a man ... who can tell the difference between a dime and a fifty cent piece—but is useless for occasions of more serious moment."[13] His failures in this regard were apparent to his intellectual colleagues. Late in his life, unlike Horatio Alger, Jr., he was, socially, at least, acquainted with the new movements in literature. But he was even then a living fossil, about as at home among the new wave of realism as a pterodactyl at a modern jetport. Howells described an incident that is typical of Holland's unease at the transition to modernism. At the end of an evening's literary discussion late in his life, Holland remarked as he left the company, "I have been listening to the conversation of these young men for over an hour. They have been talking about books. And I have never before heard the names of any of the authors they have mentioned."[14]

Whitman and Howells were not concerned with Holland's popularity. Incredibly, thirteen years after his death, when Mrs. H. M. Plunkett wrote her uncritical memoir *Josiah Gilbert Holland*, all of his works were still in print in various forms, ranging from duodecimo volumes at $1.25 each to his complete works in sixteen volumes.[15] His total sales were in the area of three-quarters of a million volumes. No less than Alger, he has almost heroic stature as a representative man of his age.

III   *Piety Triumphant: Edward P. Roe (1838-1888)*

Holland's doctorate has often been misstated as in divinity, as in Carl Van Doren's *The American Novel* where he is referred to as "Rev." The mistake is made because of his close association in the minds of literary historians with E.P. Roe, who was an ordained and practicing Presbyterian minister until he turned to fiction in 1871. The germ of Roe's first and most successful novel, *Barriers Burned Away* (1872), came as a result of a compulsive expedition to Chicago after the fire of 1871.[16] After wandering around the chaos of the burned city for several days, taking notes and undoubtedly muttering "Alas, Babylon" under his breath, Roe set out on the serialization of a novel intended to "justify the ways of God to man." His formula was simple: set a super-pietistic man from the God-fearing prairies in Sodom-on-the-Lake; have him rise to an Alger-like success in spite of the slings and arrows of the ungodly; then let the fire purify the most heathenish and bring out the most heroic qualities of his hero while he is rescuing and converting his misguided heroine.

It worked. The novel remained constantly in print through the remainder of the century and sold some half-million copies. Never one to overestimate his ability, Roe then carefully composed a second novel, *Opening a Chestnut Burr* (1874), and repeated his success to the tune of some 400,000 readers. All barriers thus burned away, he continued at a rate of almost a novel a year to the end of his life, his more popular works being *Near to Nature's Heart* (1876), *A Knight of the Nineteenth Century* (1877), *Without a Home* (1881), *A Young Girl's Wooing* (1884), *An Original Belle* and *Driven Back to Eden* (1885), *He Fell in Love with His Wife* (1886), and *The Earth Trembled* (1887). Alger and Holland may have outsold him, overall, but he was unquestionably the best-selling author of adult fiction of the period. His income from his writing far exceeded that of Howells, with whom he was sometimes compared by critics, always to Howells's advantage. Yet he seems to have been a remarkably likeable person, never allowing the flattery of his "literary" friends like Lyman Abbott and Julian Hawthorne to swell his head. He seems to have recognized his position as a humble journeyman author drawing his readership from those millions of Americans for whom novels—with the exception of his own—were a devil's playground of sin and seduction. In his own way, he was trying to raise the standard of their taste. For the rest of fame, he was content to cultivate his garden (and, incidentally, to write about it charmingly in five books, of which the most inviting are *Play and Profit in My Garden* [1873] and *Nature's Serial Story* [1885]).[17]

Even to a modern reader predisposed to find good in his work, Roe is a trial. More than in Alger, even more than in Holland, one has to forgive deserts of moralizing in Roe, swamps of bathos, ludicrous flights of nobility. But for the reader truly interested in the taste and culture of middle-class America in the Gilded Age, there is probably no finer source. Roe's novels are utterly contemporary; and, if they are unreal, their unreality is that of the aspiring bourgeois. Thus, one can go to Roe's novels to discover not only what events of the period captured the collective American middle-class fancy, but also what ideals and aspirations were central to the would-be-genteel middle class.

Barriers Burned Away provides good examples of Roe at his worst and at his most instructive. In a general way the novel typifies the American concern with the movement to the cities, their moral seductiveness, and the effects of the melting pot. Roe's hero, Dennis Fleet, is totally unbelievable in his virtue, his Christian forgiveness, and his too-convenient talents and taste. But his frustrations upon arrival in Chicago are as real in their way as those of the Marches in Howells's *A Hazard of New Fortunes*, his abstemiousness from alcohol is less teetotal than Colbourne's in DeForest's *Miss Ravenel's Conversion*, and his encounters with the Irish and especially the Germans, in society, low, high, and bohemian—making exceptions for his perfection of character—have the ring of truth.[18] Moreover, his rapid rise to social, commercial, and artistic success probably reflects accurately the prospects of a good, Christian, college-educated gentleman of the day. (How he achieved those college-bred attributes while his family was virtually starving on the prairies is another matter; for the real truth of such circumstances the wise reader will approach Hamlin Garland's "A Girl of Modern Tyre," for example, instead of Roe.)

Roe does well in characterizing the breadth and depth of big-city society in Chicago at the workaday level. Where he falls down is, curiously enough, exactly where his contemporary popularity began—in the exceptional, the catastrophe, the Chicago fire. One gets a foreboding of the climax of the novel at the very beginning, where Dennis's father is dying, unrepentant, on the wintry prairie. Job provides the model: the old man mutters several times that he wishes only to "curse God and die," and several of Job's comforters are evoked. But Dennis's arrival in the storm somehow produces a miraculous conversion, and the old man dies mumbling an appropriate *"Forgiven!"* The fire produces an analogous effect on a panoramic canvas. The sons of Mammon lose all and face the prospect of equality with the God-fearing herd; the only completely unregenerate atheist of the novel, Ludolph, perishes trying to rescue the articles of beauty which his taste, developed at the expense of the corruption of his soul, demands; the intemperate but noble Cronk is saved from a casual immolation by Dennis's crashing his bottle of Demon Rum; the Irish behave badly as usual; and Dennis has to rely on an Augustinian-style mystical experience on the part of the lovely Christine for her conversion after his exertions have brought about her physical survival. One can't help but wish that Roe had been around at the time of the Lisbon earthquake in 1755 to see what Voltaire might have made of him. Even the most evangelical reader would find his patience wearing thin.

Unfortunately, Roe's formula for the novel required a continued dependence upon a natural catastrophe of some sort to bring down the curtain, so the machinery creaks on and on through the canon of his writings. He did improve, however. In *The Earth Trembled*, which used the Charlestown earthquake of 1886 for its denouement, Roe managed somewhat more subtle effects. The theme of this novel is more complicated than the theme of *Barriers Burned Away*: instead of a commercial *Pilgrim's Progress*, Roe attempted in *The Earth Trembled* a study of reconstruction and reconciliation in the post-Civil War South. Because of the subtler theme, the catastrophic earthquake has subtler effects, among which direct intervention by an angry God was not included:

The nightmare aspect of what had occurred in darkness passed away, and the coolest and most learned found themselves confronted by dangers which they could not gauge or explain. Nor could the end be foreseen. If such considerations weighed down the spirits of the most intelligent men, imagine the fears of frail, nervous, women, of the children, the wild panic of the superstitious negroes to whom science explained nothing. To their excited minds the earthquake was due directly either to the action of a malignant, personal devil, or of an angry God. While many of the poor ignorant creatures indulged in what was justly termed "religious orgies," the great majority were well behaved and patient, finding in their simple faith unspeakable comfort and support. (410)

Under these circumstances, it is enough that Roe's hero, Owen Clancy, is excused his Northern sympathies by Mara for his good behavior in the crisis, and that the lovers are reunited. Roe does not even have the earthquake punish Mrs. Bodine, who has had the temerity to swear oaths, excused in her case because her late husband was an admiral in the Confederate navy. In most other cases Roe also resists the temptation to have the earthquake provide a "special Providence" for his characters' just deserts. In comparison with the precise and melodramatic uses to which he put the Chicago fire in the earlier novel, Roe's handling of this spectacular is deft.

Roe's remarkable denouements often justify themselves simply in terms of their action and excitement. His weakest point is always in his heroes, who over and over again out-Alger Alger in their pursuit of moral, commercial, and esthetic perfection. Where Alger in his best works insisted upon some element of luck in his heroes' success, Roe equates piety constantly (though unintentionally) with Mammon, and degrades taste and intelligence no less by insisting upon their being crowned commercially. His heroes do nothing for "show," and yet their most casual acts yield dividends. To the modern reader they are insufferable bores and prigs. His villains are better; they are usually victims of some qualities overdeveloped at the expense of more Christian virtues. And with the many miraculous conversions common to Roe's novels, there is always hope for their regeneration. There is little spectacular evil in Roe's works, no Robert Belchers. Evil is to him more banal, consisting, for example, in *Barriers Burned Away*, in Ludolph's unenlightened self-interest, which is singularly combined in his case with exquisite taste and remarkable commercial competence. Unlike Holland, Roe does not have his villains consume themselves with their own desire or decline into bestial insensitivity. He is not so concerned with the reform of evil that Holland saw resulting from abuse of the system as he is with perfecting the choice of the good Christian man among the snares of hypocrisy, temptation, and good old eighteenth-century "enthusiasm." His ideal, in political terms, is a Christian laissez-faire capitalism which includes paternalistic care of the poor and downtrodden. In that, he undoubtedly reflects the opinion of the great majority of the American people—in their ideals for themselves if not in their practices.

The ethic presented by these three writers was of course not unique to them. We shall discover the same trinity of success, piety, and reform underlying the action in virtually all of the novels, good, bad, and indifferent, considered in this study; nor were the more favored writers, whom we will not be considering in detail, free from the influence of the Protestant ethic. To take only the three that stand highest in current critical esteem: Twain was not personally unacquainted with the lure of the bitch-goddess, Success; Howells's

Christian socialism, in works like *The Rise of Silas Lapham*, was not qualitatively far from Holland's emphasis on reform in business practices; and James was not unaware of the possibilities of supremely "good" characters like Isabel Archer, Millie Theale, and Maggie Verver.[19] The difference is one of degree not kind, and of certain technical capabilities: the creation of drama instead of melodrama, the understanding of human psychology instead of insistence upon Ideality, the recognition of true sentiment instead of sentimentality. In the next chapter we shall consider the underside of these qualities, thereby perhaps gaining a truer awareness of the values of good writing.

CHAPTER 2

Drowning in Bathos: The Sentimental Novel

W HAT the critics and literary historians have come to call the "age of transition" between romantic and realistic fiction will remain ineluctably what it always was—an age of sentimentality. Curiously, the peaks of the fad for sentimental fiction correspond exactly with the high points of achievement in American literature generally. Sentimental fiction was most popular in nineteenth-century America during the 1850s, coincidental with what F. O. Matthiessen called justly the "American Renaissance," and the 1880s, when our literature flowered again with the most successful works of James, Twain, and Howells. Perhaps the coincident appearance is no coincidence. Perhaps the sudden appearance of a wave of unsentimental, profound writing requires an ocean of salt tears to generate itself, either by recommending itself in contrast or by shading delicately to true sentiment from the falsely sentimental. Perhaps an enlightened readership grows up, sighing, by weaning itself from the bathos of E. D. E. N. Southworth to cut its teeth on the irony and psychology of Henry James.

Distinguishing diseased sentimentality from healthy sentiment is not easy, and examiners often differ in their diagnoses. Therefore it is useful to examine an indisputable case to develop one's diagnostic abilities before turning to more doubtful patients. The pathologist of sentimentality is fortunate in having available to him the veritable archetype of the sentimental in the canon of Mrs. E. D. E. N. Southworth (1819–1899).

Mrs. Southworth came to her profession as the longest-lived, most prolific, and most bathetic of what Hawthorne called the "d——d mob of scribbling women" almost miraculously. Can we not see the hand of the Creator in those initials, standing for the homely Emma Dorothy Eliza Nevitte, but promising pre-lapsarian bliss on the title

19

pages of nearly one hundred novels? Was His hand not active in making her personally unlovely, timid, self-conscious, and cursed with a sister, Charlotte, with the reverse of all those qualities in trumps? Was He not active in bringing her together with Frederick Southworth, self-styled inventor and generally conceded ne'er-do-well with itchy feet to take him in and out of Emma's life and thrust her onto her own devices? And did He not cap His creation with a fecundity of energy that beggars belief? An ability to grind out copy for several serials at the same time while working as a teacher and caring for four children, in spite of consistently poor health and persistent eye strain ever threatening permanent blindness? Moreover, though born in the South, she supported the North in the Civil War, lived in the Northeast, South, and Midwest at various times in her life, finally settling in Washington for her last years. Thus her writing is—if not universal—at least never regional. It is hardly possible to consider Mrs. Southworth without concluding that in her we observe the apotheosis of the sentimental writer.

Most of Mrs. Southworth's production of sentimental fiction precedes the starting date of this study, but about one-third of it was written after 1865 and virtually all of it remained in print through the nineteenth century. All of it precisely fulfills the formula for the sentimental novel as described in the best study of the genre, Herbert Ross Brown's *The Sentimental Novel in America, 1789-1860*. It rests

upon a belief in the spontaneous goodness and benevolence of man's original instincts. It could point to what passed for philosophical justification in the admired writings of Shaftesbury, Hutcheson, and Adam Smith. It was informed throughout with a moral purpose to which all its other elements were subordinated. Into its capacious framework were poured the stock characters and situations dear to popular storytellers of every generation. The final solution was neatly reserved for the last chapter where the punishment was made to fit the crime, and the reward to equal the virtue. To achieve it, authors subjected the long arm of coincidence to the rack of expediency where it was stretched and fractured to suit every need of the plot. The reader, meanwhile, was made to cry—and to wait. As a "true-feeler," he was expected to match pang for pang, and sigh for sigh with the persecuted victim; he was mercilessly roasted over the slow fires of suspense.[1]

Mrs. Southworth announces time after time that man is innately good and that, if he will but have confidence in God and submit to

Him, he will inevitably find the strength and endurance to survive misfortune. For this premise Mrs. Southworth required no interpellation from worldly philosophers: her source was the Bible itself. When her saintly heroine Vivia is asked the secret of her good influence on others, she replies "holily, 'FAITH!'" Southworth's villains have all fallen from this state through the intervention of Satan; they may momentarily succeed in their machinations, but their just deserts will always catch up with them, usually in the last chapter. In the meanwhile, they have little rest. They trust no one, are kept constantly burning with unsatisfied desires, and, just occasionally enough to keep the reader guessing, sometimes repent.

As for her plots, Brown's metaphor is, if anything, an understatement. Not only is the long arm of coincidence racked and fractured, it is broken under the wheel, shaped to a Procrustean bed, and pierced most fatally by the Iron Maiden. The novels are filled with later wills invalidating earlier supposed riches or poverty, sudden storms, fires, shipwrecks, and floods all effecting peripeties of one sort or the other, attacks by wolf-packs, and arrivals in the nick of time. The wings of Mrs. Southworth's imagination will suffer no clipping by the laws of probability. Nor is her writing afflicted with the vice of understatement when the time comes to invite the reader's empathy for the long-suffering of her heroines. In the face of emotion, Mrs. Southworth's heroines are not reticent in having their feelings described: this one's bosom is oppressed to suffocation, that one's voice is choked, the other's reason is sent reeling, her blood curdling with horror. And those sensations are not always forced upon Mrs. Southworth's characters from without; on the contrary, they seem to have a positive genius for self-sacrifice. Susan Somerville of *The Mother-in-Law* (1851) not only passes on her beloved to her best friend, she acts as bridesmaid at the wedding; Kate, in *The Curse of Clifton* (1852), is positively eager to nurse her rival through the smallpox. But for all the prolonged physical and mental distress of these characters, Mrs. Southworth usually could kill them quickly, thus distinguishing herself from Poe's scribbling woman, Miss Psyche Zenobia. One anecdote is very revealing about Southworth's lack of concern for fictional euthanasia (and, incidentally, about her weakness in characterization and lack of concern about plot). When a friend criticized a character who was actually based upon himself, Mrs. Southworth is said to have replied "with a twinkle in her eye" that she would "have the gentleman shot in the next issue," and then promptly did so, even though she had to create a new hero to take his place.[2] Similarly, the murder of Kit Ken in *Brandon Coyle's Wife* is achieved so effortlessly the effect is almost prurient. The murderer first chloroforms her and then has his will:

With his left hand he invaded the folds of her cloak, and then the opening of her sack and basque, until he felt the warm bosom and the beating heart— beating slowly and feebly under the effects of the chloroform. Here he held the fingers of his left hand, while with the coolness and caution and ruthless cruelty of a demon, he guided the point of his fine stilletto, in his right hand, to the vital spot, and drove it in up to the hilt!

The slain girl shuddered through all her fine frame, and then grew still in death; yet it must have been only a mechanical spasm. She could have felt no pain, and known no change until she awoke in the upper world.[3]

Leslie Fiedler might well have gone to Mrs. Southworth for indications of the American equation between love and death, all unconscious as her representation of this equivalence is.

But it is not in these surely unintentional excursions into the realm of abnormal psychology that we discover the successes of Mrs. Southworth's writing. It is rather in her efforts at verisimilitude, at "local color," at the nuance of exact detail that she too rarely inserts amid the slings and arrows aimed at her heroines and the sighs and murmurs they provoke. These moments occur not in her settings, which are general and most often hackneyed—chasms, gorges, snowy landscapes, classical gardens—nor in her descriptions of characters, which run to what may be described as either the "well-tubbed look" for the hero, or the "apt to prove a villain" look for the villain. They are generally restricted to dialogue and, even there, to the dialogue of minor characters, usually characters with comic dialects. Still, Margaret Mitchell might have cheered the interview between a housewife and a young black girl in *A Leap in the Dark* (though the NAACP doubtless would not!):

"What can you do?"
"Mos' anyfing 'bout de house."
"Can you cook?"
"No'm. Aunt Char'ty she done de cookin' at our house."
"Ah! Well, can you wash and iron?"

"No'm. Aunt Moll she used to wash an' ir'n."

"So. Can you make beds, sweep and dust—clean house?"

"No'm. Sa'Ann an' Lizy Jane used to do dem fings."

"Then what can you do?"

"Mos' anyfing 'tall 'bout de house," doggedly but humbly persisted the girl.

"Can you wait at table?"

"No'm; Bell an' 'Gustus Caesar wait' on table at our house."

"Well, do tell me something that you can do," said Ora, smothering a laugh.

"Hi, mist'ess, I is a-tellin' of yer, ma'am! I kin do mos' anyfing 'tall 'bout de house!"

"What was your occupation at home?"

"Wot was w'ich, mist'ess?"

"What did you do at the Montgomery house?"

"Oh, mos' anyfing 'bout de house dey wanted of me to do."

"And what was that?"

"W'y, mist'ess, it was mos' anyfing 'bout de house," reiterated the parrot.

"Like what, now?" inquired Ora coaxingly.

"Stan' 'hind ole Mist'ess ch'r an' fan her, an' keep de flies offen her, and pick up her ball o' yarn, or her knittin' needle, w'en she drap it," said the girl.

"That was in the summer."

"Yes'm."

"But what did you do in the winter?"

"Mos' anyfing 'bout—"

"No, no; what did you do for your old mistress?" asked Ora, laughingly, cutting short the formula.

"Oh, stan' 'hind ole mist'ess ch'r an' han' her de tongs w'en she want to pike de fire, an' pick up de ball o' yarn an' de knittin' needle w'en she drap it, an' an'—hole de hanks w'en she gwine to wine it."[4]

Even her small success in recording negro dialect must be qualified, however, since that is the only dialect she reproduced with any success at all. When she tried the Irish, for example, the result is comic all right, but a comic mishmash of Celtic and Caledonian:

"Eh, sirs! wha the deil hae we here fra the ball?" they cried, gathering around her with curiosity.

"Off, you wretches!" screamed Faustina, stamping at them.

"Hech! but she hae a temper o' her ain, the quean," said one.

"Ou, aye, just! It will be for sticking her lad under the ribs she is here," surmised another.

"Eh, sirs, how are the mighty fa'en!" exclaimed a third.[5]

Her attempts at Jewish dialect are even worse, sounding more like overstated Dutch or German: "Zir, te zhip rollts mush. Tere vill pe a gread pig storm."[6]

Although her efforts toward realism in dialect achieved only mixed success, there was one area where Mrs. Southworth was almost always precise and effective. Her descriptions of ladies' dress might serve the cultural historian as well as the full series of *Godey's Lady's Book* to document the changing modes from the 1850s through the 1880s. Indeed, she is in some ways better than *Godey's*, since she can be precise about how some styles become *démodé*, how class is reflected in dress, and perhaps most subtle, how both haughty pride and humble pride find expression in changing fashions. Her vocabulary knows no limits in this area, and her attention to detail of hairdressing, fan usage, mourning costumes, ruffs, tuckers, and pelerines is always believable—at least to this non-expert in such matters. Similarly, though less intentionally on her part, she reflects well the extent of infiltration of foreign languages, particularly French, into American society. In this regard she is perhaps even a better source than Henry James, since his usage of French words and phrases is more subtly appropriate to his characterizations, while hers is more representative of general class distinctions.

These few examples of moments of artistic success in Mrs. Southworth's work reflect only the occasional oases in a Sahara of mediocrity. She remains, in spite of them, the virtually noumenal representation of the sentimental scribbler. With nearly one hundred titles in her canon, she really wrote only one story: the trials of perfect virtue triumphant finally over the machinations of perfect vice. She is never troubled by improbability or inconsistency of character, never understates emotion, never questions the received opinions of the values of marriage, the virtues of self-sacrifice, or the advisability of female dependence upon the male. Her works will always be the touchstone of bathos against which the writings of all other sentimentalists will be compared. Ironic as her superlative position is in this matter, we shall see that it is useful as a basis for analysis of a genre—the genre—that is most representative of the period analyzed in this study.

The lady who played Lou Gehrig to Mrs. Southworth's Babe Ruth was undoubtedly Susan Warner (1819-1885). Neither as prolific as Mrs. Southworth nor as long-lived, she nevertheless produced her almost-yearly novel through the fifties and sixties for the same readership as the Sultana of Sentimentality and vied with her for popularity. Alas, she could never really compete with Mrs. Southworth, because most of her works lacked her colleague's reassuring predictability. It would be presumptuous to say that Miss Warner had genius, but she did have at least some imagination in plotting and characterization, which left her unable to create consistently the kind of bathos that came almost reflexively to Mrs. Southworth. *Melbourne House* (1865) and its sequel *Daisy* (1868) pose the theoretically interesting problem of a congenitally saintly young lady who is unfortunately the daughter of somewhat worldly parents.[7] The implicit conflict has possibilities and fits well into the great tradition of saints' lives, a genre which has attracted writers as dissimilar as Flaubert, D. H. Lawrence, and Somerset Maugham. How "obey thy father and thy mother" and yet live blamelessly? Unfortunately, Miss Warner's talents were not equal to the test posed by her original impulse. She makes Daisy, her heroine, not merely a saint but an Ultramontane, holier than the Pope, while her parents—whom the author clearly wants the reader to despise—come to seem almost too permissive in their failure to curb their daughter's eccentric dogmatism. When Daisy refuses to obey her mother's request to sing a secular song on the Sabbath, the jig is up; priggishness is not sanctity, in spite of Miss Warner's intention that we understand it to be so. The problem is compounded by the Southern antebellum setting. Daisy prides herself in leading prayer meetings of the family's slaves, and sees no inconsistency in the institution itself. Mrs. Southworth avoided that particular swamp of the bathetic because of her pro-Northern sympathies—and that fact alone might account for Miss Warner's runner-up position with regard to her.

Leagues behind Southworth and Warner in the bathos sweepstakes comes a crowd of writers, male and female, who are kept from finishing in the money by a fortunate if too occasional propensity to lard their sentimentality with a touch of realism, insight, or originality. Their example bears out Mrs. Southworth's accomplishment: it is difficult to be perfectly consistent, even in mediocrity. Mrs. A. D. T. Whitney (1824–1906), for example, trails Mrs. Southworth in her initials and in her total output, but what is more important, she almost always manages something at least a little out of the ordinary in the appurtenances of her fictions. *The Gayworthies* (1865) is filled with Southworthian self-renunciation—of Gabriel Hartshorne for his father, of Joanna Gayworthy for her sister—but some of the minor characters are sharply drawn and the village and seaport life is occasionally comparable to Sarah Orne Jewett and Mary Freeman in local color. The only real folks in *Real Folks* (1872) are the minor characters. *Sights and Insights* (1876) is equally sentimental, but gives a fresh look at American perception of European travel. Mrs. Whitney's career was essentially downhill into bathos. While her earlier novels all have some life to them, her later works are unrelievedly sentimental and doctrinaire. By the time of *Bonnyborough* (1886) she was, according to a review in *The Overland Monthly,* quite overcome by "disastrous sentimentalism and mannerism."[8]

Jane Woolsey Yardley is both quantitatively and qualitatively out of the running in the bathos concourse. Modest in her productivity, she managed to produce works which, while bearing all the stamps and hallmarks of the sentimental novel, were yet marked by their author's individual touch. *Little Sister* (1882) is an often-understated history of a widow's wooing. *A Superior Woman* (1885) is comparable in its portrayal of bourgeois New York life to Howells's efforts to do the same thing for Boston in *The Rise of Silas Lapham.* Ellen Warner Kirk (1842-1906) also flirted occasionally with the Howellsian example, in *The Story of Margaret Kent* (1886), for instance. That novel is an analysis of a generally unhappy New York marriage which probably should have ended in divorce but did not; the influence of *A Modern Instance* is plain. More often Mrs. Kirk is Southworthian, as in *Through Winding Ways* (1879), which carries supremely noble characters through catastrophe after catastrophe. In *Lesson in Love* (1881), her impulse is from Jane Austen—the story concerns a twenty-year-old girl who loses her scruples about marriage to an older lawyer—but her technique is pure Southworth. Some of her later novels were published under the pseudonym H. Hayes, and represent a serious effort to produce a hard-edged realism. *Sons and Daughters* (1887) is one such effort, attempting an honest look at society in the Philadelphia suburbs, but the attempt is submerged in the sloppiness of the sentimental handling of the heroine. *Queen Money* (1888) is a somewhat more successful representation of the Gilded Age, but here again Mrs. Kirk's effort to suggest nuances of morality and guilt fails by reason of the expectations of the Age of Southworth.[9]

The other writers in this group would probably be shocked to see their names appear in a chapter initiated with Mrs. Southworth's Edenic acronym. These writers were at least conscious of their craft, aware of the direction fiction was taking, and contemptuous of writers like Mrs. Southworth. Whatever avant-garde notions they had of themselves, however, they acceded to the tastes of their age only too well. Mrs. Albert Payson Terhune, who wrote under the pseudonym "Marion Harland," belongs in the group only because she wrote too much. In occasional novels, like *Jessamine* (1873) which is redeemed by a subtle portrayal of a promiscuous young man, and *A Gallant Fight* (1888) which almost unconsciously justifies infidelity, Mrs. Terhune rises above the commonplace of the sentimental novel. But only a few moments in these novels are real, and they are the exception among the thirty-odd novels produced by her too-industrious pen. George Fleming attempted to conceal the feminine touch of Julia Constance Fletcher (1858–1938) under a neo-Jamesian style in a series of novels on the international theme, of which *Kismet* (1877) and *Andromeda* (1885) are the best.[10] She should not be dismissed lightly, since no less a writer than F. Marion Crawford believed she should be listed among the one hundred best American writers.[11] Time has revealed, however, that the Jamesian touches are barely visible under the shadow of Mrs. Southworth.

Not all the sentimentalists were women, of course. But relatively few male writers wrote enough of this kind of trash to be considered here. Let our token male be John Townsend Trowbridge (1827–1916). Although more versifier than novelist, he wrote two novels that attained considerable popularity in their time. *Lucy Arlyn* (1866) out-Southworths Southworth in the woes heaped upon the heroine, the deep dye of her "spiritualist" seducer, and the calamitousness of the ending. The sporadic efforts at presenting the local color of the upstate New York setting do not redeem the novel's other faults. *Farnell's Folly* (1885) is somewhat more successful in its rural New York local color and is less painfully sentimental. The obscene pride of Ward Farnell is reminiscent of Holland's Robert Belcher, and could stand no less well as a type of the Gilded Age. Trowbridge is also remarkable for the chutzpah of his autobiography, *My Own Story* (1903), which would seem to place him as the foremost author of the time and the center of literary society of the whole Northeast.[12] His comments on Whitman's failure to accept his "improvements" upon his poetry define his character beautifully, as does his description of the two (!) *faux pas* at the Whittier Birthday Dinner. It is in all a remarkable document, epitomizing the level of mediocrity attained by writers of the Gilded Age.

Sentimentalism did not die out with Mrs. Southworth (indeed, it is alive and well and living primarily in television studios in New York and Hollywood), but it took on a new form in the last decade of the nineteenth century and the first twenty years of the twentieth. The novels of Edgar Fawcett (1847–1904) are as sentimental as anything Mrs. Southworth wrote, but they are turned against the upper classes in their social satire and lack her Christian earnestness. Equally sentimental are the novels of Irving Bacheller (1859–1950), especially *Eben Holden* (1900), *Vergilius* (1904), and several other historical novels describing the early years of the republic.[13] But all the works of both these writers include some sort of "redeeming social importance," to borrow a phrase justifying another genre of sub-literature. The same may be said of the works of dozens of other writers postdating Mrs. Southworth: while their characterizations and underlying purposes are thoroughly sentimental, some other value— satiric, historical, sociological—shines through. The old justification, sobs and sighs for their own sake, became not enough. Sentimentalism survives, but the sentimental novel as Mrs. Southworth knew it is dead. *In pace requiescat.*

This chapter cannot end without some consideration of the effects of the sentimental upon the best writers of the period, since that is a subject most often neglected by their hagiographers, if not their critics. Perhaps Mrs. Southworth herself had no influence on James and Twain and Howells and Crane, but the readers she shared with them certainly did.[14] Twain's case shows the most obvious examples. Although he parodies the type of the sentimentalist poet in the character of Emmeline Grangerford, he is not above profiting from his audience's taste for the sentimental in Jim's description of his daughter's deafness, for example, or in the bathetic scene in Chapter 35 of *A Connecticut Yankee in King Arthur's Court* when the young mother about to be hanged gives up the baby to the priest. Only Howells's best novels are free from sentimentality entirely, while his less well known works—the novella *A Fearful Responsibility* (1881), for example—are sometimes downright Southworthian in their sensibility. Stephen Crane's *The Monster* redeems itself from sentimentality by toying with the grotesque, as does Frank Norris's *McTeague*.[15]

The great example of the sentimental raised to a literary level, of the fine line between profundity and the bathetic, is in Henry James. What is it in the portrayal of Catherine Sloper of *Washington Square*, for example, that distinguishes her from whole platoons of Southworthian heroines no less deceived by seducers quite as villainous as Morris Townsend? Plainness of face is not unheard of among Mrs. Southworth's heroines, nor are imperfect fathers. The difference is certainly only one of degree. In the much-admired late *nouvelles* like "The Altar of the Dead" and "The Beast in the Jungle," James dwells with a Southworthian voluptuousness on the refined sensibilities of Stransom and Marcher. Only his satiric undercutting of their characters separates them from their sentimental models, and only his internalization of the stresses upon them adds a subtlety missing in Mrs. Southworth's characters. And the novel that many critics consider his greatest, *The Wings of the Dove*, curiously echoes Mrs. Southworth's comment about one of her long-suffering and self-sacrificing heroines, Alice Garnet, in *The Discarded Daughter*: "I often compared her to the dove, folding her wing over the mortal wound, to hide it from all eyes."[16] If such comparisons be blasphemous, so be it. No reader can range very far in this sub-literature of the sentimental without concluding that the good writing of the age has more in common with such trash than it has with writing of another age. What becomes exciting to such a reader, familiar with the context of sub-literature, are the strategies and techniques used to overcome or subvert these limitations. These will be the center of our concern in the chapters that follow.

CHAPTER 3

The Decline and Fall of New England

THE "American Renaissance" of the 1850s was essentially a New England phenomenon. Martin Green's *The Problem with Boston* to the contrary notwithstanding, the difficulty of understanding what happened in New England in the fifties is not why the results were not better, but how such a remarkable group of writers came to flourish in one period. The answer to that question—and the answer to the even more difficult one that follows: why New England art declined after 1865—may be deduced, I believe, by a consideration of four eminent New England writers whose works span the period and place of this study and go beyond it, and who speak directly of the roots and the decline of New England greatness. Arlo Bates, Robert Grant, Howard Sturgis, and George Santayana all share in having been nurtured in the best intellectual tradition of New England; they share no less in their concern for its artistic decline and in their representativeness of that decline.

I *Dionysos in Philistia: Arlo Bates (1850–1918)*

The decline of New England after 1865 can best be explained by the clear case of a writer coming from what Oliver Wendell Holmes called the "brahmin class," who had all the advantages—educational, cultural, social—of that class, but who nevertheless failed to achieve the kind of success that Hawthorne did. Arlo Bates is precisely that man. Born of a family that arrived in New England in 1635, educated, like Hawthorne, at Bowdoin College, and quickly entering into the literary life of Boston after his graduation, his career as a brahmin was capped by his being named professor of English literature at Massachusetts Institute of Technology in 1893. Yet he was far from being a stuffed shirt, was blessed with a sense of humor and a belief that literature should be professed with enthusiasm as a bringer of joy.

Moreover, though his upbringing was brahmin, his experience was of the newer breed of *literateur*, via journalism. He was editor of the Boston *Sunday Courier* from 1880 to 1893, and earlier had been associated with various reformist publications. And, if his writings may be used as evidence for his biography, he was apparently not unconnected to bohemian society or unsympathetic to newer voices and iconoclastic views. Author of more than twenty books, ranging from the lightest fiction to serious studies of literature, he is central to the question of what happened to Boston primarily because of a trilogy he wrote on that very subject. Three novels, *The Pagans* (1884), *The Philistines* (1889), and *The Puritans* (1899), are centered in the art world of Boston, but, like James's *Roderick Hudson* and *The Princess Casamassima*, they express through the metaphor of art and the artist the problem of literature and the writer.[1]

The last two volumes of the trilogy carry the major characters of *The Pagans* through their fated trials; the first novel states in detail and depth what it was that caused the dissociation and displacement of art and literature in Boston. It is an incredibly fine evidentiary document and no less intriguing as a novel. "The Pagans" are a group of seven artists who have established a loosely organized society which meets convivially once a month. Their "patron saint" is the Egyptian goddess Pasht, a cat-headed goddess of war and libraries whose head, in the Way Collection of Egyptian sculptures in the Boston Museum, still exhibits that "faint smile beneath which lurks a sneer" (23). Their cohesiveness as a society comes from their opposition to what they sense is the increasing philistinism of Boston, as represented by an arch-philistine named, significantly, Peter Calvin. At the center of the novel are two stories that complement each other and explain the breaking up of the society: a young artist of promise, Arthur Fenton, drifts into philistinism via a just-barely-believable marriage to Calvin's niece, Edith; a young sculptress, Helen Grayson, resolves a tricky moral dilemma involving herself, her sculpting master, Grant Herman, his jilted fiancée of years before, Ninitta, and her estranged husband, Dr. Will Ashton, to nobody's satisfaction (except perhaps exponents of renunciation as a way of life, like Henry James).

But plot is less important to this novel than to most. The two stories serve admirably as *ficelles* upon which Bates hangs epigrams, conversations, and extremely telling images of the confrontation between the new wave of ideas and the old standards of transcendentalist Boston. As we might expect, Emerson stands at the center of the conflict. The Pagans depend heavily upon his thought—his ideas on originality, his reaction against puritanism, his identification of subject and object—but they must reject him as a personal guide. How the times have worked against Emerson is amply demonstrated in a conversation between Rangely, a playwright, and Helen Grayson:

"Emerson was great," he said, "Emerson often recalled Goethe in Goethe's cooler and more intellectual moods; but Emerson lacked the loftiness of vice; he was eternally narrow."

"'The loftiness of vice,'" echoed the hostess. "What does that mean? It sounds vicious enough."

"Emerson," Rangely returned, "knew only half of life. He never had any conception of the passionate longing for vice *per se*; the thrill, the glow which comes to some men at the splendid caress of sin in her most horrible shape. Do you see what I mean? He couldn't imagine the ecstasy that may lie in mere foulness."

"No," replied Helen, "I'm afraid I don't quite see. Though I am sure I ought to be shocked. Do you mean he should have been vicious?"

"Certainly not; but it was his limitation not to be tempted; not to be able to project himself into a personality which riots in wickedness far more intensely than a saint follows righteousness."

"If you mean that he could not have been wicked if he tried, that, I own, was in a sense a limitation."

"Yes; and a fatal one. No man can be wholly great who understands only one half of human impulses." (80-81)

The problem is that though the characters here tellingly reject Emerson's incomplete experience of human motives, the plot itself implies that Bates could not bring himself any more than Emerson could to a real examination of those motives. Thus, although real human passion is implicitly at the root of the problems the characters encounter, Bates attempts no explanation of that most salient factor. One could easily duplicate Rangely's remarks on Emerson for Bates himself; Helen's rejection of Grant Herman's passion for her and her own positive response to it are as coldly intellectual as anyone could wish. And the only explanation given for Arthur Fenton's marriage is as chilly as it is unlikely. Will Ashton explains it to Helen:

"He married her because he fell in love for no reason but the weakness of our sex."

"Love seems generally to be regarded by the masculine mind in the light of a weakness."

"Isn't it?" her husband returned. "Love is the condition of desiring the impossible, and if that is not a weakness, what becomes of logic?" (191)

Lust is rarely so prettified by logic, a logic further muddled by Arthur, who has already said that he "asks forgiveness for his virtues and thanks the gods for every vice he can cultivate" (51). No, no, Arlo: it is all talk, and you are as unacquainted with that "passionate longing for vice *per se*" as any denizen of Boston's or Concord's transcendentalist circles of the half-century before you.

The same inconsistency between precept and example is to be found in the novel's examination of the principles of art. Arthur Fenton is epigrammatical on the subject, but the ideas are far more dependent upon Emerson than upon Oscar Wilde:

What nonsense it is . . . to talk of any man's originating any thing. Why, when even Adam couldn't be made without material, what are we, his descendents, that we should hope to create? The authors of this old wisdom that we revamp to-day copied somebody further back, and those in turn put down what the masses felt; collected the foam which gathered in the yeasty waves of their age. Every truth comes to the people first if they could only recognize it when it comes. It is evolved by the friction of the masses, just as a fire is set by the rubbing together of tree boughs in primeval forests. . . . The longer I live the less faith I have that a man evolves any thing from his inner consciousness. Fancies are only the lies of the mendacious brain, which perceives one thing and declares to us another. . . . The age blooms once into a great man as an aloe into a crown of bloom. . . . But that depends upon whether a man goes direct to Nature for inspiration . . . or sets himself to get a living by filching the good things his neighbors have won from her. (87–89)[2]

Even more striking than Bates's Emersonian view of mimesis is his espousal of the transcendental concept of the identification of subject and object as experiential phenomena. Here the immediate cause is remarkably *not* of Emerson's age, but of Emile Durkheim's age of decadence and anomie. Arthur Fenton is again the speaker, but we may see him here as voicing the moderate view, since he only contemplates suicide, while two other characters of the novel actually accomplish it. The center of his attention is a vial of Prussic acid upon which is inscribed "Death foils the gods."

It is a comfort to me. . . . It means an end of everything. It means annihilation; it means getting rid of this nightmare of existence. I can remember when I dreaded the idea of annihilation, but I have come to feel that it is the only good to be desired. To be done with everything and to forget everything! Don't you see, Helen; I should never be satisfied with any thing short of omnipotence and omniscience, and annihilation is the only refuge for a nature like that. I want to be every thing; to feel the joy of the conqueror and yet not miss the keen, fine pang of the conquered—Lowell says it somewhere; to be
        'Both maiden and lover'—
I forget it—'bee and clover,' you know; to be the 'red slayer' and 'the slain' both. Do you wonder I want to keep this? (99)

Just as the novel identifies puritanism and philistinism as the life-destroying forces that the Pagans, with their Emersonian creed, struggle against, so it tells—and, more important, *demonstrates*—the failure of the transcendental vision to cope with the new circumstances of Philistia and Calvinism armed with immense economic power and self-righteousness. The dissolution of "The Pagans," the pathetic emasculation of Arthur Fenton at the hands of his puritanical wife and her philistine uncle, and the failure of Helen and Grant Herman to seize what joy of life they can are all a result of the baleful influence of the Emersonian doctrine of compensation. The Pagans carry on, divided and uncertain, because their art is more important to them than commercial success. Arthur survives through this novel (though not through the second novel of the trilogy, *The Philistines*) because his artistic sensitivity continues in spite of his self-destructive moral obliquity. When his wife upbraids him for the suicide of Dr. Ashton, he "looked at her with intense irritation, and an inward curse that he had ever married her. He sipped his coffee; he noted with admiration the rich, glowing hues of the dull blue bowl of nasturtiums which adorned the table" (224). And when Helen and Grant Herman separate, they remain so united that, in the last words of the novel, they "clung together by their glances until distance shut them from each other's sight" (275).

When old beliefs fail there is always hope that the new beliefs will take their place. Perhaps that was so in the world at large, but not in

Arlo Bates's Boston. One by one the possibilities are struck down. The possibility of a rapprochement between art and morality is always present in the novel, never better stated than in Grant Herman's reassuring comments on taste: "Taste is sublimated morality. It is the appreciation of the proportion and fitness of all things in the universe, and of course it is above simple morality, for that is founded upon a partial view. Taste is the universal, where a system of morals is the local" (253). A glimmer of hope there, no doubt. But if the proposition is possible, Arthur's marriage to Edith provides an ideal test case; both are intelligent, and though diametrically opposed on the question of morality and art, surely some synthesis is possible other than the selling out of one or the corruption of the other. But, no. Bates is unequivocal in his presentation of their two points of view in perfect balance and with no compromise possible.

"We do not agree, Edith," he said with cold deliberation, "and unless you broaden your views, I am afraid we never shall. You are a dozen decades behind the day, and are foolish enough to take all your church teaches you in earnest. Religion should no more be taken without salt than radishes. The church inculcates it to excuse its own existence, but you certainly are reasonable enough to outgrow this old-fashioned Puritanism."

"Arthur," was her answer, "we do not agree, and if you wait for me to come to your standards, I am afraid you are right in saying that we never shall; and, indeed, I hope you are right. It makes me more unhappy than you can think," she continued, her eyes swimming with bitter tears, "that we are so far apart on what I must believe to be vital points; on truths which I believe, Arthur, with my whole soul—as you would, too, had you not carefully educated yourself into a doubt which cannot make you better or happier." (206–207)

If rapprochement is impossible, the novel shows endlessly that giving oneself over to sin and/or art for sin's and/or art's sake is no more viable. A hardier collection of virtuous people than these Pagans is impossible to imagine. Ninitta was definitely Grant Herman's *fiancée,* not his mistress, in Rome, and he is certain of her continued purity since then; he and Helen Ashton behave incredibly morally (not to say incredibly). Indeed, Helen Ashton and her separated husband are the closest the novel presumes to rakishness, she because she lives separately from her husband, he because he does not interfere with the suicide of a friend and then determines to cheat a cancer by taking his own life. As a great sinner he reminds one of St. Augustine. And yet he is clearly patterned after Hawthorne's Chillingworth in his cold detachment toward his friends and his wife. The realistic manner of this novel simply will not support a villain of the proportions of Chillingworth. In this creation and in the novel as a whole, Bates falls between the two stools of the old romantic tradition and the newer realism.

His typically New England failure to adopt the new realism may best be seen in his efforts to produce some local color for the novel. Ninitta provides the occasion for a visit to Boston's North End, but Bates and his characters are so patronizing that the expedition resembles nothing more than a Junior League slum party. Here is Bates speaking in an authorial voice: "The poorer classes of foreigners in any city are led by similarity of language and occupations to gather into neighborhoods according to their nationality, and the Italians are especially clannish" (164). With the creator so patronizing, one can imagine how his creations behave:

Edith meanwhile was not idle. She applied herself to hushing the boisterous children, and to bringing something like quiet out of the tumult of the crowded room. She assisted the girl with her maccaroni [sic], gravely listening to the principles which governed its equitable distribution, with her own hands giving the grimy little children the share belonging to each. An air of comfort seemed to come over the frowsy room after Edith had quietly set a chair straight here, picked up something from the floor there, and arranged the ragged shade at the window. Even the little Italians, half barbarians as they were, felt the change, and were more subdued. (166)

Bates is never more obnoxious than he is in this scene; but what a terrible failure for a writer who goes out of his way to espouse a bohemian artists' community against the forces of philistinism!

Arlo Bates was probably as talented a writer as ever lived in Boston. Endowed as he was with sympathy for the new views and respect for the past, his failure was perhaps predictable, but is no less pathetic for that. It was not merely that he was caught between two worlds, "one dead, one powerless to be born," but that others, like Howells, like Crane, who had not had his "advantages," were not so crippled with deference toward a past which had lost its relevance. He is to be admired for his balanced treatment of what was the central problem of his age, but one cannot but wish that he had taken some kind of stand. What he would have lost in terms of intellectual honesty he would have more than compensated for in artistic vigor.

II   *Defender of the Faith: Robert Grant (1852-1940)*

Arlo Bates was born too early to escape the baleful influence of the New England past; Robert Grant, we might say, lived too long. Unlike Bates's, Grant's family arrived in Boston after the Revolution, and his family tradition had only a lowland Scots presbyterianism rather than New England puritanism to live down. But otherwise Grant was more of a brahmin than his shorter-lived contemporary. His education included Boston Latin School and Harvard for an undergraduate degree, a Ph.D. in philology, and an LL.B. The two men belonged to many of the same clubs, but Grant, as a successful lawyer, city and state official, and judge, probably looked down on the journalistic background of Bates; while Bates might well have had Grant in mind for the character of his arch-philistine, Peter Calvin.

Grant, like Bates, was enormously talented as a writer. Unlike Bates, he had no philosophical problems. He writes with an Augustan assurance in defense of the old values. His bugbears are the kinds of moral laxity let loose by the unrestricted freedoms found in a democracy, the bitch-goddess of success, and the failure of the *aristoi* to fulfill the obligations of their positions. From his first major work, *An Average Man* (1883), through a series of philosophical essays, *The Opinions of a Philosopher* (1892), and *Search-Light Letters* (1899), some twenty novels and several volumes of verse, to his ratification, in 1927, with A. Lawrence Lowell and Samuel W. Stratton, of the verdict convicting Sacco and Vanzetti, he never once strayed from the path of righteous defense of what ought to be.[3] Like a good Augustan, his chief weapon was satire, his manner an impeccable prose style, his stance an absolute assurance of the rightness of his views. His best works are superbly crafted: his characters subtly developed, his settings realistic yet pointed, his plots believable, his moral crises strikingly pertinent. In all ways but one, he is a major writer. All he lacked was human sympathy. Indeed, had the history of the past one hundred years not been one of increasing liberalism in North America, Robert Grant would undoubtedly be considered a major literary figure. As a spokesman for tough-mindedness and a defender of the old values, he cannot be approached.

Like Howells, he came to serious fiction through light domestic social satire. His first novel was entitled *The Confessions of a Frivolous Girl* (1880). *An Average Man* is his first study of the horrendous effects upon character of the relentless pursuit of success at any cost, a theme which he was to take up over and over again in his later works. *Face to Face* (1886) owes a good deal to John Hay's *The Breadwinners* (1884). It too was published anonymously, perhaps because of the satiric portraits of some of Grant's Newport neighbors, perhaps because of its serious examination of the confrontation of capital and labor, but the secret of its authorship was not kept as well as Hay's (or Henry Adam's authorship of *Democracy* [1880]).[4] Grant was never again to conceal himself behind his views, even though, as we shall see, his views were far from popular.

His best novel was undoubtedly *Unleavened Bread* (1900).[5] Howells's influence is apparent: Grant's heroine, Selma White Babcock Littleton Lyons, is a feminine Bartley Hubbard. But she owes as much to Flaubert's Emma Bovary as to anyone else. She is a complete creation, with every feminine strength and weakness imaginable, with all the wiles, aspirations, ideals, moral obliquities, and inconsistencies discoverable at a hoedown, a fashionable *soirée*, or a government reception. She is so human that her author's obvious dislike for her is all the more reprehensible. Grant unquestionably intends us to agree, for example, with his moral censure of her use of contraception after the death of her child, her divorce of Babcock after his infidelity, her hounding of Littleton to death because he cannot betray his artistic principles and design an architectural monstrosity for a wealthy vulgar patron, and finally her urging Lyons to betray a deal he has made with a public utilities scoundrel and vote his conscience on a crooked bill. We don't. Grant is too good a writer to descend to didacticism, believing undoubtedly that the clarity of his case against Selma's shallowness and hypocrisy will carry the day with his readers. It doesn't.

Selma's second husband, the architect Littleton, is close to Grant's ideal of character. He loves Selma from afar while she flirts with him egregiously and marries him the moment her divorce becomes final. Grant has no criticism for his ingenuousness, but he is a trifle hard on

Selma's honest feminine duplicity. When the two of them arrive in New York, Littleton sets Selma straight on the social proprieties, in what must be Grant's own voice, with an assurance which is belied by what follows. Walking down Fifth Avenue, Selma is stunned by the magnificence of the houses. She asks who lives there.

> "Oh, the rich and prosperous."
> "Those who gamble in stocks, I suppose." Selma wished to be assured that this was so.
> "Some of them," said Littleton, with a laugh. "They belong to people who have made money in various ways or have inherited it—our well-to-do class, among them the first families in New York, and many of them our best citizens." (115)

Selma is unsatisfied with this answer and draws out a lengthier justification; Littleton is not loathe to give it:

> "You mustn't pass judgment on them too hastily," he said. "New York is a wonderful place, and it's likely to shock you before you learn to appreciate what is interesting and fine here. I will tell you a secret, Selma. Every one likes to make money. . . . Yet it is the fashion with most of the people in this country who possess little to prate about the wickedness of money-getters and to think evil of the rich. That proceeds chiefly from envy, and it is sheer cant. The people of the United States are engaged in an eager struggle to advance themselves—to gain individual distinction, comfort, success, and in New York to a greater extent than in any other place can the capable man or woman sell his or her wares to the best advantage—be they what they may, stocks, merchandise, law, medicine, pictures. The world pays well for the things it wants—and the world is pretty just in the long run. If it doesn't like my designs, that will be because they're not worth buying. The great thing—the difficult thing to guard against in the whirl of this great city, where we are all striving to get ahead—is not to sell one's self for money, not to sacrifice the thing worth doing for mere pecuniary advantage." (116)

And he continues in the same vein at great length, justifying the advantages of the rich and powerful and modestly eschewing his own and Selma's possibilities of achieving their state.

So far so good. It all rings a bit hollow, however, when the one example that Grant presents of anyone actually achieving this stature happens to be the Littletons' neighbors, Gregory and Flossie Williams. Flossie knows her place, and is socially reticent until she makes enough money to earn a position that allows her to mingle with her distant relatives, the Morton Prices, who represent the *gratinée* of New York society. But she achieves this success through the stockjobbing of her husband! No wonder Selma is confused, not to mention the reader. When Williams overextends himself and his brokerage fails, Selma feels somewhat self-righteously triumphant; when she then encounters an unbowed Flossie in a high-class restaurant, she is stunned. Gregory Williams escapes his firm's disaster and bounces back, in the great American tradition, and apparently with Grant's approval. The firm's fraudulent activities were laid upon Williams's partner, but Selma guesses shrewdly that Williams "must have known" what his partner was up to; her then husband, Lyons, agrees: "'It would seem,' he said, 'as if he must have had an inkling, at least, of what was going on'" (399). But with no evidence to link him to the fraud, Williams survives, escaping any censure from characters having the author's sympathy. One wonders how Grant would have responded to Watergate; no, one knows.

The final crisis of the novel is even more telling. Selma's third husband, Lyons, owes his political advancement to the governorship to the support of an influence-peddling utilities magnate, Horace Elton. In return for his support, Lyons has promised to sign an apparently innocuous bill which will give Elton the power to buy up a number of independent utilities for a song. Another member of Lyons's party (the Democratic Party, of course) has discovered the weakness of the bill and hopes to parlay his criticism of it into a senatorial appointment, which Lyons and Selma also covet. If Lyons signs the bill, he will not get the appointment; if he does not sign it, he will break his promise to Elton. Selma "convinces" him that he must not sign the bill. He is appointed Senator. Horace Elton understands. And the Lyonses presumably live happily ever after, if life with a difficult woman like Selma can ever be happy. Grant, here as always, lets the actions speak for themselves, never injecting a hint of the didactic in what he considers a self-evident irony. Sordid the incident is; but self-evident it is far from being. The final irony comes down to Grant's version of Republican morality in the mere presentation of this situation as his climactic moral failure—which he entitles "The Success." Howells's wisdom in giving Silas Lapham a clear-cut moral problem for his "rise" is the more telling by comparison with *Unleavened Bread.*

Actually, Grant's own moral and political obliquity only improves on the subtlety of this novel, adding a retrospective twist to what remains one of the best novels of the period. Selma is a major creation in her lifelike blending of strengths and weaknesses. Her drive for success at any price, yet her feminine longing for support, make her the true predecessor of those myriad bitch-goddesses of twentieth-century fiction.[6] She is totally capable of standing on her own. She succeeds as a schoolteacher, as a journalist, as a public figure, as a social climber—but in each case she accedes to her feminine need for a man to support and be supported by. All her individual successes as a woman tire her and bore her; it is still a man's world she lives in. The parallel cases that Grant presents only prove the point. Mrs. Taylor is just more subtly manipulative than Selma, while Mrs. Earle earns no sympathy from her creator simply because her mannish Lesbianism goes too far. Grant is not concerned that it is forced on her by a society totally unsympathetic to her needs. Flossie Williams seems to have Grant's complete sympathy, but only because she follows the rules of social progress; she has none of Selma's independence. Although Grant reveals on almost every page a thoroughgoing misogyny, he builded better than he knew. No modern reader can observe the women of this novel without sympathizing with them all and wishing that the men would handle things a bit better.

Although *Unleavened Bread* is surely Grant's best novel, it is not because the others that followed are not fine. They are all successful in various ways. *The Undercurrent* (1904) and *The Orchid* (1905) are both pointed satires aimed at the supposed moral superiority of high society, tested in both novels by the question of divorce. The real motive—the worship of money—is made limpidly clear, but, as usual with Grant, without a hint of didacticism. *The Chippendales* (1909) examines the traditions of Boston society that Grant knew only too well.[7] It is free from both the artlessness and the moral earnestness of Bates's *The Philistines* and *The Puritans*. With the surgical precision of the satirist, Grant slices through the protective layers of puritanism in Boston society to lay bare the tumorous hypocrisies. The old tough-mindedness has turned into a virtue of negation: "What a Bostonian will not do has ever been perhaps his highest title to distinction." The sensitive introspection of the Mathers and Sewalls has become a fear of criticism from unsympathetic outsiders. The old independent spirit that made life miserable for a succession of colonial governors and that led to the Revolution has become, in the generally sympathetically drawn young lawyer, Henry Chippendale Sumner, a grotesque tilting at moral windmills. The old great issues which drew out the worst and best of Boston—witchcraft in Salem, liberty for the colonies—are now trivia: the censoring of a nude statue of the Bacchante, the acceptance of a family whose fortune is based upon the discovery of "Electric Coke." Sympathetic as he is in general with the best qualities of the Boston mentality, Grant cannot help but illustrate in the novel how tenuous these qualities have become. His society's dilemma is in many ways his own; although the satire is finely drawn, the values it seeks to support are no longer as certain as they once were. Thus, his subtlety can work against him for the modern reader, who can better appreciate Bates's more simplistic moral stance.

Grant's later novels lack some of the subtlety of the earlier ones, the more apparently because they are as comparable to them as sequels. *The High Priestess* (1915) is as misogynist as *Unleavened Bread*, but Mary Arnold is wishy-washy in comparison to Selma Lyons. *The Bishop's Granddaughter* (1925) is a gentle satire on divorce in comparison to *The Orchid*. And *The Dark Horse* (1931), intended as a sequel to *The Chippendales* and illustrating the unholy alliance of Boston society to the new political structures of Massachusetts politics, succeeds only in showing how comparatively out of touch with new ideas Grant had become since Marquand's *The Late George Apley* followed it by only a few years. Nevertheless, in terms of the excellence of his style and the life of the characters he created, Robert Grant deserves to be rediscovered as a novelist. Certainly *Unleavened Bread* is too good a novel to be restricted to courses on "women in literature" and the like. Halfway between Howells's *A Modern Instance* and Dreiser's *Sister Carrie*, it is more forthright than the one and more subtle than the other.[8] The fact that it remains out of print is evidence only of the parochialism of modern scholarship and criticism.

III   Attenuation: H.O. Sturgis (1855–1920) and George Santayana (1863–1952)

Henry James has well documented his reasons for his flight from Boston, personally in his Notebooks and publicly in his essay on

Hawthorne. His case was anything but unique. To fill out this chapter on the decline of New England fiction, we must range farther and farther afield to discover representative men who are writers of genius but who were not crippled and silenced by the stifling atmosphere of Boston. Both Sturgis and Santayana serve the function well, illustrating the attenuation of the moral power that was puritan Boston at the end of its age.

Howard Overing Sturgis went James one better: he managed not even to be born in Boston. His father was. Russell Sturgis was of old Boston stock, and, though the money he made allowed his son to spend most of his life as an English gentleman at Queen's Acre, Windsor, the moral tradition he passed on to him was as Bostonian as Beacon Hill. Had he not chosen to live in England, we would doubtless not have Sturgis's novels to read. His delicate genius simply could not flower in the rougher climate of Boston; while surrounded by the needlepoint and woolwork he loved so well, the talk and companionship of fellow geniuses like Edith Wharton, Henry James, and Gerard Hopkins, and a society more tolerant of his epicene tastes, Sturgis developed a sensibility that could uniquely embroider English characters with puritan morality. Dilettantes in Boston produced no lasting work; Howard Sturgis created three novels, of which one, *Belchamber* (1904), is unquestionably a classic.[9]

A New England conscience is the most striking attribute of Charles Edwin William Augustus Chambers, Marquis and Earl of Belchamber, Viscount Charmington, and Baron St. Edmunds and Chambers, for all the Englishness of his names and titles. Called "Lord St. Edmunds" in his childhood, he was nicknamed "Sainty" half-derisively early, and the appropriate name stuck. For, in his sexlessness, his constant introspection, his moral vigor, his Emersonian self-reliance, he is far more a latter-day version of the New England saint than he is representative of the inheritance of the Norman conquest. Although Sturgis is unsparing in his criticism of his hero, pointing out his weakness and ingenuousness at every occasion, Sainty stands a breed apart from the collection of knaves and fools surrounding him. Life tempers him from his birth as a delicate child to his extraordinarily loveless marriage to bring forth from him beatific acceptance of himself, his lot, and the imperfect world of titled English society. He has been compared with early heroes and heroines of Henry James, but he more closely resembles

Milly Theale of *The Wings of the Dove* than any other character.[10] He raises the concept of renunciation to a peak found nowhere else in fiction.

Sturgis tells the story with masterful control, a fine insight into character, and some deft psychological touches, notably the creation of Sainty's *doppelgänger*, his cousin, Claude Morland. Claude is everything Sainty is not: handsome, worldly, shrewd, uncluttered by the dictates of *noblesse oblige*. He crosses Sainty's path again and again, squeezing out the secular juice from experience and leaving Sainty the spiritual pulp; his moral fall and earthy rise exactly complement Sainty's tempering into finely hardened spiritual steel. Sturgis doubtless did not intend an allegory, but Claude's continental finesse, contrasted as it is with Sainty's New World earnestness in an English social setting, produces tropes that work on various socio-logical and philosophical levels. In all of them, Sainty's essential New England spirit shines through. He, of the highest class in the novel, is the only democratic thinker; he alone values money for what it can do for others; he alone is content to develop his inner self at the expense of what the world thinks of him; he alone is capable of the kind of love that he is fated never to have.

Sturgis's master in fiction was Henry James, and James could find no encouraging words for *Belchamber*. Tongue-tied by the shibbo-leths of technique, James could not see through the apparent ingenuousness of Sturgis's nineteenth-century style of narration to the heart of the novel's success as symbolism. His failure to do so doomed Sturgis to a lifetime of dilettantism, and the sterility that resulted from his failure stands for the effeteness of even the best of the New England creative tradition at the time. In the 1850s a small group of writers could band together in the harshness of the New England climate, temporal and intellectual, and, in spite of the lack of almost all the elements necessary for the creation of art, create. At the end of the century the finest creative mind New England ever produced, Henry James, had to exile himself from his homeland and then, when he encountered another self as spiritual as his own, could not experience that "shock of recognition" that made Hawthorne's contact with Melville so productive. In Sturgis's failure to continue writing after *Belchamber*, we can discern the hardy stock of New England creativity gone sterile from attenuation, as much through James's effeteness as his own.

The influence of Howard Sturgis did reach out and connect with the story of *The Last Puritan* (1935).[11] Sturgis is mentioned in both the Prologue and the Epilogue of Santayana's "Memoir in the form of a novel," and Santayana's debt to him is apparent. He mentions with affection his "friend and quasi-cousin . . . host and hostess in one, who held court in a soft nest of cushions, of wit, and of tenderness, surrounded by a menagerie of outcast dogs, a swarm of friends and relations, and all the luxuries of life" (7). There the idea for the novel is born, and when it is concluded, Sturgis is again credited with "a lot of good things" (418) put into the mouths of the characters. His influence was even more profound than these admissions suggest. Indeed, one might say that *The Last Puritan* is a "Belchamber Revisited," with its beatific hero recognized for the Boston brahmin that he is at last.[12] Santayana's puritan, Oliver Alden, is simply another version of Sainty Belchamber, with his New England roots made manifest instead of implicit.

The curious history of this unique novel and its contents amply justifies our going beyond the final date of this study to examine it. For, if we can see in *Belchamber* the native stock of New England grown effete and attenuated, Santayana's classic is an extraordinary example of what may bloom from an exotic graft. Santayana himself, as his name suggests, was no ordinary Boston brahmin. Born in Madrid, he spent his early years in Avila before coming to Boston in 1872. From that date, however, his education was fairly typical of the Boston intellectual: Boston Latin School, Harvard, study in Germany, Harvard Ph.D. in 1888. From 1888 to 1912 he was a colleague of William James and Josiah Royce, but his interests continued outside of philosophy, including poetry and criticism. Like Bates and Grant, he was a Renaissance man in the variety of his interests; like Sturgis, he was fundamentally committed to rumination over esthetics and ethics. Nothing in his early years except his New England experience can account for the remarkable production of his only novel when he was over seventy years old. As a document of its age and place, *The Last Puritan* is unrivaled except perhaps by *The Education of Henry Adams.*[13] Both works are deeply concerned with the mixed blessings of the heritage of New England character; both are written in a flawless style that can range equally happily from pure comedy (Oliver Alden's first passionate kiss destroyed by the flavor of cucumbers and sardines) to the most complex ethical examination

(Oliver on his inability to love an individual woman because of his too highly developed *agape*); both present a panorama of the nineteenth century viewed by characters who are the best the century can produce and who conclude, self-confessed, that they are failures.

All of the other works we have considered in this chapter which deal with the New England character are mere sketches or gross caricatures compared to *The Last Puritan*. Their puritan characters are types; Oliver Alden is the archetype, laid bare by hundreds of incidents—cruxes, all of them—which delightfully expand our knowledge of his magnificent potential and crushingly imply his inability to act upon it. We see him first turn the pages of Walt Whitman to the passage from "Song of Myself" and read "'I could turn and live with the animals, they are so placid. . . . They do not weep for their sins. They do not make me sick discussing their duty to God.'"[14] "Dope," Oliver thinks. "The Lilies of the field." His response is amplified by his father's comment: "I like the first three words: *I could turn.* Deeply felt. They would mean conversion, repentance. They might have been spoken by Buddha or by John the Baptist" (223). We see him responding to the love for life of his cousin Mario (who owes a lot to Sainty's cousin and double, Claude, but is much more richly and complexly drawn) with an exactly balanced mixture of admiration and contempt, and a feeling of guilt for both responses. We see him over and over again determining the most difficult, the most painful course of action and choosing it deliberately, like a moth the flame. When he is told, "you admit you love all these things, and yet you abandon them, while you cling to your old resolution, although you hate it," the "words pleased Oliver immensely. They were not a compliment. To be complimented was to be told what other people valued, not what you really were. Here at last was a recognition of his true nature. What a relief, what an encouragement, to be enlightened and confirmed in his self-possession, in his integrity!" (395) Paradox piles upon paradox as Oliver Alden's ethical nature is distilled painfully in the alembic of his experience. By the time the reader has finished the novel, he knows *everything* there is to know about this exceedingly complex man, who has been laid bare to such a degree that Lambert Strether, for example, in comparison, seems a pasteboard figure.

The novel of New England character could go no further. As Santayana states, there will be other puritans, but Oliver Alden is the apotheosis of the type. And the type is nothing if not self-defeating, self-consuming. Going back as far as Sylvester Judd's *Margaret* and Hawthorne's "The Artist of the Beautiful," we can observe a continuous process at work through fiction of the type until *The Last Puritan*: a refinement of sensibility until feeling becomes all in all; a refinement of ethics until action is impossible; a refinement in esthetics until the beautiful all but disappears.[15] This finest of New England novels is, then, just as self-defeating as the character of Oliver Alden. The revels are ended; no other work of the type need ever be produced.

IV Outside the Main Stream: A Survey of Lesser New England Writers

Meanwhile, back in New England, while the better writers struggled with their crippling inheritance from the puritan past, a lesser breed made do with lesser subjects. Julian Hawthorne (1846-1934) tried to struggle out from under his father's shadow with some thirty books, of which about half were novels, and a plethora of short stories and criticism. *A Fool of Nature* (1896) more nearly escapes from the sentimentality that crippled his writing than any other of his books. Perhaps his failure can best be seen in his greatest success: his measurements were kept at Harvard for years as the most perfect attainable for male physical development. Louisa May Alcott (1832-1888) had a less famous father and a greater success with *Little Women* (1868) and the various sequels it spawned. It certainly dealt with middle-class life in a manner quite different from that of writers like Mrs. Southworth, but Alcott's use of realism to increase sentimentality was too perverse to be favored by any but children and gushing girls. She had her influence and her followers, however. The best of these was undoubtedly Henri Dauge, a pseudonym of Henrietta Hurdy Hammond (1854-1883), whose *A Fair Philosopher* (1882) out-Alcotts Alcott in the closeness of Drosée and Jo, their innocence of worldliness, their ethical ruminations, and their living happily ever after.[16]

A tougher mentality is apparent from the beginning in the works of Donald Grant Mitchell (1822-1908). His early writings by Ik Marvel precede the opening date of this study and are a questionable blend of fiction and the familiar essay, but he did write a novel, *Dr. Johns*

(1866), which is one of the more successful studies of New England character. The period of the novel is the twenty years after the War of 1812, but it is not only an historical novel. In the character of the clergyman (drawn from Mitchell's own father) and the conflict of heterodox ideas with Connecticut orthodoxy, Mitchell struck the tonic chord of New England fiction. In particular, the character of Adele contrasts richly with that of Dr. Johns, a charming collision between the irresistible world of Voltaire and the immovable morality of Jonathan Edwards. The same kind of conflict lightens *The Autobiography of a New England Farmhouse* (1865), by Nathan Henry Chamberlain (1830-1901), a work which deserves better than the obscurity into which it has fallen. Covering the same sweep of time as Sylvester Judd's *Margaret*, it avoids that novel's dreaminess for a harder-edged contrast between the ages of the tough-minded puritan and the liberalism of the New England Unitarian of the mid-nineteenth century. A quite different but no less salient factor in New England life is central to *Sam Shirk* (1871) by G.H. Devereux (d. 1878).[17] Here it is the wild nature of savage New England that is the center of interest: hunting, logging, Indian life, all described with a sympathy for wildness that Thoreau confessed to in wanting to eat the woodchuck raw. The New England inheritance is apparent no less in this work than in studies of puritanism; Oliver Alden was as uncertain about what his response to nature should be as he was over more ethical questions. In *Sam Shirk* the reader is untroubled by ethics. The physical pleasures of life in nature are all in all.

Another kind of "natural" life is presented in *The Broughton House* (1890) by Bliss Perry (1860-1954).[18] The village of Broughton is more than one hundred miles away from Boston in the Berkshires, and is centuries away from the concerns of writers like Bates and Grant. Such villages were undergoing a pathetic change—the uprooting of the best young men and women who went west leaving only dregs behind. The phenomenon is described brilliantly in the works of Mary E. Wilkins Freeman. That aspect of life in western Massachusetts is not central to Perry's work. He stresses instead the nostalgic view of rural life, complete with "unforgettable characters," and especially the contrast between the unsophisticated village folk and the travelling men and vacationing urbanites who meet them on their own ground. Perry was no less a brahmin than Grant or Bates, a critic and an academic, but unlike them he turned away from the problems of his day in this work to indulge in a misty, glowing kind of genre painting.

There were as well whole handfuls of lady authors who happened to be from New England but who might be better considered in the previous chapter, so dominant is their sentimentality over their New England settings and characters. With names like Matilda Bright, Antoinette Blackwell, and Adeline Trafton Knox, their works are justly forgotten by all but the inveterate hunters of "first editions" in used book stores—alas, they rarely achieved the glory of a second edition. Nevertheless, some of them have a measure of distinction simply because of the nature of the New England heritage. Kate Carrington's *Aschenbroedel* (1882), for example, might stand as an antidote to Grant's *Unleavened Bread* in its simple (and, it must be admitted, simplistic) description of how stifling New England provinciality can be to an intelluctually curious young girl. Kate Carrington was no less stifled by the poor reception of this book; it was not reprinted and she wrote no others. More successful was Jane G. Austin (1831-1894). She wrote historical novels primarily and most successfully, but always with a New England setting. Her tendency to idealize historical characters, like Miles Standish in *Standish of Standish* (1889), probably worked to her advantage in terms of contemporary popularity, but makes her unreadable now. She was a true member of Hawthorne's "d——d mob of scribbling women," writing dozens of juveniles and nonfiction works along with her historical fiction and the odd novel. *Mrs. Beauchamp Brown* (1880) is typical of her nonhistorical fiction. In a coast-of-Maine setting chosen for its picturesqueness, she gathers an improbable crew of types and puts them through a range of catastrophes that would warm Mrs. Southworth's heart. Caroline G. Curtis (1827-1917), who also wrote under the pseudonym of Carrol Winchester, escapes the Scylla of sentimentality only to be wrecked on the Charybdis of dullness. Nevertheless, *The Love of a Lifetime* (1884) does describe New England village life with a certain realism. Caroline Chesebro (1828?-1873) does that and adds psychological verisimilitude on the old New England problem of the expiation of guilt in *The Foe in the Household* (1871).[19]

Others could and perhaps should be mentioned, but the point of diminishing returns has been reached. The good writers of New England, Mary E. Wilkins Freeman, Sarah Orne Jewett, and the great, Adams, James, struggled over that intangible, the New England heritage, using the tools of the new realism with some success. It took a great or at least a good writer to meld such intractable materials to such a demanding technique. The failure of the lesser breed is the more obvious because of the difficulty. Perhaps the case of Elinor H. Porter's (1868-1920) great success with *Pollyanna* (1912) illustrates the difficulty.[20] In an age grown sick with introspection, in the city that was the center of William James's philosophy of pragmatism, in the intellectual milieu that gave birth to Irving Babbitt's distrust for all new ideas, large numbers of people could respond to the "new idea" of Pollyannaism in spite of its ludicrous inapplicability and the sub-literate presentation of it by its author. Boston and New England had fallen on evil days indeed, and were not to recover. The literary center had moved elsewhere, as we shall see, and those who were left behind, like Mary E. Wilkins Freeman's heroines, dragged out their pathetic lives with only their dignity left to supply the pathos.

CHAPTER 4

The Rise of the South

TO turn from the writers of New England in our period to the literature of the post-Confederacy South is the most abrupt about-face possible. It is to abandon a culture in decline to embrace one in ascendence; to give up in despair on an ethical tradition grown too heavy to support its new evolutionary structures and to embrace another generating itself from nothing; to move from contemplation of a species in the process of extinction to wonder at the phoenix. In both cases the period 1865–1920 was a period of transition, but for New England the transition was to virtual extinction, while for the South it was to a flowering of incredible richness. For New England we could observe a distinct trend toward attenuation and decline in a series of minor writers all struggling with the problem of the heritage of puritanism. For the South we should be able to detect the evidence of a struggle toward the light.

From the ashes of the defeated South rose three separate and distinct strains of fiction, all of them quite different from the kind of fiction emanating from New England. Robert Underwood Johnson, who, as associate editor of *Century Magazine*, was instrumental in supporting and publishing many of the new voices of the South after the war, defined that difference:

These writers and their successors have excelled in the direct narrative style. I account for this by the fact that the South was not affected by the subtleties of Emerson or Lowell or by the other transcendentalist influences of New England literature. These did not come into its ken for those influences were related for the most part to the Abolition movement. Rather, the writers of the South derived their style from Thackeray, Macauley, Addison, and the other essayists of the Spectator type. This made them, first of all, good storytellers.[1]

He is certainly correct, and the only criticism one could have of his statement is in the unaccountable absence of the name of Sir Walter

51

Scott from his list of progenitors of the Southern writer. For it is Scott who was the principal source of the first and most important strain of the new Southern fiction, running straight from George Washington Cable through William Faulkner and including all the major writers. This is storyteller's fiction, filled with a sense of place and race, often concerned with the historical past, but dealing with it as usable myth rather than history. It is no accident that Cable intended to use the title "Jadis" for his first collection of short stories, which was published as *Old Creole Days*, as it is no accident that Faulkner hedged his fiction in biblical echoes and Thomas Wolfe developed an epical style.[2] Their concern with history is in event, and usually symbolic event, which can be converted for whatever psychological or sociological purpose they wish.

Distinct from this main stream of development but contributing to it after the period covered in this study are two subordinate lines of development, in which the minor Southern writers may be found. One, and by far the more important, was an insidious "boring from within"—the rewriting of history as romantic fiction. Thomas Nelson Page was the chief practitioner of this kind of fiction. Appearing to accept the fact of the South's defeat and the end of slavery, Page and others of his type then cast a romantic glow over the old plantation life, the epic struggle of the war, and particularly the relationship between the blacks and their white masters. The strategy is as old as the Trojan War, and worked as wells for the Southern writers as it did for Homer and Vergil. Let the winners write the histories; the losers have the advantage of the pathos of defeat for their romances. And what modern's vision of the antebellum South does not more resemble Margaret Mitchell's than that of the historians?

The second line is more direct, less successful, and harder to assess objectively. These were the writers, chief of whom is Thomas Dixon, Jr., who steadfastly held to the old ideas of race and Southern chivalry, who failed even to give lip-service to the concept of reconstruction. Fear of the black is the only constant in their works. Paternalism is possible for them, but only with the threat of the lash behind it. Blacks are divided into "good niggers" and bad, and the smell of racism is obvious in the animal and jungle imagery associated with the black wherever he is mentioned.

The constant in all three strains is history. History as myth, history as romantic shading, or history as angry self-justification—these seem fine distinctions, but they are clearly marked in the sundry works emanating from the post-bellum South. The South, even more than New England, had a mixed blessing of tradition and heritage to live down. The fact of slavery was more open and obvious than the puritan heritage, and led to more open and obvious fiction. Not that introspection and renunciation are not to be found here (Faulkner's *The Bear* is closer to Walden Pond than to Dixon's Piedmont, South Carolina), but in the minor writers of the period of our interest the capacity for subtle examination of this heritage was not yet quite possible. The main pleasure in reading these works is to watch it develop.

I   *Unreconstructed Rebels: Prenatal Pangs*
of The Birth of a Nation

The list of Southern writers who managed to carry an unreconstructed attitude through the postwar period *and* who wrote in a way to reveal that attitude *and* who managed to publish those writings is not a very long one. It is reasonable to suspect that there may be dozens of unpublished manuscripts tucked away in desks below the Mason-Dixon line which long ago made unsuccessful rounds of the Northern editors. Even the most liberal Northern editors, like Richard Watson Gilder of *The Century*, refused manuscripts that did not show a reconstructed mentality, while accepting works that tacitly presented the concept of negro racial inferiority.[3] For a Northern publisher to accept a work that had a reactionary tone on race relations required either unusual merit in other areas or pro-Southern sympathy on the part of the publisher. Lippincott of Philadelphia was often accused of just such sympathies immediately after the war, and the publication of the works of John Saunders Holt (1826–1886) might serve as evidence of Copperhead tendencies. Not that Holt's novels, written under the pseudonym of Abraham Page, are devoid of unusual merit: they are quite extraordinary in their simple style and self-assurance. Holt is a kind of slave-holding Eric Hoffer. In *The Life of Abraham Page, Esq.* (1868) and *What I Know about Ben Eccles* (1869) he presents a thesis about human development that has its attractions.[4] In brief, it is that to be a gentleman is the chief, the only value in life. So far so good. Henry James would agree. But Holt is somewhat too provincial in his outlook. He goes on to "prove" that such self-development is only possible for the Southerner, and requires the institution of slavery, which is therefore totally justified as a means to this desirable end.

Holt himself is not nearly the provincial that Abraham Page is. Through his service in the army—with Jefferson Davis in the Mexican War, as an officer of Mississippi troops in the Civil War— he had seen something of life outside the kind of country-squire existence he gives his spokesman character. Nevertheless, the novels are completely self-assured and self-justifying. His idea of culture is provincial ease and contentment. It is possible that just such works as these raised the ire of the Radical Republicans of the North to pursue the disastrous and devastating results of the Reconstruction Acts.

Less provocative to Northern feelings but probably no more reconstructed than Holt were the novels of Francis Christine Tiernan (1846-1920), who wrote under the pseudonym of Christian Reid. Born in Salisbury, North Carolina, and very much a Southern lady (she was for some years national vice president of the United Daughters of the Confederacy), she wrote novels which only happen to be laid in the South, in which race as a problem is nonexistent. Miraculously, she achieves the *status quo ante bellum* merely by fictionalizing it as so! By the intensity with which flirtations are pursued on hotel verandahs in such novels as *A Daughter of Bohemia* (1874), one could never guess that either racial or sectional tension had ever existed in the South. Negroes are present in the background, but not even as local color, and the staple of most Southern novelists of this period—the Northern man or woman who is won over by the charm of Southern character—is also missing. One finds more precision in the settings of her non-Southern books, several of which are placed in Mexico. In short, Christian Reid's novels are more a throwback to the writings of the old South; they have more in common with Augusta Evans, for example, than with Thomas Dixon, Jr., or with the unreconstructed racism of the one novel of William Falkner (1825-1889), whose *The Little Brick Church* (1882) was a direct reply to Harriet Beecher Stowe's *Uncle Tom's Cabin*— and probably an embarrassment to his more famous great-grandson.[5]

All of these writers prepared the way for the culmination of this type of fiction in Thomas Dixon's *The Leopard's Spots* (1902) and *The Clansman* (1905).[6] Although Dixon is the subject of a book-length study in this series, some mention must be made of his work here as it relates to the development of Southern self-consciousness about the question of race and tradition. He goes far beyond any previous writer on race; there is simply no precedent for the virulence of his characterization of negroes in either *The Leopard's Spots* or *The Clansman*. In his one-sidedness on this question, he stands alone among the writers of the South. Indeed, his race hatred is so great it leads him to perpetrate such melodramatic monstrosities as the famous scene in which Dr. Cameron sees burned into the eyeball of Mrs. Lenoir the rape of her daughter Marion. Aside from that *idée fixe*, his writing is typical of the New South style of fiction. His historical revisionism—typified in the conversion of Abraham Lincoln into a Southern sympathizer, indeed, from the subjective point of view of Mrs. Cameron, a Southerner—had its echoes in the works of Joel Chandler Harris and other Southerners. His defense of slavery by virtue of a comparison with Northern hypocrisy was a typical Southern argument. His emphasis on the tradition of Scottish covenanters as the Southern heritage which is responsible for the founding of the Ku Klux Klan strangely echoes a comment Herman Melville made in a "Supplement" attached to *Battle-Pieces*. Melville paralleled the situation of the Southerner to what "Burns, Scott, and the Ettrick Shepherd [James Hogg] felt for the memory of the gallant clansmen ruined through their fidelity to the Stuarts—a feeling whose passion was tempered by the poetry imbuing it, and which in no wise affected their loyalty to the Georges, and which, it may be added, indirectly contributed excellent things to literature."[7] One might even say that Dixon's at least partially sympathetic portrait of the arch-Radical Republican Stoneman was an effort at reconciliation of the two sections, as were, of course, the two sets of lovers, typically found in this sort of fiction. Thus, Dixon is far from being exceptional in his writings—except for his reactionary theory of race. Once again we have a proof of what Hannah Arendt called the "banality of evil."

II   *The Reconciliators*

That the Civil War was the most important event in American history is borne out by the literary concern which became almost an obsession in the fifty years following the war for the reconciliation of the two sections. American writers North and South at last had their "gesta Americana" as source material for romance, a material much more pliable than anything the frontier could offer. That the material was a cliché from the very beginning was not important. What novelist, looking around for a subject, could resist the lure of "Paradise Lost" for the Southerner? Derring-do with J.E.B. Stuart or Stonewall Jackson? Brother against brother, father versus son, or the overcoming of "pride and prejudice" of the sections? Cut a pattern, choose a fabric, stitch it together, and novel writing became as easy as dressmaking. The classic creations, John DeForest's *Miss Ravenel's Conversion from Secession to Loyalty*, and Margaret Mitchell's *Gone With the Wind*, span our period and more, and serve as benchmarks for the lesser works, of which we can give only a sampling.[8]

To begin with, there were the trans-sectionals: Northern writers like Albion W. Tourgee who spent time in the South and Southerners like George Washington Cable who came North. The impulse to write fiction was almost irresistible for such favored persons. William Mumford Baker (1825-1883), for example, was a Northern minister with no apparent inclinations toward fiction before the war. But, having remained in Texas with his flock through the conflict, without compromising his anti-slavery and anti-secessionist principles, he would have committed an act of heroism had he remained silent about his experiences. His half dozen novels on the subject of sectional reconciliation are undistinguished but typical of the genre. *Colonel Dunwoddie, Millionaire* (1878), for example, describes the social and financial success of a chivalrous Southerner in the North after the war. Baker parodies some of the qualities of the stock Southern colonel, but with sympathy, and stresses the theme of the reconciliation of the two sections. *A Virginia Inheritance* (1888) by Edmund Pendleton (1815-1910) is a better novel, with a broader scope and wider range of characters, but the story itself is as hackneyed as it could be. It concerns the dispossessing of a Virginia family by a Northern cousin and includes the obligatory scene of the Southerners charming the devil out of a cold Northerner who arrives prepared to despise them. When the scene then shifts to the emigration of the family to New York and their discomforts there, the novel attains a dimension not often found in this kind of writing. Pendleton had a larger sympathy than most of the trans-sectionals, having come from a Virginia family, although born in the North and serving with a New York regiment in the war. Katherine Sherwood Bonner McDowell (1849–1883) serves well as our final example. She was born in Holly Springs, Mississippi, and spent her life in the South until 1873, when she moved to the very sink of Abolitionism, Cambridge, Massachusetts, where she served for several years as the secretary to Longfellow. Under the pen name of Sherwood Bonner she wrote *Like Unto Like* (1878), which is as reconciliatory as the title suggests.[9] Indeed, her respect for the character of Northerner and Southerner alike knew no bounds.

Most of the minor writers from the South who specialized in the theme of reconciliation—Grace King, Mary N. Murfree, Thomas Nelson Page—are the subjects of book-length studies in this series, but a few who are almost as important as writers and who were certainly prolific should be mentioned here. Mary Greenway McClelland (1853–1895) knew the foothills of the Cumberland Mountains of Virginia from her youth and did for them in a dozen novels what Mary Noailles Murfree did for the hills of Tennessee. Her best novel is *Jean Monteith* (1887), a sensitive study of the legacy of the war on a young girl.[10] The local color is well drawn, and there is no cheap effort to achieve effects through dialect.

John Fox, Jr. (1863–1919) found in the Cumberland mountains of Kentucky what Mrs. McClelland saw across the state line in Virginia, but, since Kentucky did not secede and was spared the rigors of radical Reconstruction, his consideration of post-bellum social problems is less mordant. Beginning with *A Mountain Europa* (1894), through *A Cumberland Vendetta* (1895), to his immensely popular *The Little Shepherd of Kingdom Come* (1903), Fox was more concerned with detailing the beauties of the Kentucky landscape and insisting upon the ideals it fostered in those fortunate enough to live there than he was with examining the social problems incident upon the conclusion of the war. These problems are not absent in the novels, however, especially in the conflict of *The Little Shepherd of Kingdom Come*, where the force of law on the one hand and tradition on the other divide Chad Buford's family and friends as Southern or Union sympathizers. *The Trail of the Lonesome Pine* (1908) is more modern in its theme and subject, and still appropriate to the region it describes.[11] Fox represents the forces transforming the New South through a young Kentucky engineer struggling against the old feudal society. The blend of picturesque realism and personal idealism that he achieved in the novel was rewarded by an even greater popularity for that novel than he had achieved with *The Little Shepherd of Kingdom Come*, helped along, no doubt, by the popularity of the song, "The Trail of the Lonesome Pine."

Like John Fox, Francis Hopkinson Smith (1838-1915) came from a border state, in his case Maryland. But Smith's ties with the North were much closer than Fox's, and his writings about post-bellum Southerners in a series of novels about "Colonel Carter of Cartersville" reflect a larger sympathy for the Northern point of view. Smith was an engineer and engaged in construction work for the government for much of his active life (his greatest accomplishment was the Race Rock lighthouse); the connection gave him sympathy for the new industrial mentality of the Northeast, the drive and force of industry, and even, to some extent, the sophistries of business. Smith wrote a number of novels besides the Colonel Carter series, of which the best is probably *The Tides of Barnegat* (1906), but his creation of the indomitable colonel with his dreams and chivalry of a past age was his comic masterpiece.[12] Colonel Carter could have stepped from the novels of Thomas Nelson Page (who was a good friend of Smith); his darkies love him and continue to call him "marster," which Smith describes as "a title the days of freedom had never robbed him of." In turn, he is paternal with them—perhaps the foremost example of literary paternalism toward the black race outside of the works of Page.

But it is Smith's treatment of Colonel Carter's rapprochement with the ways of the industrial Northeast that distinguishes his work. Stockjobbers with names like "Klutchem" provide the conflict in Smith's Carter novels, but turn out not to be such bad chaps after all. Innocently they violate the Colonel's moral code, always at the edge of a fatal duel; innocently they crush his business plans for his "garden spots" or his "airline railway," but they are always won over to his chivalric viewpoint in the end. Clearly, what Smith intended was that the injection of Southern ideals and chivalry into Northern business practices represent the purest of marriages possible for the creation of a new American dream. Colonel Carter is the catalyst in these novels, which are really about American business and Northern society. Only he never changes; and always his innocent morality triumphs. It is all a fantasy, but a delightful one.

A most unusual strategy for the novel of reconciliation was adopted by Marion C. Legaré Reeves (1854–1898), who wrote under the pseudonym Fadette. As her maiden name suggests—it is one of the best known in cultured and intellectual Charleston society—and her *nom de plume* proves, she was no provincial Southern apologist. In *Ingemisco* (1867) she took the type of a Southern Scotch covenanter family and placed them abroad for a Grand Tour, thereby substituting one problem of conciliation for another. *Randolph Honor* (1868) and *A Little Maid of Acadie* (1888) are more conventional but still have a level of sophistication unusual in this kind of writing.[13]

Sophistication is not what one thinks of first when reading the novels of Julia Magruder (1854–1907). In her twenty-odd novels, almost all of which deal in one way or another with the problem of reconciliation, no attention seems to be paid to style, to complexity, to subtleties of any kind. What is different about her writing, and what makes her novels fascinating to read, is that beneath her simplicity, beneath the banality of her "one woman, at least two lovers" plots, she was really trying to find the answer to the dilemma of the postwar Southern girl, drawn one way by the pull of tradition and the other by what she sensed was the modern world. Her first novel has the clearly conciliatory title *Across the Chasm* (1885) and deals, predictably enough, with a Southern girl, Margaret Trevennon, who spends a winter in Washington studying Northern manners.[14] She is shocked primarily by Northern snobbishness, the concern over deciding "whom to treat civilly and whom to snub." Margaret has learned democracy by proximity with her black servants and is so sure of her gentility that the question has never occurred to her before. It is a charming paradox, akin to the old anecdote about Jefferson's walking to his inaugural being proof of his aristocratic bearing, not his democratic principles.

Unfortunately, Miss Magruder has not thought through the nuances of this position adequately, with the result that the reader sees condescension where she intends him to discover high-mindedness. Margaret is too thoughtless, too much an unquestioning product of her Southern heritage to gauge the relative merits of her simplicity in comparison to the social subtleties around her. As a first effort at the quintessential conflict of character of this type of novel, however, *Across the Chasm* succeeds rather well. It was followed by a deluge of novels by Miss Magruder on the theme of reconciliation, all with essentially the same plot, but each in turn becoming more complicated in the characters presented to the reader. *A Sunny Southerner* (1901) is representative.[15] First published in the *Woman's Home Companion* (1899), it is "magazine fiction" in the fullest sense: no hint of style or subtlety, straightforward characters, simple plot. Perhaps partly for those reasons, it is a fine and conclusive example of the novel of reconciliation.

The plot is simple. Honora Chiltern is supervising the reconstruction of her Southern family mansion, Chiltern Hall. She has hired a Northern architectural firm to design a building in the "new" style over the objections of her traditionalist father. As a result, the old plantation is humming with Northern workmen, including a laborer going under the name of Steele who seems more of a gentleman than his position would indicate, and a foppish young architect named Henry Barrett who, we are assured, is of the "Barretts of Albany," an old family. There are no surprises in the plot: Steele turns out to be Steele van Bertlandt and very much a gentleman, while Barrett is revealed as a social climber. Honora makes the obvious choice in the end, after the usual number of peripities. What is different about this novel is its details. Honora is a "new woman"; she uses slang like "I sized him up," and "that's rather too big a contract," for "I judged his character" and "that's too much to expect." She is also a complete democrat, has read Fiske's *Old Virginia and Her Neighbors* and subscribes to his theory of the middle-class origin of the "first families."[16] She is in constant conflict with her family over these matters, and manages to hold her own.

Steele is a less well realized figure. He disguises himself as a laborer to do research for a book which he hopes will aid the workingman's cause. His reading includes Henry George's *Progress and Poverty* and Kidd's *Social Evolution,*[17] but one never feels that his "radicalism" is anything more than "radical chic." When Honora's last protest to him is that she wishes that he were only a workingman because "it would be so sweet to have to struggle and suffer," his gentle reproach is "Am I less a man because I am a gentleman?" He is probably the best man she could get in such a novel, but one can't help but feel that she is compromising her ideals, even when he jokingly protests to her:

Have patience, my child; you may yet see me working by the day to support you, when I've used up all my patrimony in the way I determined to use it on the day when it came into my hands. This scheme of helping and protecting laboring men is the object to which I have vowed to devote my life, and you are the only woman in the world whom [*sic*] I believe could help me in it. (190)

The socialism is grotesque, the classlessness a facade, but however crudely, Julia Magruder has in this novel made the connection between three separate conflicts which were to bulk large in the twentieth century: she reconciles sectional conflict, economic and class conflict, and sexual discrimination in one pair of lovers. That truly is efficiency.

After the writers who made a career of novels of reconciliation comes a congeries of writers North and South—but mostly from the South—who cannot resist the odd novel of the type or the occasional situation based on the idea of reconciliation. Lydia Maria Child (1802–1880) moved from her rather successful novels of Greek and New England history to try one abolitionist propaganda novel, *A Romance of the Republic* (1867). It is about as reconciliatory as radical reconstruction was, in spite of occasional sympathetic touches. *The Little Joanna* (1875), by Elizabeth Whitfield Croom Bellamy (1837–1900), who wrote under the pseudonym Kamba Thorpe, is a novel of the New South in the old manner. It tries hard to be more than a juvenile novel by alluding to the fallen state of the South, but the problem is never central. *The Colonel's Opera Cloak* (1879) by Christine Brush (1842–1892) is more successful. It deals with the problems of an impecunious Southern family in the North, and by keeping the touch light and only implying something of the problems of reconciliation and the difficulties of unskilled Southern gentry, makes its point well. The only novel written by M. Jacqueline Thornton, *Di Cary* (1879) centers specifically on the misfortunes of a few Virginia families ravaged by the concluding battles of the war and the excesses of reconstruction. The novel is a defense of Southern resistance to reconstruction, but has a much less strident tone than the novels of Dixon. James Maurice Thompson (1844–1901) cut his teeth on the novel of reconciliation with *His Second Campaign* (1883) before he went on to better things in satire and historical fiction, notably *Alice of Old Vincennes* (1900). *His Second Campaign* effectively contrasts the idyllic life of some North Georgia hill people with the greater sophistication of the North. Amanda Minnie

Douglas's *Osborne of Arrochar* (1890) is a bit unusual, since it is set in Maryland after the war, when that very much anti-abolitionist society was converting to the spirit of the New South without the spur of reconstruction to urge it on. And finally there is William Perry Brown, whose *A Sea-Island Romance* (1888) summarizes all of the clichés of the reconciliation novels of the eighties. To that most Edenic of southern paradises, Sea Island, Georgia, come two families to be neighbors. The head of one family is an ex-planter and colonel from the South, the other an industrialist and ex-general of the North. (Even the ranks are clichés; a Northern colonel would be out of place.) The two families feud because the Northerner wants to exploit the phosphate on the island, the Southerner to protect its natural beauty. Their children play out a Romeo and Juliet drama which is threatened by a storm at sea, and the two fathers are reconciled as they pray to the same God to preserve their children. It is not the best of these novels by any means, but one would have to search long for anything more typical.[18]

III   *Into the Twentieth Century*

This survey of the two confluent streams that together fed the more prominent Mississippi of Southern writing from Cable to Faulkner helps to explain the sudden arrival of maturity in Southern writing from the 1920s on. To begin with the negative, the vein of reconciliation as theme had simply worn out by then. Like Julia Magruder—in choice of subject matter if not technical subtlety— William Faulkner, Thomas Wolfe, Robert Penn Warren, Ellen Glasgow, and the others that followed were forced to discover combinations of conflicts of the modern era to blend with the special problems of their section. The result was greater psychological complexity and a more satisfying character development. The minor writers also fixed a certain typology on the subordinate characters of the South—the Negro mammy, the comic fieldhand, the white mossback—which could be manipulated by writers of greater genius to surprise their readers' expectations. The effect is rather like that Shakespeare achieved with his manipulations of Plautan characters made common coin of drama by his predecessors and contemporaries.

Most important of all, these writers succeeded in what they

attempted to do—they reconciled the two sections of the country to each other and rewrote the history of the South. They did not deny the failures and the inadequacies of the prewar society, nor excuse the excesses of the reaction against reconstruction, but they managed to cast such a romantic glow over the whole area, people and customs, that the new historians with their more proletarian and econometric approaches have not the slightest chance of converting popular belief to the reality of Southern history. Myths are more powerful than history, as the relative importance in Western culture of Paul and Tacitus proves. The Southern writers of the twentieth century are no more than the apostolic succession of the mythmakers who preceded them.[19]

CHAPTER 5

Social Satire in the Gilded Age

THERE was, of course, much to satirize in the Gilded Age. Just as the Civil War "released" the South from its bondage to an antiquated social order and expelled it willy-nilly into the modern age, so the rest of the country found itself after 1865 with its great moral preoccupation vanished, free to pursue more secular matters. These, as is usual after a bloody war, turned out to be money, pleasure, and social advancement—exactly the usual grist for the satirist's mill. If we add to this context the other salient factors of the period—the dominance of sentimentality in fiction, the ubiquitousness of the Protestant ethic, and the rawness of the new money and the new social hierarchies it spawned—satire is almost too easy, like shooting passenger pigeons with a cannon. For it had the effect of allowing the great writers of the period to "throw away" their satire, to condense it to epigram, as in Henry James's succinct summary of the intellectual capacity of the hero of *The Bostonians*: "Basil Ransom had read Comte—he had read everything"; or to use it casually, as in Howells's soft-pedaled treatment in *A Hazard of New Fortunes* of the vulgarity of Fulkerson, in order to concentrate on the development of a complex character.[1]

The easy availability of subjects for satire tended to make the next rank of writers concentrate their fire on the more serious issues, like politics and the extremes of economic and social deprivation. These writers are therefore more properly discussed in the last two chapters of this work. These exclusions leave an enormous residue, however. As sentimentality faded in popularity (or became *infra dig*) for that mass of "d——d scribbling women" Hawthorne complained about, they easily shifted their attention to the social abuses so prevalent and visible around them. Thus there remains more than a sufficiency for this chapter of social satirists who had something to say, who wrote well at least some of the time, and who are, nevertheless, forgotten today. What they had to say was generally critical of the power of money to corrupt, of social stratification to abase, or of the seeking of pleasure to pervert normal human development. They said it in novels set in American cities from New York to California and among sights familiar to American tourists all over the world. And, more often than not, they said it from the mouths of characters who are little more than types, who are set in stock situations, and who accept without criticism the general validity of the three parts of the Protestant ethic—success, piety, and reform. Their novels are a comparative pleasure to read today—comparative to the sentimen-alists—but what they leave unchallenged by their satire gives their measure as much as the abuses they attack.

I   Mercator for the Gilded Age:
Charles Dudley Warner (1829-1900)

If the "Howells revival" ever succeeds—if Howells ever achieves the status of a "living" writer, like James and Twain, instead of the cold, dead position he has among professors of American literature as the "Dean of American letters"—then a Warner revival may not be far behind. Charles Dudley Warner was everything Howells was—and a little less. Indeed, he seemed to dog Howells's footsteps, succeeding him at *Harper's* at the "Editor's Study" in 1892. Like Howells also, he came to fiction through the travel book (if we exclude his early collaboration with Twain on *The Gilded Age* [1873], which has little to recommend it beyond its giving a name to the period). His early travel books, from *Saunterings* (1872), through *My Winter on the Nile* (1876) and *In the Levant* (1877), to *Our Italy* (1891), allowed him to develop a capacity for wry observation of character and place that is far superior to the adolescent boisterous-ness of his collaboration with Twain. It was not a very long step from this kind of writing to completing the persona of fiction in *Their Pilgrimage* (1886), a book bridging travel writing and fiction in exactly the manner of Howells's *Their Wedding Journey* (1871).[2] Warner mastered the technique no less well than Howells: nearly equal parts of place and character; the place seen through an innocent, often a foreign eye, and interpreted by a sympathetic, humane, slightly conservative spokesman who sees through the hypocrisies, small and large; a counterpoint provided by several type characters, of which usually two are female, one incredibly innocent, the other archly worldly.

In *Their Pilgrimage* the emphasis is barely on place, generally the watering resorts of the wealthy and fashionable of the Northeast, ranging from Newport Beach to Bar Harbor, Maine. But in spite of the fact that the book was written expressly to accompany the engravings by G. S. Reinhart, Warner's fictional characters and their witty and sensible commentary make the work an effective piece of satiric fiction. He had to change little but his emphasis from place to character to move up to the trilogy that crowned his career, *A Little Journey into the World* (1889), *The Golden House* (1895), and *That Fortune* (1899).[3]

Time and the critics have not been kind to Warner's trilogy, which was intended to be an epic work describing the creation, perversion, and destruction of a great fortune based on stockjobbing, preceding Norris's effort at the same sort of thing about wheat. There is no doubt that each novel individually is flawed. *A Little Journey into the World* suffers from slow development, a narrator whose commentary intrudes too regularly upon actions that really need no comment, certainly not his heavy-handed irony, and from a failure to explain satisfactorily the moral dissolution of its heroine. In *The Golden House*, authorial intrusion is even more disturbing, since it definitely goes against the grain of the action, and the "just deserts" it proclaims ring hollow, smacking of the wish-fulfillment plots of Mrs. Southworth. *That Fortune* is patently unbelievable in its insistence that ideals gained through exposure to great literature at an early age can persist through the trials of maturity in a setting where they are ridiculously inappropriate.[4]

Taken together, the effect of the three novels is rather different. It is true that one has to forgive much. No modern reader can resist skimming the many pages of authorial commentary that interrupt the movement of the plot and add nothing but the obvious, however wittily pronounced, to the thematic development. In the first novel Warner was clearly aiming at something like the effect of the chorus in Greek drama; the commentary is individualized, set clearly in the moral certitude of "Brandon" (for which read the social milieu of the Warner family in Nook Farm, outside of Hartford), and had specific reference to the social rise and moral decline of Margaret Debree, an erstwhile member of that circle. Most of that justification disappears in the second and third novels, and it is inadequate in the first. If didacticism is, as many think, the curse of the nineteenth century, here is its full noxious flower. One can not excuse the fault in Warner, but there are extenuating circumstances. His intrusions are often witty and bitingly ironic. Moreover, he had a cause which he must have believed amply justified these lapses from what he knew was the approved technique of his day. He remained a moral idealist to the end, and fought with this and other techniques in the three novels against what he saw to be an amoral or even immoral realism in literature. Perhaps he can be forgiven a fault that he shares with writers as varied as Hawthorne in his almost gloating intrusion over the death of Judge Pynchon in *The House of the Seven Gables* and Baudelaire in a poem like "Correspondences."[5]

What remains of the three novels is well worth reading. The mortar that holds them together is one character who is central to no single volume but is, nevertheless, the protagonist of the trilogy. Carmen Eschelle is the woman Rodney Henderson should have married in *A Little Journey into the World*, but he does not correct his error until the last paragraph of that novel. She then takes a back seat to her husband's financial manipulations and their effects upon the hero and heroine of *The Golden House*, Edith and Jack Delancy, until the end of that novel, when she successfully betrays Henderson's intention of leaving his money to charity. She is then forced into a marriage with her co-conspirator, Thomas Mavick, in *That Fortune*, only to watch the money disappear at the hands of an even more unscrupulous operator. Had Warner published the three novels of the trilogy together as one massive triple-decker, Carmen would be commonly compared to Becky Sharpe. She is completely unscrupulous, marvelously resilient, and utterly charming.

Moreover, the three novels together do succeed in developing a coherent theme which is epical and American. The first novel illustrates what scruples must be overcome in the gaining of a great fortune, how larger ideals must be subverted to defense of the nuclear family, and how, under these circumstances, ideals can be made to appear to support the most morally obtuse intentions. The second volume deals directly with the social responsibility that large amounts of money bring and the inherent conflict in the very concept of philanthropy. *That Fortune* resolves the contradictions most happily with a redefinition of culture that separates that much-abused concept from the world of money entirely. Each of these themes is also present in the other two novels, but in those it is presented contrapuntally. Thus, though the three novels seem structurally loose, they actually form a lengthy three-act tragicomedy of American high finance—no mean accomplishment. Dos Passos' *USA* reaches no higher and no lower on the American social scale for its material, is hardly less didactic, and is structurally less well organized.[6] All Warner really lacked to produce a great book was a technique to match his moral earnestness, to disguise it in a "newsreel" instead of intruding it authorially.[7]

Of the three novels, *A Little Journey into the World* is the most interesting, probably because the full conception of the trilogy is implicit in it. Carmen Eschelle is fully developed at her first appearance in the novel. At the opera (Wagner), she appears in vivid contrast to Margaret Debree in her sophistication, wit, and easy relationship with two men, Henderson and the English earl-to-be, John Lyon, whom Margaret has just refused to marry. Her quick eye senses the relationship, and she pursues her intuition in a social call. She is on such easy terms with Henderson that a modern reader would assume that they were lovers, which of course was far from Warner's intentions. She loses him even though he knows that she would make a better wife for him:

In all his schemes he found the thought of Margaret entering. Why should it not have been Carmen? he sometimes thought. She thoroughly understood him. She would never stand in the way of his most daring ambitions with any scruples. Her conscience would never nag his. She would be ambitious for a career for him. Would she care for him or the career? How clever she was! And affectionate? She would be if she had a heart. (139)

The concept Warner here develops is an important one. Although the American young-man-on-the-make would do well to marry a worldly woman, he does not. Instead—because of the reading of too many novels? because of the Puritan heritage? because of an unconscious desire to corrupt purity? surely not—he chooses the Iron Maiden to test against his will. He does so because he sees woman's duty as the civilizing of men, and he imagines no conflict between this duty and the making of a great deal of money. The theme of woman's role as civilizer is developed indirectly in the novel, but it is the dominant motif. Margaret chaffs a foreign visitor that it will take another century to civilize men because it is so difficult to "get the cruelty and love of brutal sports out of them," to which he replies, "Then you'd cease to like us. Nothing is so insipid, I fancy, to a woman as a man made in her own image (254)." At the end, the role of woman as civilizer is used as the key to the moral compromise of Margaret's relationship with her husband. She comes to see her role as civilizer to be subsumed in a larger role as the end product of the civilizing process. The conclusion is given in her own words in one of Warner's most telling images:

"See that flower before you.... See the refinement of its color and form. That was cultivated. The plant came from South America. I don't know what expense the gardener has been to about it, what material and care have been necessary to bring it to perfection.... You cannot put any of your mercantile value on it. Well, that is woman, the consummate flower of civilization. That is what civilization is for." (349)

Margaret's decline in sickness follows shortly, melodramatically, after this scene. Duration of bloom is not a quality sought after in hot-house societies. The less sensitive plant, Carmen, endures through three volumes. Margaret is the victim of a specifically American misconception typified by the slogan, "Why not the best?" Idealism betrayed into a context of materialism is surely the worst— and the most American—of faults.

The corruption of Margaret into bloom and death is contrasted with the selfless love in poverty and squalor of Ruth Leigh and Father Damon of *The Golden House* and the intellectualized ideality of the love between Evelyn Mavick and Philip Burnett in *That Fortune*, and, of course, the lesser domestic felicity of Carmen with Rodney Henderson and, later, Thomas Mavick. Margaret is the only tragic character of the three novels, and thus the center of everyone's attention. But surely Warner intended her as but one example in a myriad of cases exploring the relation between private lives and social responsibility. She is no Isabel Archer, nor was meant to be. Rather, in terms of the three novels, her role is to "swell a scene or two," and perhaps, to play "sometimes the fool."

The satire in these three novels is hardly at all dependent upon the larger structure of each novel or the trilogy. Warner is best in the telling satiric scene—a conversation with a young Adventist aboard a train, a "dunking" baptism in the chilly Connecticut River, a conversation between Carmen and Jack Delancy detailing the nuts and bolts of social climbing, scenes on Wall Street, at the opera, at various watering places. One of the best, because it is consistently understated, occurs in *A Little Journey* at a garden party in Lenox, where Margaret chats with Mr. Summers Bass, a writer of the realistic persuasion. He tries to impress her with the details of his craft:

"See that young woman upon whom the sunlight falls standing waiting her turn. See the quivering of the eyelids, the heaving of the chest, the opening lips; note the curve of her waist from the shoulder, and the line rounding into the fall of the folds of the Austrian cashmere. I try to saturate myself with her every attitude and gesture, her color, her movement, and then I shall imagine the form under the influence of passion. Every detail will tell. I do not find unimportant the tie of her shoe. The picture will be life."

"But suppose, Mr. Bass, when you come to speak with her, you find that she has no ideas, and talks slang."

"All the better. It shows what we are, what our society is. And besides, Mrs. Henderson, nearly everybody has the capacity of being wicked; that is to say, of expressing emotion." (243)

When she leaves him, he surreptitiously enters into his notebook the phrase "the prosperous propriety of a pretty plutocrat," which he intends to use in his forthcoming novel, "The Last Sigh of the Prude."

Warner could never be considered even an important minor novelist; he too generously emphasizes his faults in his trilogy. But he does range farther among the social levels and pick out more of the foibles of the period than any of the social satirists below the level of Howells and James. He successfully refrains from picturing his capitalist villains as the epitome of evil, in the manner of Holland, and he is neither the mossback that Robert Grant proclaims himself to be nor as morally uncertain as Arlo Bates is at his best. Having given the name to the Gilded Age, he managed to write one of the best delineations of its worst qualities. Comparing his trilogy with Howells's *A Hazard of New Fortunes* or James's *The Princess Casamassima* would serve no useful purpose.[8] Those novels are on a plane Warner never approaches. But perhaps in the very crudeness of his earnest moral position he more closely represents his age than they, all burdened with talent and genius as they are. His is the middle ground of the faulty moralizer, Juvenal for the philistines, who probably understood him better for the fact that he never rose above their appreciation.

II *Sitting Ducks: Social Satire about New York*

A simple listing of the works that satirize New York society in the last half of the nineteenth century and beginning of the twentieth would probably run nearly to book length. A city that could bring together Harry Thaw and Stanford White along with Evelyn Nesbit, that could send Gorky home because he was travelling with his mistress, that could sponsor tenement reform but deny the East Side to "literature" for Stephen Crane, is too easy a target. Southern writers could not resist; when they wanted to justify their "peculiar institution," a quick look at New York snobbery made the point. Regionalists, realists, and naturalists all drew from the joint-stock material of a society universally scorned and jealously admired for its effete, snobbish, and parvenu qualities. Edgar Fawcett (1847–1904) made a career out of some forty-odd novels and plays ridiculing the pretensions of what O. Henry came to call Baghdad-on-the-Hudson. It is an embarrassment of riches. What follows, therefore, is merely a sampling of some representative types of social satire aimed at the sitting ducks of New York society.

The seductive allure of New York society as a subject for satire may be seen in the late career of William Starbuck Mayo (1811–1895), who will always be best known by his exotic satires in the manner of Melville's *Mardi, Kaloolah* (1849), and *The Berber* (1850). These works allegorize satire on American society, but Mayo dealt more directly—and brilliantly—with New York in *Never Again* (1873). Abandoning his earlier technique of indirection, Mayo cut right to the center of the question of the power of money to establish the hierarchy of New York society and set a standard of irony that few of the satirists who followed him could reach. Since he had himself experienced varied societies, primitive and civilized, during his travels in Africa and the Near East and residence in New York, he wrote with a cosmopolitanism appropriate to the eclectic tastes of New York social climbing. Less cosmopolitan but no less biting in their satire were the New York novels of Edwin Lasseter Bynner (1842–1893), of which *Tritons* (1878) is the best.[9] Bynner, like Robert Grant, was a lawyer who gathered some of the best of the raw material for his fiction in his office as legal consultant for the rich and powerful. Having practiced law in St. Louis and New York before settling in Boston, he knew firsthand three different kinds of society and could skewer the vulgarities of each. One of his New York plutocrats proclaims that his drawing room needs to be redone. He decides "to have the walls covered with Japanese stamped leather, with a dado of ebonized cherry carved in cameo, after a medieval design of hunting scenes and insignia. . . . The ceiling I shall have painted in panels and cross-hatched with ebonized moldings, while for the frieze I am going to have a facsimile cast of the Parthenon actually set in the wall." One would suspect Bynner of hyperbole if he were unacquainted with the reality of New York fin-de-siècle taste in decoration.[10]

Although she too had a good deal of cosmopolitan experience to draw from, the New York society novels of Constance Cary Harrison (1843-1920) are definitely written from within the milieu she exposes. Born of a Virginia family that descended from Thomas Jefferson on one side and the "Virginia Fairfaxes" on the other, she had impeccable social credentials when she married the private secretary of Jefferson Davis, Burton Harrison, moved to New York City, and soon rose to become a leader of its society. Her first efforts at fiction, *Golden Rod: an Idyll of Mount Desert* (1880) and *The Story of Helen Troy* (1881), are anything but satiric. They accept at par the superficial values of the New York drawingroom, the cottage in the Berkshires, and the Marie Antoinette style of pastoral in Maine. Hooking the right husband is sufficient justification for almost any kind of behavior. But in *The Anglomaniacs* (1890) Mrs. Harrison reveals a capacity for satire that is as striking for what it reveals about those aspects of social behavior that are acceptable and those which are not.[11] Her irony is directed at the newly rich and their efforts to gain position among older, more secure families, and particularly at the aping of English manners and styles as a short-cut to the top. This novel must surely have the lengthiest and most detailed analysis of the advantages and disadvantages of marrying a lord as a means of social climbing. Even the pursuit of a lord has its virtues, and may be used to interest eligible homegrown males, while some behavior that verged for the time on the scandalous is shown to have value in the always amusing gymnastics of social climbing. What is implicit in all this, of course, is that the game is worth the candle. It took writers less firmly ensconced in the higher tiers of society than Mrs. Harrison to question that assumption.

If the "English connection" is the major cliché of New York social satire, the young female Lochinvar riding in from the West and viewing society with a primitive eye is the next most popular. Indeed, the two are most often found together. In the novels of Mrs. Mary Elizabeth Wilson Sherwood (1830–1903) the prairie blossom more often than not gets transplanted transatlantically, to the great chagrin of the parvenus who snubbed her closer to home. Mrs. Sherwood, like Mrs. Harrison, is of the best New York society, so her satire is directed at the lower and younger reaches. In *A Transplanted Rose* (1892), Rose is an irreverent Western type who is cultivated by the best and scorned by the less secure social types.[12] The technique is pure James Fenimore Cooper translated to high-societese. *Natural* goodness like Natty Bumppo's is discernible only to the highly cultivated eye; the natural grace and simplicity of the raw, untutored girl are detected only by the socially secure member of society, while the climbers see only her indelicacies. When she marries her Englishman, of course, they all see—either to their delight or their chagrin.

To conclude this *tour d'horizon* of social satire on New York, one should return to its base—the money that built it. William Henry Bishop (1847–1928) had a career typical of the third- or fourth-drawer "literary man" of the period. He began writing as an avocation, discovered it paid well enough to eke out his own birthright to the level of a sufficiency for travel abroad, and produced kudos enough to garner him an academic post at Yale to comfort his declining years. In his fruitful years he essayed just about every style and genre possible for a man of modest talent. He was most comfortable in the standard romance of the American abroad. *Detmold* (1879) is about a young American architect in Italy. But he wrote travel works of mild scholarship—*Old Mexico and Her Lost Provinces* (1883)—and tried his hand at regionalist local color in *The Golden Justice* (1885), which is set in Milwaukee. It would be extraordinary if such a journeyman *literateur* did not try his steel on New York society. *The House of a Merchant Prince* (1882) is chiefly of interest to the Howellsians as a predecessor in several ways of *The Rise of Silas Lapham*.[13] Its central moral issue is a tricky and complex question of a forgery that was believed to have taken place, and might have taken place, but did not. Bishop's technique is also subtle and Howellsian. The connection between the making of money and the achieving of social position is omnipresent but rarely directly stated. Instead Bishop concentrates on the piling up of details that imply success and failure in society and business as parallel functions. His use of understatement and the telling detail might well have influenced Howells, since the novel ran in *The Atlantic Monthly* just after Howells left that periodical, and he must have read it.

If this section on New York social satire seems skimpy and truncated—the last novel considered was published in 1890—there is a very good reason. The conditions that allowed for naive satire of the kind discussed here, in which the basic concepts of the Protestant ethic and the correctness of social stratification remain unchallenged, were no longer possible after about 1890. As a result, the writers who were able to see the opportunity for satire were either such good writers, like Ernest Poole and David Graham Philips, that they have been analyzed in individual volumes of this series, or they found their interest turned to larger questions of social inhumanity and are considered elsewhere in this study. Probably the genre continued past 1890—probably it is alive today. But almost by definition, the shooting of sitting ducks is a sub-literary pastime. When satire attacks what is no longer germane and leaves the indefensible alone, it is no longer satire.

III   *Some Sub-genres of Satire*

American satire almost always has as its principal targets money, social position, and power. In only a relatively few novels the emphasis shifts. One subject, which follows logically after a consideration of New York social satire, is the satire of societies that are not as cosmopolitan as New York, but ape it more or less successfully. Kamba Thorpe, the pseudonym for Elizabeth Whitfield Croom Bellamy (1837-1900), disguised a writer with a deft if popular touch for the anomalies of provincial society. Her *Four Oaks* (1867)[14] examines the life of suburban society in Netherford, an archetypal habitation, which serves as an "island" in the Norman Douglas sense of the word, where people of sundry backgrounds intermingle. Mrs. Bellamy has a fair capacity to pick out the telling nuance of the climber, the husband-hunter, and the bit of local color which defines a certain kind of American society away from the centers of culture.

Philadelphia has always suffered from comparison with New York. For that reason it is a little difficult to determine if Harford Flemming's *A Carpet Knight* (1885) is really intended as satire.

Harriet McClellan's other novels are not notably satiric, but this one is so firmly set in a society which compares itself to New York and Boston in such preposterous ways that one must give her the benefit of the doubt about her intentions. One has no doubts about *A Foolish Virgin* (1883) by Ella Weed (d. 1894). The setting of Cincinnati society, so self-conscious about being "Western," so eager to entertain Boston ideas, however ludicrously they are presented, so ripe for "culture" that the heroine takes up china-painting, because "in Cincinnati one must do something," is even more of a sitting duck than New York. The same is true in spades for Marie Healy Bigot's *Lakeville* (1873), one of the first novels about social doings in Chicago.[15] In this novel the rawness of a newly emerging society is completely laid bare: the intense pursuit of money, the complete lack of cultural amenities, the creation of a social hierarchy without any cultural justification whatsoever. The local color of this novel in its "Lakeville" setting at least (the action moves to Europe in the last half) is impressive compared to the kinds of novels we have been considering.

Another sub-genre of satire is the roman à clef and a difficult one to analyze it is. To be effective satire, such works must present characters whose disguises may be pierced to reveal the real people being satirized. The reader of a later age, no longer aware of the ephemeral events which provide the keys to the novel, is at a disadvantage. Thus the reviewer of W. H. Rideing's *A Little Upstart* (1885) for the *Boston Literary World* assured his readers that "through a thin veil of fiction we discern a company of men and women, many of whom, notwithstanding their disguises, we are sure we know." Unfortunately, he did not specify his identifications, and they were lost to this reader. Miriam Belknap, the heroine, is undoubtedly a complete fabrication; but the modern reader would like to know who Rideing had in mind for the social-climbing poet, Mrs. Ames, and several other less splenetically satirized members of Boston's literary set. We are more fortunate with *Miss Bayle's Romance* (1887), an otherwise undistinguished satire by W. Fraser Rae.[16] Here the people satirized are either given their own names or easily recognized anagrams. The most interesting of these is "King Edwards" for Edward King and the Prince of Wales. Except as social chit-chat and literary gossip, however, the novel is unexceptional. It does serve as a bridge to a third sub-genre of satire to be considered, in that it is completely concerned with the "international theme," the "American girl abroad," the confrontation of American innocence with European corruption, a topic so common among novels of this period that it demands separate consideration.

Miss Bayle's Romance is based upon the real career of a Miss Chamberlain, daughter of a stockjobber from Cleveland, who had an enormous success abroad with, among others, the Prince of Wales. But, if her career is based on fact, her character is surely more derived from prototypes like Daisy Miller and Isabel Archer than from "poor real life." All the qualities Daisy revealed in 1879—her refreshing honesty, her flaunting of convention, her simple belief in her own innocence—had become clichés eight years later. Indeed, it is sometimes hard to tell what Rae is satirizing, Miss Bayle's naiveté or the exaggerated English appreciation of it. The sexes are reversed, but the clichés continue in *Almost an Englishman* (1878) by Moses L. Scudder (1843-1917).[17] In this novel two Americans, the anglophobe Ketchum and the anglophile Hill, invade England and return with appropriate marital booty. Most of the satire derives from the expectations of the English they encounter, who have conceived American manners from the works of Mrs. Trollope almost exclusively. There is a good deal of reference in the novel to spitting on carpets, although that action is never actually performed.

American social climbing abroad is the satiric subject of Lucy H. Hooper's *Under the Tricolor* (1880). The principal concern of the book is the colony of American expatriates in Paris, ashamed of their American heritage, and trying, by every device, fair and foul, including conversion to Catholicism, to break into either the English or the French resident *haut monde*. They are a pitiful spectacle, and the satire is brutal indeed. In *Bledisloe* (1887), by Ada M. Trotter, exactly the opposite is true.[18] The novel is about the stay of two lively American girls in a sleepy English town. They have a number of adventures, meet some fascinating people, and make many transatlantic friends while constantly comparing things American with things English. The satire is gentle as the characters are endearing.

In summary, a few conclusions may be made about satire in the Gilded Age. To begin with, inclusion within this category is a sure criterion for relative failure as a novelist. Social satire within the structure of the Protestant ethic became the genre for scribbling women and men, as sentimentality lost its allure with the reading public. The larger events of the period—the corruption and scandals of the 1870s, the beginning of class warfare in the eighties and nineties, the decadence of the *fin de siècle*, and the rise of anomie and *angst* as forerunners of modernity—swept the better writers of the day away from the social concerns that dominated this lighter fiction. Those who remained to work within the genre in any way revealed in the lightness of their treatment of social evils the paucity of their own moral force. What remains is anything but Augustan satire; it is rather social chit-chat written from only the shakiest perch upon the morally indefensible. It is perhaps justified in what it attacks and what it defends; the substitution of money for culture, the febrile strategies of social climbing, and the unjustified self-satisfaction of having arrived at the top will always be material for satire. But the great themes lay elsewhere, and the better writers sensed that much at least. One need not worry about the suitability of one's wallpaper when Armageddon is at hand.

CHAPTER 6

Exotics, Fantastics, and Cowboys

WHILE the mainstream of American fiction bubbled merrily along from the psychological romance of Hawthorne and Melville to the psychological realism of Howells and James, and the underground current splashed from the sentimentalists to the gossip of social satire and the novel of manners, another tradition persisted among a small group of writers but an enormous audience of readers. American literary critics and historians have never been at ease among the writers of fantasy and exotic romance, perhaps because such literature is so far from the mainstream, perhaps because its enormous popularity makes it suspect. The genre persisted into a contemporary respectability not unrelated to the fact that its most important modern practitioners are academics of flawless repute. In the period 1865–1920 it remained mostly underground, in the dime novels of the House of Beadle and its followers, and periodicals typically hidden in the corn-crib. It surfaced into respectability only occasionally during the period, notably in the works of Frank R. Stockton (1834–1902), in a spate of utopian novels in the 1890s, and in the perfection of the myth of the cowboy and the wild west. Writers in the genre are consistently underestimated by most critics, partly because their defenders so consistently overestimate them.

I Frank R. Stockton and the Romance of Fantasy

The quality most outstanding in the writings of Frank R. Stockton is a kind of boyishness, an untrammeled enthusiasm possible only for someone who, in maturity, never lost the easy expectations of youth. It is no surprise, then, to read in a lightly fictionalized biographical story which he never managed to place with a publisher that he had from the first an easy-going attitude toward life and literature that was never to leave him. He wrote in "What Can I Do for an Old Gentleman," while still in his teens, that he wished to enjoy life as he worked, not after his work was done, and he was by no means a fool—so he tried Literature. Everyone knows there are two ways by which a man can make money by the joint labor of his brain and pen. One, is to learn the business as you would a trade, and become a journalist, employed by those who will harness your Pegasus, but will at the same time provide him with oats—the other is to write what one pleases, as one pleases, and endeavour to find someone who will also be pleased with it—and pay for it.[1]

It is both Stockton's strength and his weakness that he never had to revise those attitudes. Although he seems to have drifted into writing by accompanying his engravings with texts, the truth is that he wrote prolifically from his adolescence, and managed to publish almost everything he wrote later, after he became popular. Thus his mature production seems uneven because his earliest stories were published simultaneously with some of his latest and best work.

There can be no doubt, however, about the success of the longer adult fiction of his mature years. Beginning with the loosely novelistic frame of the stories collected in *Rudder Grange* (1879) and its sequels, *The Rudder Grangers Abroad* (1891) and *Pomona's Travels* (1894)— all published serially much earlier than their copyright dates— Stockton gave free rein to an imagination that always threatened to run off with him, but never failed to delight a constantly growing readership. Imagination is the key word to describe his writing. Either outrageous and farcical settings or actions are accepted with complete aplomb, or his characters turn the humdrum into the exotic by their extraordinary behavior or perceptions. *The Casting Away of Mrs. Lecks and Mrs. Aleshine* (1886), probably his best novel of this type, illustrates the technique perfectly.[2] In the face of shipwreck and the threat of drowning, the two mature ladies draw from their treasury of middle-class skills what is necessary to survive, using brooms as paddles, breaking out sausages and cheese in the middle of the ocean—preserved, one assumes, for just such an occasion—and paying their board religiously to the absentee landlords on their desert isle—after deducting a proper amount for their housekeeping. At the other end of the scale, when they return to Mrs. Aleshine's very ordinary Pennsylvania farm with three entranced sailors in tow, the sailors determine, as a gesture of appreciation, to paint the farm in the stripes and colors of shipping companies all over the world, "until an observer might have supposed that a commercial navy had been sunk beneath Mrs. Aleshine's house grounds, leaving nothing but its smoke-stacks visible" (282). The art of understatement, dead-pan comedy in prose, found its highest development in Stockton's works.

In spite of his febrile imagination, Stockton was not immune to the dicta of literary fashions, but as one might expect, his efforts toward literary realism are somewhat halting and tentative. His best work in that vein is *The Hundredth Man* (1887).[3] Verisimilitude in that novel is created by the scenes describing the events in a New York restaurant, done very much in the style of Daniel Defoe in places (for whom, along with Charles Dickens, Stockton always professed admiration). But truth to detail about the preparation and serving of food at Vatoldi's is counterpointed by some of the wildest and most comic flights of his imagination in the story of the strike of the restaurant's waiters, who want to wear dress coats instead of aprons and jackets. It is an industrial strike as seen by Hollywood casting offices. Picketers carry signs with biblical overtones like "Eat not at the house of the oppressor!" A renegade scab is placarded, while dining:

YESTERDAY THE BOYCOTTERS GIVE ME
TWO DOLLARS
TO PLAY SHAM, AND TO-DAY I AM PAID
THREE DOLLARS
TO EAT, DRINK, AND BE MERRY. (139)

Interwoven with the scenes of the restaurant is the main plot of the novel, from which it gets its title. Horace Stratford is a wealthy modern Diogenes looking for the "hundredth man," whose humane qualities distinguish him from the other ninety-nine. His fantasy leads him to interfere with an engagement, which in turn entangles him with the novel's heroine, Gay Armatt. His redemptive manipulation of her toward a more suitable mate, Arthur Thorne, earns him the role of the "hundredth man" in his own and the reader's mind. It is all very gently comic, full of social *savoir faire*, and ripe with the kind of imaginative detail one expects from Stockton. The concerns of the late nineteenth century are all present—industrial strife, the unease of the wealthy in the face of their social obligations, the strain of the newly rich when they have no tradition to channel their ideas of *noblesse oblige*. But the concerns are transmuted in the crucible of Stockton's imagination to the farcical strike, Stratford's redemptive quest, and the final determination of J. Weatherby Stull, the secret owner of Vatoldi's, to create a "law hospital" with the earnings he has gained from his restaurant's marvelous oyster stew.

Stull's "law hospital" is typical of Stockton's prescience, more often remarked by critics in his technologically futuristic novels, like *The Great War Syndicate* (1889) and *The Great Stone of Sardis* (1898).[4] The law hospital is an act of extrapolation of present "technology" into the future no less than the others. Philanthropists had long been founding hospitals and endowing universities; Stull, with something of his creator's imagination, joins the two matrices of philanthropy as usually practiced toward the ill with his recognition of the legal plight of the poor, to invent a concept only now gaining acceptance in American society, legal "clinics" available to those who suffer most from the necessary imbalance of a capitalist economy. It is the mark of Stockton's rich imaginary powers that he virtually throws away this truly remarkable insight in *The Hundredth Man.* His invention of "negative gravity" backpacks, from which the Buck Rogers creation and the modern real thing descend, dates from 1884, but is more striking than the "law hospitals" only because of our intense preoccupation with the more flamboyant qualities of technological advance in comparison with more meaningful progress in social matters.

The Great War Syndicate, like "negative gravity," captures our imagination because of the technological fascination of inventions like the "Repeller," an ironclad ship with a long-range cannon which fires with deadly accuracy because of a computer-like aiming device. What ought to impress us about the novel is the creation of a military-industrial complex in the "War Syndicate" which is more powerful than the governments of the states in which it thrives, and which forces a *pax Americana* upon an accepting world. *The Great Stone of Sardis* is filled with technological miracles—a submarine under the North Pole icecap connected to New York by an umbilical telegraph cable, a ray for seeing through successive strata of the earth's surface—but its sociological savvy is no less striking: the hero, having discovered an enormous diamond at the North Pole, buries it to save the world from the economic disruption it would create. Comparison with F. Scott Fitzgerald's "Diamond as big as the Ritz" is inevitable; where Fitzgerald's vision is apocalyptic, Stockton's is hopeful. The good sense of Mrs. Lecks and Mrs. Aleshine persists into what for

Stockton was undoubtedly a future filled with as many possibilities as dangers. It is hard not to love such a writer, however one feels about the tough-mindedness of his vision.

Stockton has been called the "principal humorist of the genteel tradition" and accused of "letting his lively fancy go its happy way in many books, some of them dictated while he lay at ease in a hammock . . . in the midst of all the crowding issues of [the eighties]."[5] Those issues are not absent from his writing, as we have seen, but they are seen in a larger, happier context as a result of that "lively fancy." Undoubtedly Stockton's reputation has suffered simply because of the time in which he happened to be writing. Now that the pendulum is swinging back from the excesses of dogmatic realism, now that writers like Jorge Luis Borges, John Barth, and Vladimir Nabokov are the fixed points of light of our firmament (not to mention J. R. R. Tolkien, C.S. Lewis, and T.H. White), perhaps it is time for a Stockton revival. Surely the author of "The Lady or the Tiger?" cannot be considered psychologically naive, however fantastic his creation. The same is true for the sociology of *The Great War Syndicate* and the economics of *The Great Stone of Sardis*. Undoubtedly he wrote for an audience that appreciated him for the wrong, escapist, reasons, and he fell into a decline when those reasons had become suspect; now that the assumptions of both the "genteel tradition" and the "age of realism" are no longer current, Stockton deserves a rereading and reappreciation.

II   *John Ames Mitchell (1845–1918)*
and the Romance of the Apocalypse

If Stockton's happy situation allowed him to invoke and smooth over a vision of the future into purest fantasy, John Ames Mitchell's brought him closer to those who felt and feel that the American dream is nightmare. As Stockton began his career by using his talents as an engraver, Mitchell began as an artist, at Phillips Exeter Academy and Harvard and at the Ecole des Beaux Arts in Paris. Mitchell chose to "harness his Pegasus" as a journalist, however, and that rein on his fancy led him into darker valleys than any Stockton imagined. Mitchell was the founder and first publisher of *Life*, a satiric weekly which during Mitchell's tenure was more like the *Harvard Lampoon* than the slick weekly it became after it was bought in 1936 by Time, Incorporated. As a satiric publication, it was a rather scattershot affair, concerning itself as much with unburning issues like women's dress fads as with the great social problems of the Age of Transition. But Mitchell did not turn his back on the larger issues of the Gilded Age; his attacks on the giants of capital brought his magazine repeated libel suits and even the threat of physical violence toward himself. His social conscience during these years was raised to a far higher level than Stockton ever reached.

At about the age of forty-five, ripened by many years of life in New York and proximity to the centers of political and economic power, Mitchell turned more and more to fiction. His early efforts were incredibly crude, but showed from the first what direction he would take. *The Last American* (1889) is a novelette which a modern high-school sophomore might be proud to have written, but hardly anyone of greater sophistication.[6] It is written as a fragment from the journal of Khan-Li, a prince of "dimph-yoo-chur" and admiral in the Persian navy. Khan-Li is in charge of an expedition in the year 2951 which rediscovers America. His helmsman is named "Grip-til-lah" and among his companions are "Nofuhl," "Ad-el-pate," and "Bhoz-ja-khaz." Most of the humor, alas, comes from these funny names, which is perhaps the kindest thing one can say about the work. The expedition arrives in a deserted, ruined New York, and, after some rather pointless tomfoolery based on linguistic interpretation of broken inscriptions, gets down to some satire on manners, mores, and politics. American women are accused of going about too much in the world, blushing too little, and managing their own lives. Irish politicians come in for their share with the discovery of a half dollar minted in 1937, during the reign of Dennis Murphy, the last of the Hibernian dictators. Yellow journalism is scathed for providing scandal in place of responsible reporting, and the American reading public for tolerating the situation. It is all farfetched and almost embarrassing in its naiveté.

Then the ship, the *Zlohtuhb*, sets sail for Washington, where the last American is encountered. A father and his daughter create an "international incident" by serving their guests raw whiskey and then misinterpreting a courteous kiss by one of the Persians. In the ensuing struggle, the American fights gamely, but is overwhelmed. If satire is intended, it is hard to say what it is directed upon, beyond the anachronistic assumption that these Persians persist after an ultimate oil crisis.

Such senescent juvenilia are interesting only as a preparation for Mitchell's more important works, of which the best are *Dr. Thorne's Idea* (1897), a study of deviant behavior based ultimately, like Frank Norris's *McTeague*, on Lombrosso's ideas about heredity, and *The Silent War* (1906).[7] The apocalyptic vision of *The Silent War* makes the novel kin to the savage utopias of writers like Ignatius Donnelly, while Mitchell's obvious sympathy for "good" capitalists, like his hero, Billy Chapman, shows that he is not far from the Christian socialism of Howells and H. G. Wells. The central idea behind the silent war is simply a bad guess about the future of industrial relations in America. Instead of a rapprochement between big business and big labor, a single organization of workingmen called the People's League is approaching the numbers necessary to elect its own president and congress, and threatening to create an income tax, "to tax the millionaire for the benefit of the working man, instead of taxing the working man for the benefit of the millionaire (125)," as the system of tariffs did when the novel was written. Such reform is only what Billy Chapman himself had argued for among his plutocratic colleagues. But the League has fallen into the hands of a sinister Committee of Seven who, not content with their approaching victory at the polls, are attempting to hurry up the process by a particularly cold-blooded scheme of extortion. They have a list of millionaires whom they approach for a "donation" of $200,000 for the League. Those who refuse are murdered. After a few murders, the word gets around, and the treasury is filled. The murders themselves are interesting, rather like the reputed Mau-Mau terrorists in Kenya. Each millionaire is "set up" by his own servants, but slain by someone else's. Billy Chapman, as a scrupulous millionaire, is, of course, in a terrible bind; sympathetic as he is to the ends of the People's League, he can not tolerate their methods, and so refuses to pay. He is preserved by the most unlikely of coincidences, but one can hardly accuse Mitchell of manufacturing a happy ending. There is every indication that in spite of Billy's specific fate, the People's League will prevail and the Committee of Seven, with its extraordinary fund-raising capacities, will become the power behind the American government. One thinks of the news stories of the junctures among the Mafia, the CIA, and the Teamster's Union and shudders. Certainly no writer presents such a chilling picture of the relations between crime, business, and labor until Ira Wolfert's *Tucker's People* in 1940.[8]

Mitchell's radical vision is the more striking for his obvious sympathy for capitalism. Although he does caricature the greedy industrialist, banker, and Solid Citizen as foils, most of the wealthy characters in the novel (all who are given names) are quite sympathetic. They argue with the caricatures about the morality of their positions and espouse socialistic (or at least paternalistic) views. Above all, they themselves illustrate, and they urge upon the others, an avoidance of conspicuous consumption. As one of them says,

I would suggest . . . that being recognized as gamblers, you make yourself less conspicuous. Try to travel without private cars. Avoid getting the best of everything by extravagant fees. Give people of moderate means a chance to get what they pay for. (62)

On the other hand, Mitchell does not make the Committee of Seven terrifying. They are described as definitely "not anarchists in appearance." Rather, they have the air of "prosperous workingmen— or skilled mechanics," which, of course, makes their cold-blooded extortion and murder scheme the more horrendous. And their arguments, as Mitchell presents them, are unanswerable, even by his sympathetic spokesman for capital, Billy Chapman.

"The working people of this country, Mr. Chapman, are on the ragged edge of revolt. You rich men, here in the East, have no conception of the bitterness—the deep resentment—at the conditions that result in this unequal distribution of wealth. Those who work the hardest get the least."
"If you can believe that American workmen are worse off than those of other countries, you can believe anything."
"That is not the question. In a country like this, there is plenty for all; plenty of food, clothing, space and fuel, more than enough for everybody. Why should a few have not only the best of it all, but a thousand times more than they can use, while all the others, those who work the hardest, live in attics and cellars, eat the meanest food and never enough? And all in a land of plenty. You will admit there is something radically wrong when a few are amassing fabulous fortunes and many, however industrious, can barely live." (121–122)

Moreover, Mitchell again and again makes the point that extortion and murder as political weapons are merely an extension of business principles. A spokesman for the Committee of Seven makes the exact point to Billy: "We are merely meeting you capitalists on your own ground and with your own weapons. You hold us up with your trusts, your tariffs, your irresponsible and somewhat peculiar management of the people's savings. Is it not better that a dozen or more millionaires should quietly disappear, especially if they prefer death to parting with a fraction of their fortunes, *than that mobs should rule?*" [italics added] (123) The managerial quality of the last clause carries real terror in it. Both sides decry anarchy; each sees the means as justifying the end. Apocalypse is rarely so orderly and reasoned. It is a "silent war" indeed, and the more frightening for that.

Mitchell's later novels decline in their quality and their ferocity, but *Drowsy* (1917)[9] deserves some discussion as a fantastic romance in the science-fiction vein à la Frank R. Stockton. Cyrus Alton gets the nickname "Drowsy" from his tendency toward fantasizing, but he hitches that sin to the wagon of a sound technological education at Harvard and M.I.T. and develops a new "electro kinetic" force which he uses to power a spaceship. A trip to the moon yields the discovery of a long-dead civilization and, more practically, a 3000-caret diamond, which he just happens to pick up among the rubble on the moon. With his newly acquired wealth and a promise not to flood the market with more stones, he continues to dabble in science, including thought-telegraphy and the first trip to Mars. His thought-telegraph works with his beloved, and his spaceship fails, the two phenomena joining to provide a happy ending with no hint of future disruption of the diamond market or the orderly growth of technology. The novel is interesting primarily as a corrective to the reader who might have misunderstood the lesson of *The Silent War*: Mitchell's vision of the ideal future is a benign capitalism based upon the combination, typically American, of inventiveness and the laws of the marketplace as described by Adam Smith.

The two novels by Mitchell define rather neatly the two kinds of futuristic romance spawned at the end of the nineteenth century by the success of Bellamy's *Looking Backward* (1888). Like *Drowsy*, Albert Chavannes' *The Future Commonwealth* (1892) and Solomon Schindler's *Young West* (1894) are more concerned with technological marvels than with sociological problems; like *The Silent War*, Henry Olerich's *A Cityless and Countryless World* (1893) and Costello N. Holford's *Aristopia* (1895) center on the organizational and sociological changes created by new societies evolving out of the inequities of the rampant capitalism of the late nineteenth century.[10]

Of the dozens of romances of technology produced before 1920, the best were produced by a hackwriter writing anonymously for a dime novel series called The Frank Reade Library. Luis P. Senarens (1865–1939) wrote under the pseudonym "Noname" an incredible series of adventure novels for boys which anticipated the science-fiction boom of the twentieth century. He orbited one of the first space satellites in *Lost in a Comet's Tale* (1895), invented the helicopter in *Frank Reade, Jr., and His Airship* (1884), and designed the first robot in *Frank Reade and His Steam Man* (1876). His inventiveness was doubtless spurred by the formidable competition of the writers of other juveniles like the Tom Edison, Jr. series published by Street and Smith and equivalents in the Beadle series. Works for more mature readers were not lacking in predictions of airplanes, automobiles, and space travel. The journey to Mars had become almost a commonplace by the time Drowsy blasted off, while labor-saving devices in works like Chauncey Thomas's *The Crystal Button* (1891) were reducing the workday to four hours.[11]

Technological advances could create dystopias like Donnelly's *Caesar's Column* (1890) and Twain's *Connecticut Yankee in King Arthur's Court* (1889) and a few lesser works, but more frequently were combined with social advances to produce true utopias. C. N. Holford's *Aristopia* (1895) set limits on ownership of private property which effectively did away with greed. Albert Chavannes' *Brighter Climes* (1895) combined the best of socialism in production and individualism in distribution for his "Socioland" in Africa. Henry Olerich's *A Cityless and Countryless World* (1893) described a Fourieristic world of ideal communities of one thousand members each. And so, to use a phrase made current by a much later utopian, it goes. The literary value of these works is virtually nil, and their historic and sociological value is generally restricted to those who are interested in the lunatic fringe of social change. No student of nineteenth-century history and culture can afford not to read the best writers in the genre—Bellamy, Howells's *A Traveler from Altruria*, Twain's *Connecticut Yankee*.[12] But research beyond the next level, Stockton and Mitchell, is better left to the specialist and the enthusiast for utopias, science fiction, and juveniles.

III   *Towards the Cowboy: Thomas A. Janvier (1849–1913) and Mary Hallock Foote (1847–1938)*

Writers of the period did not have to go as far as Mars to find the exotic, of course. The West, with its blend of the Garden and the

Desert, its possibilities for untold wealth in gold or sudden and cruel death at the hands of savage Indians, provided an *exotica Americana* as suitable to romance and fantasy as the most esoteric utopia. The mythos of the Western novel had already been set with Cooper's Leatherstocking tales; all that the writers of the period 1865-1920 added were refinements to the genre. Nevertheless, these refinements define the transition from the romantic age to the modern age for the novel of western adventure no less well than the equivalent works of New England, the South, or the utopians.

Cooper's novels are all based upon a sophisticated vision of the contrast between nature and culture. That sophistication is continued in the writings of Thomas Allibone Janvier, particularly in his remarkably successful Western novel, *The Aztec Treasure House* (1890). Janvier's life and works divide into three neat segments: Western travels, bohemian life in New York's Greenwich Village, and travels and studies in Provence. For the purposes of this chapter, only his Western travels are directly significant, but the evidence of his good-humored appreciation of bohemianism in his first book, *Color Studies* (1885), and his later association with Mistral and the *Societé de la Félibrige* in Provence suggest the breadth of his range and his eye for the telling detail.[13]

The immediate inspiration for *The Aztec Treasure House* was undoubtedly H. Rider Haggard, especially *King Solomon's Mines* (1885) and *She* (1887).[14] In the characters gathered together to make up the expedition—an anthropologist, an heroic priest, a competent metallurgist, an ex-railway shipping clerk from Massachusetts, an Indian boy and his burro, El Sabio, "the wise one"—in the succession of dangers and mysteries, from savage Indians to mysteriously sunken cities, the style is pure Rider Haggard. But Janvier did more than merely transplant African adventure to the Southwest. His narrator, Professor Thomas Palgrave, Ph.D. (Leipsic), is a wonderful creation, doubtless drawn to some extent from Janvier himself. In the midst of whatever excitement occupies the foreground of the book, the Professor is as often as not bemused by some linguistic or anthropological aside. Indians are about to try to take his life; he muses that the expression is "an imperfectly expressed . . . concept for life can be taken only in the limited sense of depriving another of it; it cannot be taken in the full sense of deprivation and acquisition combined" (93). In the midst of a bloody retreat, he apologizes for the brevity of his account:

I cannot tell very clearly how our retreat to the Citadel was managed, nor even of my own part in it; for fighting is but rough, wild work, which defies all attempts at scientific accuracy in describing it—and for the reason, I fancy, that it engenders a wholly unscientific frame of mind. Reduced to its lowest terms, fighting is mere barbarity; a most illogical method of settling some disputed question by brute force instead of by the refined reasoning processes of the intelligent human mind; and by the anger that it inevitably begets, the habit of accurate description, is hopelessly confused. Therefore I can say only that foot by foot we yielded the ground to the enemy that pressed upon us. (342–343)

And, whenever he reaches the limit of fantastic description the reader is likely to swallow, he refers him to his soon-to-be-published magnum opus, *Pre-Columbian Conditions on the Continent of North America.*

The other characters on the expedition are hardly less well realized. The heroic priest, Fray Antonio, has a streak of pedantry that delights the narrator; moreover, his heroism itself is suspect with its almost pathological search for martyrdom. The incredibly competent engineer, Rayburn, and the comic low character, Young, are stock creations, but they succeed in surprising the reader from time to time, Young on the social structure of the Aztec society they encounter, Rayburn with some shrewd and arch comments on human nature.

The novel includes surprisingly little "local color" of the Southwest which is at all specific. The adventures with the latter-day Aztecs are located in a never-never land which is only generally remarkable as sub-tropical. There is a good deal of social comment of a vague utopian sort in the description of the Aztec society. It seems the ancient Aztecs under the wise king Chaltzantzin practiced a kind of eugenic breeding system: all persons who, on coming to maturity, were judged weaklings or cripples, were to be killed. As soon as the law was in effect the weak-kneed liberals began tinkering with it, changing it after Chaltzantzin's reign to create a class called "Tlahuicos," who were to be permanent slaves and the pool from which the human sacrifices were drawn. One would think the Tlahuicos as a breeding pool would create an inferior society, but that was not the case. Developing over the centuries as a separate caste, yet reinfused with each generation of cripples and weaklings, the Tlahuicos had become a proletariat bubbling with revolutionary fervor, and with a natural connection to a "liberal" wing of the ruling class—the relatives of each generation's weaklings and cripples. The revolt turns out to be abortive, however, since the army remains loyal to the despotic priest-captain. All of this is interesting in itself, but it is made more so by the comments of Young and Rayburn, likening this rather exotic society to standard American politics. The priest-captain "goes in for Boss management and machine politics . . . as straight as if he was a New York alderman or the chairman of a state campaign committee in Ohio. . . . Where our chance comes in is in having the respectable element, the solid men who pay taxes and have an interest in decent government. . . . They may not pay taxes here, but that's the kind I mean," says Rayburn (232). It is likely that Janvier intends some sort of political comment with the Tlahuicos, perhaps alluding to the situation of the blacks in America, perhaps directing some satire toward liberal reformers. If that is the case, he has not succeeded in making any point very well, since everyone seems to lose in the end except the intrepid foursome.

It is too easy to poke fun at this novel, and it is unfair and unwise to do so. For all its faults, it succeeds admirably as a romance of adventure and develops some thought-provoking ideas about ancient Indian culture and the clash of that culture with the modern ethos. The blend of archaeology, sociology, and derring-do that Janvier managed with this novel was not to be seen again in the genre until Willa Cather's *Death Comes to the Archbishop*, where, to be sure, it was done much better.[15] *The Aztec Treasure House* is valuable as a pioneering work, and remains well worth reading.

At the opposite extreme from Janvier's adventure novel is Mary Hallock Foote's sensitive study of Western life in the mining camps, *The Led Horse Claim* (1883).[16] Where Janvier's writing is all mystery, suspense, and violent action, Mary Hallock Foote retells the Romeo and Juliet story in a setting remarkably apt for it—rival mines on opposite banks of Led Horse Gulch, Colorado. The plot itself is fatuous, in large part through no fault of Mrs. Foote. Her original story had the lovers separating at the end, but a happy ending was forced on her by her editor.[17] The setting is authentic and extremely well realized. Mrs. Foote had been living in Leadville, Colorado, where her husband was a mine manager, for years. And if as a woman she could perhaps not observe, let alone write about, those segments of crude Western society which provided the staple for Joaquin Miller or Bret Harte, her astute observation and recording of the problems of genteel living in such raw surroundings is the more interesting.

The two novels together represent the parameters of Western fiction. Janvier's writing involves myth, action, esoterica; Mrs. Foote's precise observation, manners, the exoteric made interesting by its curious setting. The two possibilities of technique were to be continued in Western novels through the period to 1920, with only the occasional writer able to combine them effectively, as Owen Wister did in *The Virginian* (1902), and Eugene Manlove Rhodes did in a series of novels.[18] Favoring either a mythic quest or local color, the "cowboy novel" developed into a distinct genre between these two antithetical directions. And, while the foremost practitioners of the genre have been well studied in this series, several noteworthy writers somewhat below the level of Wister and Rhodes demand our attention.

IV   *Pioneers of the Cowboy Myth*

In spite of precursors like Cooper's *The Prairie* (1827) and Washington Irving's *Adventures of Captain Bonneville* (1837), the "cowboy novel" as developed in the twentieth century was essentially fixed as a genre in the 1890s and 1900s.[19] Its earliest manifestations are not novels, but histories of the brief epoch during which the cowboy of myth and movie came closest to existing: the years 1865–1880, when all the "events" of the cowboy novel were briefly present: the Great Cattle Drive, the extermination of the buffalo and the Indian, the great popular expansion westward and the subsequent closing of the range. The cowboy figures in all aspects of this period. Although he is most prominent in the cattle drive and the closing of the range, he lends his type to the hunting of the buffalo and the genocide of the Indian.

It is almost impossible to discover the inventor of a cliché like the cowboy; there are too many parts to the production-line model added by too many different hands to allow the historian to determine specific origins. Therefore it is probable that Emerson Hough (1857–1923) added little to the archetype of the cowboy, even though his *The Story of the Cowboy* (1897) is the first and among the best of the early descriptions of the cowboy type, and he certainly did not allow mere facts to interfere with his mythic creation.[20] *The Story of the Cowboy* is hackwork from beginning to end, totally dependent upon secondary sources and extremely uncritical in its handling of those sources. Hough's purpose is clear from the very first words of his introduction—to raise a monument to the type of the cowboy which would persist into an age when he was no longer present:

> The story of the West is a story of the time of heroes. Of all those who appear large upon the fading page of that day, none may claim greater stature than the chief figure of the cattle range. Cowboy, cattle man, cow-puncher, it matters not what name others have given him, he has remained—himself. From the half-tropic to the half-arctic country he has ridden, his type, his costume, his characteristics practically unchanged, one of the most dominant and self-sufficient figures in the history of the land. He never dreamed he was a hero, therefore perhaps he was one. He would scoff at monuments or record, therefore perhaps he deserves them. (viii)

It is precisely such a figure that Hough presents to the reader—and proceeds to alabasterize permanently: "the virile figure of a mounted man. He stood straight in the stirrups of his heavy saddle, but lightly and well poised. . . . a loose belt swung a revolver low down upon his hip. A wide hat blew up and back a bit with the air of his travelling, and a deep kerchief fluttered at his neck" (viii). Such writing hardly even pretends to be anything more than fiction, and throughout *The Story of the Cowboy* Hough's eye is on the epic, the heroic, the archetypal. His consideration of "Society in the Cow Country" is a brief for a Warner Brothers set, introducing each type with statements like, "there was always a sheriff in a cow town, and he was always the same sort of man—quiet, courageous, just, and much respected by his fellow-men" (241), repeating the same kind of guff about the newspaper editor, the lawyer, the saloon-keeper, the gambler, and all the other clichés of the Western. Had he individualized his characters at all, his "history" would have been a full-fledged novel.

Not that *The Story of the Cowboy* is completely without historic relevance. Hough's description of the cattle drives is generally accurate, as are his comments on the range wars of the eighties, including a history of Billy the Kid which is remarkably unromanticized. But no effort toward historical accuracy can possibly counterbalance Hough's obvious intentions toward the picturesque in such paragraphs as this one:

It is high and glaring noon in the little town, but it still sleeps. In their cabins some of the men have not yet thrown off their blankets. Along the one long, straggling street there are few persons moving, and those not hastily. Far out on the plain is a trail of dust winding along, where a big ranch wagon is coming in. Upon the opposite side of the town a second and more rapid trail tells where a buckboard is coming, drawn by a pair of trotting ponies. At the end of the street, just coming up from the *arroyo*, is the figure of a horseman—a tall, slim, young man—who sits straight up on his trotting pony, his gloved hand held high and daintily, his bright kerchief just lopping up and down a bit at his neck as he sits the jogging horse, his big hat pushed back a little over his forehead. All these low buildings, not one of them above a single story, are the colour of the earth. They hold to the earth therefore as though they belonged there. This rider is also in his garb the colour of the earth, and he fits into this scene with perfect right. He also belongs there, this strong, erect, and self-sufficient figure. The environment has produced its man. (262-263)

Was ever a writer more self-consciously engaged in archetypal creation? Does not such writing constitute a kind of fiction, however disguised as history? And, of course, the work was incredibly successful, reprinted many times in the twentieth century and plagiarized in general and in detail by hundreds of writers, including Hough himself in later novels like *The Covered Wagon* (1922).[21]

If *The Story of the Cowboy* is mythic creation posing as history, Andy Adams's *The Log of a Cowboy* is the same thing as autobiography.[22] Adams (1859–1935) gives a name to his persona, Thomas Moore Quirk, but no commentators on *The Log of a Cowboy* have been fooled into thinking that the narrator was anyone other than Andy Adams, whose experiences of trail drives exactly correspond to those of the *Log*. What no critics have noticed is that Adams uses the same archetypal techniques as Hough, except that his Tom Quirk and colleagues are individualized to the point of having names and escaping the "earth-colour" implications so patent in Hough's description.[23] They are nonetheless complete archetypes, romantic versions of what such revisionist histories as Frantz and Choate's *American Cowboy Myth and the Reality* (1955) have shown to be entirely the creation of nostalgic and romantic imaginations.[24] Tom Quirk is no more Andy Adams than Ishmael is Herman Melville—which is to say, of course, that he is something more. Through Tom, through the other characters in the *Log* and the stories they tell around the campfires, myths, not history, come into being.

The *Log* is filled with details about a specific trail drive from the Mexican border through Texas and the plains to Montana—but so is Faulkner's *The Bear* about a specific hunt.[25] The *Log* records faithfully virtually every kind of event possible on such a drive, river crossings, stampedes, debauches in towns along the trail, information about the handling of cattle specific enough to generate a textbook on the subject—but so does *Moby-Dick* on whaling. When all the details and trifles are added together with the epic setting and underplayed but heroic style, it becomes clear that the purpose of the book is not to detail a historical phenomenon but to generate a continuing myth. Instead of a stuffed carcass in a museum, Hough and Adams give us live wings for our imagination. Ours and central casting's.

And therein lies the difficulty. If Oedipus is a myth, so is Mickey Mouse, and, somewhere in between, Rip van Winkle. There are Mickey Mouse cowboys, a plethora of them. Frank H. Spearman (1859-1937) created a true archetype with *Whispering Smith* (1906), whose title character speaks so softly that he is given this soubriquet despite his accomplishments with a six-shooter.[26] Alas, throughout the novel all he does is whisper and shoot villains until the reader could hardly care less. So much for Mickey Mouse. The Oedipuses of cowboy fiction are to be found in works by writers like Zane Grey, Eugene Rhodes, and Walter van Tilburg Clark, and are therefore outside the limits of this study. But several other writers have managed to create characters of considerable mythic dimensions who are nevertheless largely forgotten.

Stewart Edward White (1873-1946) was something more than a hackwriter, though the fifty or so books released under his name would seem to argue to the contrary. His Western fiction has a definite sense of place in spite of the fact that his travels in the West were limited. But in characterization he worked well within the Emerson Hough tradition of the man produced by his environment. In particular, his first three novels, *The Westerners* (1901), *The Claim Jumpers* (1901), and especially *The Blazed Trail* (1902), present the archetypal Western hero—a man thoroughly schooled in his craft, self-reliant in the Emersonian tradition, always quietly confident of his ability to cope with the unexpected, and answerable only to his own conscience in moral matters—that is, willing to take the law in his own hands, usually by way of a Colt .45. The variations on this theme are endless, in White's novels of the West and in the genre as a whole, but the main characteristics of the Western hero remain constant from Natty Bumppo to Shane and Destry, and White was not the one to experiment rashly in this field. A later trilogy based on California history, *Gold* (1913), *The Grey Dawn* (1915), and *The Rose Dawn* (1920), shifts the emphasis from the Western archetype to the influence of place upon character, but these are perhaps not properly cowboy novels.[27] White also wrote adventure novels about Africa and works on spiritualism, but his Western books are the basis of his reputation, and they are eminently readable.

Two otherwise quite minor novels illustrate how the cowboy hero's willingness to stand outside the law marks the major area of influence of this genre upon modern literature. Charles C. Park's *A Plaything of the Gods* (1912) is based upon the real life of Joaquin Murieta, the California bandit.[28] The novel traces Murieta's life from his early days as a devout Catholic to his conversion to a blood-thirsty bandit intent upon revenging the wrongs done him and his Spanish colleagues by the American invaders of California. The emphasis in the novel is always on the factors justifying Murieta's behavior and the quality of fairness that he presents as he administers his own brand of justice. In one sense, the novel harks back to the old Robin Hood ballads, but in tone it is much closer to the modern cult of the anti-hero that is best illustrated in the movie *Bonnie and Clyde*. In the growth of that genre the cowboy novel is central, marking the line of descent from Emerson's comment that he would prefer to be "the devil's child" than submit to moral judgment other than his own, through Twain's Colonel Sherburn, to Berger's Little Big Man, to mention only the most "western" of the modern examples. Self-reliance and transcendentalism may mark the beginning of the tradition, but it is the American frontier and the cowboy myth that allowed it to develop.

Roger Pocock's *Curly* (1905) illustrates the other value to be derived from the cowboy myth.[29] This novel is virtually a Populist tract in its insistence that the large landowners, the banks, and the politicians are leagued against the poor farmer-cowboy, who must turn outlaw in order to survive. The satire is not subtle here, but the technique is pure. Through the innocence of the cowboy and his innocent eye, the hypocrisy of society can be laid bare most effectively, and the cowboy's resort to extralegal practices seen only as his marching to a different drummer. Thus the genre has enriched the modern complex novel with its expansion of the transcendental paradoxes first proposed early in the nineteenth century.

CHAPTER 7

The Political Novel

IN 1870 Mark Twain visited Washington, attended several sessions of Congress, and met with President Grant in the White House. The experience was, he noted, "a perfect gold mine" for fiction. He mined the ore with Charles Dudley Warner for *The Gilded Age* (1873) without refining it very much, but set a tone for the topical aspects of the political novel which was to last until the first World War.[1] For Twain and Warner the conflict between ideality and corruption centered on the politics of Reconstruction, with its equal opportunities for the perfecting of the state and the "general grab." But, although *The Gilded Age* is firmly placed in the topicality of post-bellum scandal, it presents through the characters of Laura Hawkins and Senator Dilworthy the generic conflict of the need for power to do good versus the inevitability of corruption. Washington, for all its vulgarity, its rootlessness, its antipathy for culture (a "select reception" is one in which there are only "invited guests"), draws Laura like a magnet with its waves of amoral energy. To convert that energy to social reform seems to her one of the most meaningful ways to spend her life—and almost leads her to disaster at and in the hands of Dilworthy.

The pattern has been repeated over and over again during the past century by writers as various in their talent and political persuasion as Henry Adams (*Democracy*, 1880) and Henry James (*Pandora*, 1884) to the latest clutch of post-Watergate romans à clef.[2] Unfortunately, the problems of writing a topical novel about politics in Washington make it difficult for even the best writers to succeed. As Joseph Kraft noted in a review of post-Watergate fiction,

The best novels are made of more common clay than presidents and senators . . . The egoism of the famous makes war on Trollope's iron dictum that "there must be love in a novel," for the great love chiefly themselves. High public events tend to undermine the requirement that in fiction character is fate. Events, far more than character, determine action.[3]

Thus even the best writers, Twain, Adams, James, recognizing that their efforts were unsuccessful, turned to other topics for fiction (or, in Adams's case, to other forms—the *Autobiography*—to examine the topic).

So the lure of "the gold mine" was meretricious, a lode of fool's gold at best. As we have seen, the minor writers of our period chased the vein assiduously. Southern writers particularly found it hard to resist the impulse to scathe the North by attacking the most southern of its cities in novels written about the Reconstruction period. Robert Grant took some of his best shots at "the democracy" in *Unleavened Bread*, only to be impaled, finally, on the ambiguity of the ethic he assailed.[4] There is probably a political reason behind these failures, deducible especially from Grant's example. While the ethic of the reading public and the majority of writers was staunchly conservative, and the political attitude crying to be pilloried in political novels was populist corruption, all of the political *energy* and, finally, social benefit was mingled inextricably with that corruption. It is from this crucial ambiguity that Grant's protrait of Lyons in *Unleavened Bread* fails fatally; Thomas Dixon's portrait of the radical Republican Stoneman falls apart even more disastrously through the same fault. The ethos of politics is simply too complex to yield to the surgeon's scalpel of satire.

From the period 1865-1920 we will examine four works of political fiction which represent the problems of writing such fiction and some solutions to those problems. It will be clear that the quality of these novels varies considerably and that none is totally successful. But each illustrates the problem of the relationship between political activity and individual morality, public and private behavior, and the question of "engagement" of the author. Quality usually depends on the writer's ability to recognize the complexity of the political process and to eschew satire at the expense of the basic moral ambiguities involved: contact with and belief in the wisdom of the untutored and unwashed multitude; log-rolling and compromise; and, yes, bribery and corruption. Political fiction, like politics, is no place for the moral absolutist.

I *Frances Hodgson Burnett (1849-1924)*, Through One Administration *(1881)*

No political novelist—not Henry Adams, not even John Ehrlichman—had a better background for a novel about Washington than Frances Hodgson Burnett. Of fairly cultured English background, with all that implies toward her acceptance in polite American society, married to a professional man with a turn for research and scholarship, and a near neighbor and friend of the Garfield family, she had access to both the "best" and the most powerful social circles in the capital. Her use of this background material is exceptional; everything is understated, and the reader is given the distinct impression of the provinciality of Washington, of its absorption in the pointlessness of politics, office-seeking, and log-rolling, without any appearance of effort on Mrs. Burnett's part. Rarely does one read a book with such apparently effortless blending of the specific and the universal as in *Through One Administration*.[5] The "one administration" is unnamed, a cycle of growth and change for the characters, unquestionably political in that it destroys here, brings success and happiness there, but the reader does not know even if it is Democratic or Republican!

The plot centers around Richard Amory's corruption and moral destruction over the "Westoria" land claim, certainly a typical boondoggle of the time, but the introduction to it and the step-by-step disintegration of Richard are handled so delicately that the effect is anything but portentous or caustic, with never a hint of satire or moral unction. Richard's involvement comes out of his romantic attachment to the original story of the lands; at his deepest and darkest period in the lobbying for the railroad connection that will either make him rich or destroy him, his pleading is always touched with an element of truth. When the inevitable bribe passes hands, it is thrown into the fire unopened, and we never know what or how much it was. And Mrs. Burnett is careful to point out that the essential problem of lobbying is psychological—determining who must be bribed, who can be moved by reason or scruple, who can be badgered—and that these categories are constantly shifting.

Political reality provides a deep and subtle background for the events of the novel, a rich texture without easily definable shapes and forms. For example, although there is never a mention of party affiliation of any of the major or minor characters, the novel constantly suggests the high visibility, the eminence, and the possibility of power, notoriety, or fame that comes from high position. When Bertha is threatened with social ostracism, it is the wife of the Secretary of State, the highest cabinet position, who comes to her aid. Power—almost always in its potential rather than its kinetic form—underlies every action of the novel. It is present on the streets and in the drawing rooms, and has its own fascination:

It was the rule, and not the exception, that in walking out he met persons he knew or knew of, and he found it at no time difficult to discover the names and positions of those who attracted his attention. Almost all noticeable and numerous unnoticeable persons were to be distinguished in some way from their fellows. The dark sinewy man he observed standing on the steps of a certain family hotel was a noted New England senator; his companion was the head of an important department; the man who stood near was the private secretary of the President, or the editor of one of the dailies, or a man with a much-discussed claim against the Government; the handsome woman whose carriage drew up before a fashionable millinery establishment was the wife of a foreign diplomat or of a well-known politician, or of a member of the Cabinet; the woman who crossed her path as she got out was a celebrated female suffragist, or female physician, or lawyer, or perhaps that much-talked of will-o'-the-wisp, a female lobbyist; and eight persons out of every ten passing them knew their names and not a little of their private history. So much was crowded within a comparatively limited radius that it was not easy for any person or thing worthy of note to be lost or hidden from the public eye. (155)

It is this context of power, eminence, energy that electrifies the otherwise mundane materials of the central plot of the novel. Philip Tredennis, a character much like Dobbin in Thackeray's *Vanity Fair*, returns to Washington after eight years on the frontier to discover that Bertha Herrick, the young lady he should have pursued before he left, has married a moral lightweight, Richard Amory, and has a social butterfly named Lawrence Arbuthnot fluttering about her flame. Scandal seems inevitable. Tredennis vows to devote himself to the well-being of his lady fair, à la Sir Launcelot, and hovers about her for the remainder of the novel, protecting her reputation, saving her from adultery with Arbuthnot only to make her wish for the same fate at his hands! Meanwhile, Richard, having become deeply committed financially to a land scheme, urges Bertha to lobby for him with several interested politicians. When the bubble bursts, Richard is disgraced but Bertha, staunchly defended by Tredennis, is not.

This mush is made more than palatable by the political context. Tredennis, as a natural man more at home in a tepee than at a soirée, provides an essential moral counterweight to the very subtle relation-ships among the more sophisticated. Indeed, it is hard to imagine that Mrs. Burnett did not intend a rather sly parody of the "verray parfit gentle knight," like Holland's Jim Fenton of *Sevenoaks*, since Tredennis is *so* good and *so* pure that it is clear to any reader that his martyrdom is inevitable.[6] Without Tredennis, the novel, which was widely criticized for its "dangerous tendencies,"[7] was probably unpublishable; with him shining as a moral exemplar, Mrs. Burnett was free to explore the subtle shadings of Washington morality.

A moral chiaroscuro is evident in all parts of the relationship between Richard and Bertha Amory and Lawrence Arbuthnot, and its operative theme is one appropriate to the capital city—the need for "having an object." The concept is first raised in relation to Arbuthnot, who is presented as the typical victim of the imperma-nency and relativism of politics; having failed to get an important position with the new administration, he is always aware that the position he does hold is neither permanent nor related to his level of competence. His response to this condition of anomie is to reject all political values and to live only a social life, and that devoid of passion. His momentary temptation to seduce Bertha once past,

he was not fond of affairs, and even his enemies were obliged to admit that he was ordinarily too discreet or too cold to engage in the most trivial of such agreeable entanglements.

"If I pick up a red-hot coal," he said, "I shall burn my fingers, even if I throw it away quickly. Why should a man expose himself to the chance of being obliged to bear a blister about with him for a day or so? If I may be permitted, I prefer to stand before the fire and enjoy an agreeable warmth without personal interference with the blaze." (345)

How Washingtonian it seems to have discretion or coldness as a substitute for virtue—which explains the public's relative tolerance for the occasional sex scandal that is exposed in Washington.

Richard Amory is an even more complex character than Arbuth-not. Instead of having no "object," he has many. Like so many of Henry James's villains, he is an *amateur*, with collections of various kinds serving his need for an objective in life. He is of the natural *aris-toi*, having money, social position, and a beautiful and charming wife: hence he is pointed out to visitors to Washington as one of those who naturally exercise power. He is certainly not an evil man, and his moral crime is really social. In his eagerness to push his land scheme to a successful conclusion, he makes two errors. First, he invests too heavily in it himself (thus committing the "crime" of an unbalanced portfolio), and second, he uses his wife in the process, attempting to turn her from a "prominent Washington personality" into a "female lobbyist," an epithet used often enough in the novel to deserve the quotation marks as a euphemism for "prostitute." His problems arise from his inability to see the full complexity of the political process; like the satirist, he is searching for a simple evil. The success of his scheme comes to depend upon one man, Senator Blundel, whose influence must be gained to push the decision through. Richard's co-conspirator, Planefield, urges him to see Blundel to "settle what is to be done between you." Richard ingenuously takes this expression to mean that he must bribe Blundel, and he remarks scornfully to Planefield, "Have they *all* their price?" "No," Planefield replies. "If they had, you'd find it easier. There's your difficulty. If they were all to be bought, or none of them were to be sold, you'd see your way" (383). Blundel remains enigmatic to the end, destroying Richard by doing nothing—letting the bill die in committee, but with the suggestion that it might be resurrected next year for reasons which he does not divulge—but aiding in the social resuscitation of Bertha— also for reasons which he does not divulge. He is the compleat senator.

The most complex and interesting character of all is Bertha Amory, a heroine who shares some of the qualities of Henry James's best creations.[8] The subtleties begin with the first suggestion of the problems of her marriage. Her father says that she has "made the mistake of merely marrying the man who loves *her*," instead of waiting for the man she could love fully. Thus the implication of her part in the failure of her marriage is present throughout the novel. Her unhappiness with Richard leads her to provoke Arbuthnot to adultery and to virtually confess her desires to Tredennis. But her most revealing scene is played out with another woman, Mrs. Sylvestre. Letting her hair down with one who has also suffered from men, Bertha truly reveals herself; then, as Mrs. Sylvestre gradually draws Arbuthnot to herself, Bertha's mixed feelings are most humanly presented. This entire section of the novel is remarkably deft in its handling of psychological subtleties that few male writers could understand, let alone represent.

When the plot circles around the political realities of the novel, Bertha's character is equally complex, her moral obliquities equally subtle. Her "crime" as a "female lobbyist" is merely to extend her invitation list to include those congressmen and senators who can aid Richard's project. Her unease about the situation derives not from the social inferiority of those whom she has to invite—no one spits tobacco on her rug, as they did for Mrs. Trollope—but from the hypocrisy underlying the invitations and the fact that they are forced upon her. Even there, subtleties remain. When she makes Richard specifically compel her to invite certain persons to one of her soirées, she feels a sense of blessed relief (as though the reader were to act as a Nuremberg judge to whom she could say, "I was only following orders"), and when she is quite specifically directed to vamp Blunden, she is compared to a sacrificial dove. Blunden's response to her is also subtly conveyed: he knows he is being vamped; he enjoys it immensely; he does not want the enjoyment to end, but he does not intend to vote for Richard's bill either. By publicly supporting Bertha during her social crisis, he achieves all his ends and more. Richard deserts her for a lonely remittance-man's exile in Paris, where he is "exceedingly popular in the American colony," and where he plans vaguely to have his wife rejoin him some time. Tredennis dies his inevitable martyr's death. Arbuthnot marries Mrs. Sylvestre. The society remains closed and contented. Why some critics consider the novel a tragedy escapes this reader.

Through One Administration is unquestionably Mrs. Burnett's best work of fiction; as a political novel it compares favorably with the best political novels of the period; as a novel of manners it is comparable with the best of James and Howells and Edith Wharton. It has probably not received the critical respect it deserves because of Mrs. Burnett's later works, notably *Little Lord Fauntleroy*, which tarred all her earlier work with its notoriety.[9] It is so good a novel that one would expect that Mrs. Burnett would go on to even better works, an *a fortiori* case to be derived from the examples of *The Gilded Age* and *Democracy*. The reason Mrs. Burnett did not pursue excellence in the novel was, quite simply, the difficulties she had with this one, so far ahead of its time it was. R.O. Beard, for example, criticized *Through One Administration* as a work which flirted with adultery as a viable phenomenon, and presented sympathetically neo-sacrilegious statements like "The worst punishments in life are the punishments of ignorance," and "All men are born free and some equal." What probably hurt Mrs. Burnett even more, and was primarily responsible for her retreat from serious fiction, was the fact that her respected and respectful editor, Richard Watson Gilder, for various reasons, sided with her critics and admonished her for subjecting him to "the only serious, dangerous, and at the same time correct criticism" he had then received as an editor.[10] Chastened, Mrs. Burnett never looked back; otherwise the superb intelligence that created the juvenile masterpiece, *The Secret Garden*, would have written masterpieces for adults.[11]

II *Tales of Two Bosses*: The Honorable Peter Stirling *and* The Boss

Through One Administration is really a novel of manners in a political setting. *The Honorable Peter Stirling and What People Thought of Him* (1894)—to give the novel its full but seldom used title, by Paul Leicester Ford (1865–1902), is a truly political novel— some believe a roman à clef based on the life of Grover Cleveland— with many of the trappings of the novel of manners.[12] The central novelistic question upon which the plot revolves is whether the sterling of Peter Stirling—his New England background, his Harvard education—will shine through the necessary crudity of his Democratic politics to satisfy the need for a marriage and a happy ending. The true center of the novel is the central political question of the fiction-reading public of the nineteenth or any century: how to reconcile the principles of democratic government with its practices. Ford plays upon the differences between novelistic and political readings of the novel. His well-mannered characters, for example, are always crediting Peter Stirling with a kind of hypocrisy of *noblesse oblige*, which Peter constantly denies, asserting his real position through paradoxes which are far over their heads. Criticized about the sorry state of national affairs, Peter replies,

"Things are in bad shape and getting worse."
"But Peter," queried the woman, "if you are the leader, why do you let them get so?"
"So as to remain the leader," said Peter smiling quietly.
"Now that's what comes of ward politics," cried Mrs. Pell. "You are beginning to make Irish bulls."

"No," replied Peter, "I am serious, and because people don't understand what I mean, they don't understand American politics."

"But you say in effect that the way you retain your leadership is by not leading. That's absurd!"

"No. Contradiction though it may seem, the way to lose authority is to exercise it too much. Christ enunciated the great truth of democratic government when he said 'He that would be the greatest among you shall be the servant of all.'" (241-242)

Framed between the Irish bull and Christian paradox, there is the truth of democratic politics. It is precisely this kind of political realism—balanced, profound, subtle, in sharp contrast to a mannered society—that Ford manages to create in this novel, just as Mrs. Burnett produced her social realism in a political context.

Curiously, Ford denied at the outset of *The Honorable Peter Stirling* that he intended a realistic study of American politics. He implied instead, through a minor character, that he was only writing a romance, and he made all the standard criticisms of the realists while doing so:

By all means let us have truth in our novels, but there is truth and truth. Most of New York's firemen presumably sat down at noon today to a dinner of corned beef and cabbage, But perhaps one of them at the same moment was fighting his way through smoke and flame, to save life at the risk of his own. Boiled dinner and burned firemen are equally true. Are they equally worthy of description? (3)

It must be admitted that there are about equal parts of boiled dinner and burned fireman in *The Honorable Peter Stirling*, but the wise reader quickly learns how to skip over the burned fireman passages. These are the passages concerned with Peter's incredible nobility of character. The reader is asked to swallow whole, for example, Peter's willing assumption of guilt for the sexual sin of a rival, along with other "burned firemen" of equal nobility, all, doubtless, to prepare him to accept the most charred fireman of them all: Peter's eventual Humbert-Lolita marriage to Lenore D'Alloi.

As for the boiled dinner, the novel has enough for any appetite. Once we accept the unlikelihood of Peter's New England background and Harvard education, his rise in New York ward politics seems likely enough. His sympathy is first invoked over issues so basic they are indisputable. His first involvement with his ward is to insure that its children will have pure milk to drink. Successful in that, he is drawn into the question of saloon closures and comes to see that as open-and-shut as the pure milk issue: if the rich man is to have his club, why should not the poor man have his saloon? The novel proceeds step by step to Peter's arrival as The Boss of a Democratic machine that makes him the most powerful man in the state of New York, and—if those who see the novel as a fictionalization of the career of Grover Cleveland are correct—as a natural candidate for the presidency of the United States. En route, Ford explains a great deal about how the machinery of Democratic politics operates from the interesting point of view of Peter's access to both classes. At his worst, Ford makes Peter sound like a lecturer in Political Science 101 as he explains political reality to the elite: why the "better classes" should not govern, why reform movements fail, why bosses are necessary. More often, Peter illustrates his lectures with his own practical experience, the details of which are often fascinating. We see him in the saloons, which he fights to keep open partly for the rightness of his argument that they are the equivalent of the rich man's clubs, partly also because they are the base of his power. We feel the weight of the votes he controls in his quiet dealings with other powerful men on issues which will doubtless make some of them rich. And we observe his tortured feelings as colonel of militia organized to keep the peace during a strike, when he orders his troops to fire on their fellow proletarians in the interest of a Higher Order.

Thus, like Mrs. Burnett, Ford proves himself to be no absolutist in either fiction or politics. The odors of boiled dinner and burnt firemen seem as inextricably mingled as the question of good and evil in Peter's descants on the subject:

"Do you really think people are so bad, Peter?" asked Lenore, sadly.
"No. I have not, ten times in my life, met a man whom I should now call bad. I have met men whom I thought so, but when I knew them better I found the good in them more than balancing the evil. Our mistake is in supposing that some men are 'good' and others 'bad,' and that a sharp line can be drawn between them. The truth is that every man has both qualities in him and in very few does the evil overbalance the good. I marvel at the goodness I find in humanity, when I see the temptation and opportunity there is to do wrong. (284)

As in Mrs. Burnett's novel, there are no villains in *The Honorable Peter Stirling*. Ford's intention is rather to explain to the novel-reading but politically conservative public this new phenomenon of American politics. Peter prefers to be called the "leader" but understands when his critics call him a "boss." Since both epithets are tarnished from our perspective (albeit one of them primarily in German translation), the novel is still pertinent. Indeed, in its central crisis, Peter's strikebreaking with the militia and his explanation of it, this novel speaks for political liberalism about as well as any such document written in the last century. Peter tries to avoid violence at all cost and is injured trying to stop it when it breaks out anyway. Ford's comment explains the liberal position that Peter constantly represents:

Underneath that great dun pall lay soldier and anarchist, side by side, at last in peace. The one died for his duty, the other for his idea. The world was none the better, but went on unchanged. (340)

It is the impracticality of ideals of all sorts, of the right and the left, that Peter strives against. He is sympathetic to socialism, even to anarchism, since he "sees the fearful problems which [the radicals] think their theories will solve" (351) and recognizes the historical necessity of change toward a more equitable distribution of wealth. When ideal leads to confrontation, to escalation, and finally to violence, he then places himself in harm's way in an effort at compromise. Thus his wounding in the battle with the strikers is the key to his character; he is finally not just a compromiser but a Redeemer. It is doubtless for that reason that Ford wanted his novel to be considered a romance, and the wise reader will take it that way. Politics in the U.S. are not yet ready for Christ as The Boss.

In complete contrast to *The Honorable Peter Stirling and What People Thought of Him* is *The Boss, and How He Came to Rule New York* (1903) by Alfred Henry Lewis (1857-1914).[13] The differences are indicated in the titles. The name Peter Stirling, with its implications of the rock upon which the Christian church was built and the stability of silver as a means of exchange, is in violent contrast to the unnamed but vulgar "Boss." The subtitles contrast too. Ford's interest is in explaining the subtle differences between the popular opinion and the real Peter Stirling; Lewis is writing a "how to" book, a recipe for political power.

The two novels differ in every other way as well. Ford's style is a genteel third-person narration in the language of polite society; Lewis's is a first-person narration with a lilting hint of Irishness in the voice of the title character, and more than a little vulgarity in the slang of most of the low-life characters and the verbal eccentricities of the higher-class characters. Ford, although writing a romance, at least gives lip service to the laws of probability and pays some attention to consistency of character and motivation. Lewis couldn't care less about such niceties. Ford concerns himself with and attempts an explanation for the philosophical and ethical backgrounds of the phenomenon of Bossism; Lewis gives a practical and amoral recipe for becoming a boss. In short, the two books ought to be read together, as antidotes for each other and for the sheer enjoyment of the contrast. Yet the sense one has at the conclusion of either work is quite similar, to paraphrase Marlowe:

> A god is not so glorious as a Boss,
> I think the pleasure they enjoy in heaven
> Cannot compare with Bossly joys in earth.
> To wear a crown enchased with pearl and gold,
> Whose virtues carry with it life and death;
> To ask and have, command and be obeyed;
> When looks breed love, with looks to gain the prize—
> Such power attractive shines in Boss's eyes.
>
> *(Tamburlaine, Part I*, I, v.)

Looked at cynically, *The Boss* is merely an unzipped version of *Peter Stirling*. The one thing Peter never does is anything improper. He takes no graft, accepts no bribes, uses his power of coercion only to win men to his benevolent schemes. *The Boss* is not so wishy-washy and Sunday schoolish. The first job the narrator gets through his association with Tammany Hall is a clear-cut case of coercion. Big Kennedy, the Ward Boss, goes to a German grocer and demands he give the narrator a job. The grocer demurs. He has no "wacancy."

"Then make one," responded Big Kennedy coolly. "Dismiss one of the boys you have, d'ye see? At least two who work for you don't belong in my ward." As the other continued doubtful Big Kennedy became sharp. "Come, come, come!" he cried in a manner peremptory rather than fierce; "I can't wait all day. Don't you feed your horses in the street? Don't you obstruct the sidewalks with your stuff? Don't you sell liquor in your rear room without a license? Don't you violate a dozen ordinances? Don't the police stand it and pass you up? An' yet you hold me here fiddlin' and foolin' away time!"

"Yes, yes, Mr. Kennedy," cried the grocer, who from the first had sought to stem the torrent of the other's eloquence. "I was only tryin' to think up w'ich horse I will let him drive alreatty." (43)

One always has the feeling that Peter Stirling never drops his velvet gloves, while in Lewis's novel the naked power of the Boss is always present.

Both novels are anchored in political reality, but *The Boss* has none of the cosmetic touches that made *Peter Stirling* acceptable to the genteel reading public. Take the question of reform movements. Ford is certainly skeptical about their efficacy. A character who is educating Peter on the subject states the situation very clearly:

"If [a party] has a long tenure of office it is generally due to distrust of the other party. The natural tendency otherwise is to make office-holding a sort of see-saw. Let alone change of opinion in older men, there are enough new voters every four years to reverse majorities in almost every state. Of course these young men care little for what either party has done in the past, and being young and ardent, they want to change things. The minority's ready to please them, naturally. Reform, they call it, but it's quite as often 'Deform' when they've done it." (107–108)

The phenomenon is summed up more succinctly by Big Kennedy in *The Boss*:

"This whole reform racket . . . is, to my thinkin', a kind of pouter-pigeon play. Most of 'em who go in for it simply want to swell 'round. Besides the pouter-pigeon, who's in the game because he's stuck on himself, there's only two breeds of reformers. One is a Republican who's got ashamed of himself; an' the other is some crook who's been kicked out o' Tammany for graftin' without a license." (164–165)

There is, of course, a world of difference in those two views, though substantively they are very similar.

The most striking quality of *The Boss* is its celebration of the joy of politics, quite apart from any and all questions of morality. The subject is first broached by Old Mike, the oldest of three generations of ward heelers in the novel. He is queried by the "reputable old gentleman," who represents what Lewis calls "mugwump" politics, on his views of "political economy."

"I should think," said the reputable old gentleman . . . "that if you ran from tyranny in Ireland, you would refuse here to submit to the tyranny of Tammany Hall. If you couldn't abide a Queen, how can you now put up with a Boss?"

"I didn't run from the Queen, I ran from th' laws," said Old Mike. "As for the Boss—everything that succeeds has a Boss. The President's a boss; the Pope's a boss; Stewart's a boss in his store down in City Hall Park. That's right; everything that succeeds has a boss. Nothing is strong enough to stand the mishtakes av more than one man. Ireland would have been free th' long cinturies ago if she'd only had a boss."

"But do you call it good citizenship," demanded the reputable old gentleman, not a trifle nettled by Mike's hard-shell philosophy of state; "do you call it good citizenship to take your orders from a boss? You are loyal to Tammany before you are loyal to the city?"

"Shure!" returned Old Mike, puffing the puffs of him who is undisturbed. "Do ye ever pick up a hand in a game av ca-ards?" The reputable old gentleman seemed properly disgusted. "There you be then! City government is but a game; so's all government. Shure, it's as if you an' me were playin' a game av ca-ards, this politics; your party is your hand, an' Tammany is my hand. In a game of ca-ards, which are ye loyal to, is it your hand or the game? Man, it's your hand av coorse. By the same token, I am loyal to Tammany Hall." (57–58)

The pleasure of politics, the playing of the hand of "ca-ards," is shown in the novel through a series of hilarious anecdotes and cynical but good-humored discussions. The story is told, for example, of how Big Kennedy thwarts a reform movement by running the "reputable old gentleman" himself as his own reform candidate, then defeating him at every point after the election on the viability of reform. It is during this election that the reputable old gentleman's son, Morton, rises to prominence through his ingenious political stratagems. When he discovers that there are 300 black voters in the ward, he "votes" all of them by using only a handful of Negro women in bib overalls. They "all look alike." Graft is handled just as straightforwardly. When Morton decides he wants to make his fortune with a street railway, he approaches Big Kennedy for the franchise. Kennedy demands 40 percent of the common stock.

Young Morton drew in his lips. The figure seemed a surprise. "Do you mean that you receive four millions of the common stock, you paying nothing?" he asked at last.

"I don't pony for a sou markee. An' I get the four millions, d'ye see! Who ever heard of Tammany payin' for anything!" and Big Kennedy glared about the room, and sniffed through his nose, as though in the presence of all that might be called preposterous.

"But if you put in no money," remonstrated young Morton, "why should you have the stock? I admit that you should be let in on lowest terms; but after all, you should put in something."

"I put in my pull," retorted Big Kennedy grimly. "You get your franchise from me."

"From the City," corrected young Morton.

"I'm the City," replied Big Kennedy; "an' will be while I'm on top of Tammany, an' Tammany's on top of th' town." (182)

When the narrator in his turn becomes Boss of Tammany, he is no less quick to take graft than was Big Kennedy. Once again it is Morton who presents him with a scheme. This time it is to job the stock of a rival street railway. Morton buys in quietly before Blackberry Traction begins bargaining with the Boss for new franchises; he encourages them to think their plans will meet with success, and lets the word leak out. Morton then sells short when the stock peaks and the Boss refuses their request, and holds short for its fall, picking up a cool million for the Boss on each transaction, even though Blackberry Traction is exactly where it was when the operation started, and nothing is changed at all. The incident is only one of many examples of the Boss's following of Big Kennedy's advice on the taking of graft—that a good cook in money matters ought not to fail to lick his fingers. Thus, only two kinds of graft are considered in the novel—graft which is taken to expedite legitimate city affairs, and graft which is really a confidence trick in which would-be swindlers are swindled. The novel does not defend graft in politics *per se*, but it certainly puts it in the most flattering light possible.

Another striking aspect of the novel is its consideration of the *realpolitik* of Bossism. Old Mike, Big Kennedy, and the narrator, each in his turn, pass on the wisdom gained in the crucible of their political experience. In general, it is cynical, bitter, mordant advice, but it is leavened with humor and serves as an antidote to a foolish

altruism. In *The Honorable Peter Stirling*, Peter impresses Leonore
D'Alloi because he has set up a fund to lend money to members of his
ward. She offers to contribute to the fund, and he demurs, since, as he
says, the money goes out on loans, never gifts, and as a result, the
modest fund he began with years ago is now much larger and still
growing. The conversation gives him an opportunity to moralize over
the relative value of gifts and loans in terms of character-building.
Huck would say he was all full of tears and flapdoodle. In *The Boss*
the narrator also sets up a fund to lend money to members of his
ward, and prefers the loan to the gift. His reasons are perhaps more
honest. As Old Mike says, "it's better to lind people money than give
it to 'em. You kape them bechune your fingers longer by lindin" (56).

Old Mike condenses his advice to his son, just before his own death
and his son's election as Boss of Tammany, to a single paragraph
remarkable in its wisdom:

> "Jawn," he said, "you'll be th' Chief of Tammany. The Chief, now fightin'
> for his life, will lose. The mishtake he made was in robbin' honest people.
> Jawn, he should have robbed the crim'nals an' th' law breakers. The rogues
> can't fight back, an' th' honest people can. An' remember this: the public
> don't care for what it hears, only for what it sees. Never interfere with people's
> beer; give 'em clean streets; double the number of lamp-posts—the public's
> like a fly, it's crazy over lamps—an' have bands playin' in every pa-ark. Then
> kape the streets free of ba-ad people, tinhorn, min', an' such. You don't have
> to drive 'em out of town, only off th' streets; the public don't object to dirt, but
> it wants it kept in the back alleys. Jawn, if you'll follow what I tell you, you
> can do what else ye plaze. The public will go with ye loike a drunkard to th'
> openin' of a new s'loon." (155)

Big Kennedy's advice to the narrator upon his succession is much
more detailed and Chesterfieldian. Some of the pithier comments go
well beyond politics:

> "Never give a man the wrong office; size every man up, an' measure him for
> his place th' same as a tailor does for a suit of clothes. If you give a big man a
> little office, you make an enemy; if you give a little man a big office, you make
> trouble." . . .
> "Say 'No' nineteen times before you say 'Yes' once. People respect th' man
> who says 'No', and his 'Yes' is worth more where he passes it out. When you
> say 'No', you play your own game; when you say 'Yes' you're playin' some

other duck's game. 'No' keeps; 'Yes' gives; an' the gent who says 'No' most will always be th' biggest toad in his puddle." . . .

"Always go with the current; that's the first rule of leadership. It's easier; an' there's more water downstream than up." . . .

"Always pay your political debts; but pay with a jolly as far as it'll go. If you find one who won't take a jolly, throw a scare into him and pay him with that. If he's a strong, dangerous mug with whom a jolly or a bluff won't work, get him next to you as fast as you can. If you strike an obstinate party, it's the old rule for drivin' pigs, If you want 'em to go forward, pull 'em back by th' tails. Never trust a man beyond his interest; an' never love the man, love what he does." (208-209)

At the novel's conclusion, when the narrator considers with his cronies how his life has been spent, there is no need for advice, but there is also no suggestion of repentance or reconsideration. The central image that Lewis presents is a comparison between the modern city dweller and the savages who lived there before him, not at all uncomplimentary to the savages. In this light, the last comment on The Boss, that he is an atavism, is not necessarily uncomplimentary either:

This once Boss, silent and passive and white and old, and waiting for the digging of his grave, is what breeders call a "throw-back"—a throw-back, not of the generations, but of the ages. In what should arm him for a war of life against life, he is a creature of utter cunning, utter courage, utter strength. He is a troglodyte; he is that original one who lived with the cave bear, the mastodon, the sabre-toothed tiger, and the Irish elk. (329)

It is worth noting that all the species mentioned are extinct, while the Boss lives on.

Both *Peter Stirling* and *The Boss* are romances, but of antipathic types. Peter is simply the Naturally Good man of romance in a political setting. The Boss is a "throw-back," all right, but a throwback to our first chapter—he is a Horatio Alger character in politics—no less romantic, but on a different social and literary level. So the bribe-taking, the vote-swindling, the apparently amoral or immoral practicality of *The Boss* are all no less romantic than the altruism of *Peter Stirling*—they are simply of a different class, one which is much more "upwardly mobile," and therefore less likely to be hypocritical about appearances and reality. Both novels are unsuccessful at describing the reality of politics, but they miss the target on different sides. *Peter Stirling* substitutes altruism for self-interest and thus hits the target of what politics ought to be in an ideal democracy; the Boss functions from self-interest alone certainly, but demonstrates an almost inhuman competence in all his political manipulations, and thus describes a perfect totalitarian society. Unfortunately (or fortunately), the United States is neither, and thus both novels fail as novels, while being perfectly satisfactory as romances. They also present a lesson for any would-be political novelist: it is much easier to treat of politics in a never-never land of ideal democracy or perfect savagery than in the imperfect real world of America between the wars.

III   *Toward Political Reality:*
I. K. Friedman (1870-1931)—The Radical *(1907)*

The closest approximation to a realistic and successful political novel in this period is Isaac Kahn Friedman's *The Radical*.[14] This novel has a great deal in common with the others we have examined in this chapter, but it also profits from certain qualities unlikely to be found in much of the writing of the period. Like *The Honorable Peter Stirling*, the main character, Bruce McAllister, seems motivated more by his ideals than by self-interest. But Friedman does not make the mistake of having Bruce lecture the other characters about what politics ought to be, nor does he give him a New England-Harvard background. Bruce is called "the butcher boy" in his ward, and his prudent and abstemious conduct is more naturally come by: his father deserted his family when he was sixteen and Bruce was left in charge of keeping them out of the poorhouse. He chose politics as "the easiest way to lift himself and the family out of the pit." He is no plaster saint. Bruce "slipped in that ooze and filth" of ward politics more than once, but "two inward voices" called him onward—one of them "selfish ambition," the other concern for his class. The dual motivation works in the novel adequately. We learn that Bruce had "soiled his hands with the slime-covered gold that finds its way into politics; he had grafted with the worst and best of them" (20-21). But most of this money, we learn later, was to support the family, to pay for a sister's art lessons and the postgraduate education of a scientifically minded brother.

Those are rather minor techniques to gain sympathy and belief in Bruce. The main one is simpler and much more brilliant. Friedman rarely lets us see Bruce succeed at anything, and all his successes which we do see are undercut by failures resulting from them. Certainly one of the most provoking characteristics of Peter Stirling is that success crowned his every activity, from naming the governor of his state to attracting the nymphet, Leonore. The same is true of the Boss of Lewis's novel, except that he is taken in by a scheming son-in-law, quite unbelievably, at the end. Friedman uses this technique to gain verisimilitude for his character almost as well as Mark Twain used it in *Life on the Mississippi* to create humor. In the first scene of the novel we see Bruce apparently triumphing over a Republican rival, Hammersmith, at a debate, only to get sodden drunk afterwards and to lose the election anyway. The rest of the novel is primarily concerned with his efforts to get his anti-child-labor bill passed, first in the house, then in the senate, only to have it declared unconstitutional by the Supreme Court. In the process, Bruce has his moments of triumph, but they are few and unsatisfying, as he is gradually convinced that he is powerless to change things. At the end of the novel, he resigns his senatorship to take his cause "out on a fair field before the people," because, as he comments ambiguously, the White House "has both a front and back door" (362). We are present at the fictional birth of Populism.

Another reason for the success of this novel is Friedman's handling of the minor characters, political and nonpolitical. Some of the political minor characters are merely stereotypes: "Sir" Anthony Wyckoff is villainous commerce, a blend of Morgan, Vanderbilt, and Rockefeller; Ardmore is gentility too weak to preserve honor; and so on. But many are much more than that, and some are positive gems. Georgia Ten Eyck is a scheming woman who will do anything to make her father President, including marrying herself off to a politically powerful person. But, although she is totally at odds with Bruce's intentions, she compliments and admires his speeches and his political manipulations. Even more striking is Bruce's mentor and protector in politics, Fiske, who pursues his own goals avidly but honestly, following generally liberal principles. Yet it is he who supplies the Brutus-stroke to Bruce over a military bill which would allow the use of militia to break strikes. Bruce is of course dead against the bill; Fiske ponders at length, and finally comes out for "law and order." Bruce resigns shortly after. It seems that this one action is finally responsible for "radicalizing" Bruce, but all comments about Fiske through the novel are generally respectful, and his actions bear out his honesty, humanity, and good will. Peter Stirling *talks* of how he meets more honest than dishonest people in politics; Friedman illustrates the phenomenon with living characters.

Friedman's other successes with minor characters are hardly less striking. He has a real female lobbyist in Fanny Scollard, who almost succeeds in seducing Bruce, and whose drift into prostitution is alluded to forthrightly. Her wastrel brother Brant Scollard is also well described, and the state of the family as a whole, as minor officeholders in bureaucratic Washington, is presented in a much less melodramatic manner than Mrs. Burnett managed the equivalent in *Through One Administration*. The press is well represented by Bruce's crony, Ed Butler. A truly minor character, he is instrumental in only one scene, in which he serves as a human "bug" to blackmail a group of senators when he overhears their confidential remarks. Butler's motivation is part friendship with Bruce, desire to get a good story, and plain human curiosity.

Almost completely outside the political framework of the novel is an extensive subplot of the conflict in art and taste between romanticism and realism. Rossiter Rembrandt Dickinson is a crotchety, egotistical painter whose intolerance for "pretty" art is matched only by his contempt for politics and anything else that interferes with his life. His introduction to Bruce's sister Elaine is to gratuitously insult a sculptured nymph she is working on by suggesting that she do it in chocolate cream, it is such a confection. His own work runs to laborers in mills, on canvases too large for ordinary rooms, with figures which are, like his own personality, "overpowering, huge, domineering." He is equally opposed to mammon. When someone suggests to him that he might do better by painting a Diana or an Orpheus because such pictures "take" with the public, he launches into a tirade:

"Takes! takes! You can't serve the Almighty and the almighty dollar, woman! What do I care what takes! That's not my purpose on earth! Enough milksops have put Orpheus to twanging his harp—no wonder he flew to Hades for refuge. And Diana has been hunted enough; let her rest! I know what I'm about. Rossiter Rembrandt Dickinson wants to paint contemporary life; I don't steal my inspirations from Greece. I work like a slave for 'em here, and now. (119)

The Radical includes several indications that Friedman had read his Henry James well—and distinctly rejected him as an influence.[15] R. R. Dickinson is about as unlike Roderick Hudson as a painter could be, and his philosophy of taste and art, with which the author seems to be in total sympathy, leaves little room for the ideal. Friedman's metaphor of art seems to imply that the artist/novelist must first tell truth, always tell truth from his very individual point of view, and finally tell truth with a distinctive, possibly even eccentric style. The metaphor describes this novel rather well, especially its style. Friedman's style, like R. R. Dickinson's, when he is describing matters of national import, is "overpowering, huge, dominant," given to Homeric epithets, extended (and sometimes mixed) metaphor and simile. When this style is used for trifling matters, it reads something like a parody of James:

"Do you like pictures?" she asked suddenly. It was to break the ice into which he was to fall, while she, as it were, was to stand on the shore and watch how he disported himself in the uncomfortable situation. (50)

More often it is used to describe the powerful influences at work in government and the subtle and complex effects they render:

At a few minutes to twelve, their hands in their pockets, in strolled the gods themselves, chatting as they moved over the affairs of Olympus and the deeds of puny mortals, crawling like ants on the mundane sphere far, far below. Each particular divinity found his desk in one of the concentric rows that circle the wide dais where Jove himself, wielding a presidential gavel, sat enthroned.

Once in their desks the senators, who have certain dimensions and attributes in common with mortals, busied themselves with their private correspondence, deaf to the clamor of the clerk droning on and on through a list, high as Olympus itself, of pensions, memorials, petitions, reports, bills—all that vast river of legislation—presto! our mountain is turned into water!—that flows on silently and without interruption into the limitless sea made by the outpouring that has gone before it. (217)

Such casual metaphoric shifts are not infrequent when Friedman considers the subject of power in America, particularly when he describes his *bête noir*, his capitalist of capitalists, "Sir" Anthony Wyckoff:

The President leaned on our merchant king for advice, believing that whatsoever was bad for Sir Anthony was bad for commerce, and *vice versa*, and that in any way to disturb the business and vested interests of the country was to severely injure the fortunes of his party. When Sir Anthony spoke, commerce spoke, which after all was the only voice worthy of a consideration in the United States. (174)

The second example must be one of the most extended, confused, and confusing analogies ever written; it too is about Wyckoff:

Scientists tell us that if a pea is placed at the side of a cocoanut, the relative size of the sun and the earth will find their just proportions represented, and if one takes our United States Government, the money it controls and expends, the number of people it employs, and places it beside Sir Anthony's Universal Trust, the same pea and the same cocoanut will do to show how one shrinks in importance beside the other. Anthony, then, would be richer and more powerful than the government; he would have a larger majority of its voters on his pay roll, and he intended to have the government run to suit himself. The milk in the cocoanut, to say the same thing differently, was in no way designed for the fattening of the despicable little pea; but, on the other hand, to extend the figure of speech a little further, the cocoanut had certain little designs whereby the pea was to serve its ends. The sun, huge as it is, and the earth, small as it is, are of mutual [?!] benefit in our vast solar system, and both help to keep the whole in motion. Surely, if the cocoanut is kind enough to keep its place and distance, and does not roll over and crush the pea out of existence, the latter ought to show its thankfulness by sundry little deeds of kindness. (152–153)

One can only guess at how angry Friedman must have been to commit such an atrocity, especially when one considers that his prose, when not applied to the robber barons of commerce, is usually quite simple and clear.

The problem, of course, arises because Friedman, unlike any of the other writers considered in this chapter, was *engagé*. His passionate interest in the populist cause did not allow him to write a subtle novel of manners in a political setting, like *Through One Administration*; his rejection of liberals like Fiske is a rejection of the romance of idealized politics like *The Honorable Peter Stirling*; and his recognition of the relative powerlessness of the true democrat when in opposition to the combined force of business and government led him to reject the easy cynicism of *The Boss*. Both his force and his failures as a novelist stem from this one factor, a passionate involvement with the social and economic plight of the poor. Because of that, the novel, bad as it is, serves as a bridge to the last chapter of this study, in which the phenomenon of engagement is often the unifying factor for works as various in style, technique, and social problems as the four works examined in this chapter were for everything except their common subject.

CHAPTER 8

Toward the Modern:
Some Reluctant Innovators

THE period from 1865 to 1920 has long been known as the Age of Transition—from Victorian to modern, from romantic to realistic, from sentimental to scientific. Few situations in life are more difficult than living in periods of transition; one is reminded of the ancient Chinese curse, "may you live in interesting times." If one is living in interesting times, the key to "success" is to choose the right movement and to back it wholeheartedly. The moderate Christians in ancient Rome who were too rational to seek martyrdom, the Mensheviks of 1917—their names were writ in water. In an age of transition the virtues of restraint, prudence, and reason may be crippling deficiencies.

The writers to be considered in this chapter are among the finest discussed in this work, but they are all failures from the modern critics' point of view. Each is an experimenter of sorts; each contributed in some way to one or another of the "new waves" in fiction that marked the Age of Transition. Each failed to commit himself beyond reason and prudence to what must have seemed a dubious cause. Some may have failed for lack of talent or genius as well, to be sure, but most did not. They were simply unable to free themselves from their Victorian upbringing, their belief in romantic ideals or the primacy of sentiment. They were victims of their age. Had they been living in any period but one of transition, their talents would surely have earned them a modicum of recognition as minor but important writers. But the modern temper is so self-righteous that most of them are simply ignored, denied even the scorn that H. L. Mencken cast on Howells, for example, merely because their support of modernity was too timorous.

While the contents of this chapter will be critical and judicious, a certain tone of advocacy will be inescapably present. These novels deserve reading for more than antiquarian, sociological, or historical reasons. They are good novels. Now that the hard dogmas of realism have softened, now that critics are coming to realize that the house of the novel has many mansions, these are the kinds of works that, along with the writings of Robert Grant, H. O. Sturgis, Frank Stockton, and others who have been considered in earlier chapters, ought to be known to literate readers of the novel. Their failure to be "modern" is in the sense that word had twenty or thirty years ago, and the values present in them are more and more coming to be appreciated again.

I have, rather artificially, divided this chapter into two parts: experiments in style and experiments in content. It should be understood that the two parts overlap considerably.

I *In the Wake of James and Howells: The New Style*

The followers of James and Howells are easily discerned. Like their masters, they are cosmopolitan in their personal lives, thoroughly professional as writers, apt to chose rather ordinary and banal material for subject matter and to treat it with an impeccable style. The two finest practitioners of this kind of realism, hardly less proficient than James and Howells themselves, were Arthur Sherburne Hardy (1847-1930) and Anne Douglas Sedgwick (1873-1935).

Hardy was a virtual Renaissance man. Educated in Switzerland, at Phillips Andover, and at West Point, he served in the army, as professor of mathematics at Grinnell and Dartmouth, and as a distinguished diplomat in Europe and the Near East, as well as following Howells in the editorship of the *Cosmopolitan*. His writing is no less varied, ranging from his long poem, *Francesca of Rimini*, his first published work (1878), through a half-dozen novels, several collections of short stories (among which are some exquisite detective stories featuring M. Joly, who might be a model for some parts of Simenon's Maigret), an autobiography, *Things Remembered* (1923), to a series of mathematical textbooks. Even the novels themselves are incredibly varied, including a historical novel of the time of Charlemagne, *Passe Rose* (1889), and novels set in the recent past in France and America. Of these, his best is also his first, *But Yet a Woman* (1883).[1]

This novel is remarkable first because it has no American characters in it—indeed, only one English-speaking minor character, an Englishman who is summarized in a very Gallic way as having "an accent and [living] behind a cold exterior." One might guess that Hardy was rather slavishly following some influence—Flaubert, les Frerès Goncourt, perhaps, or more directly and specifically, Ludovic Halévy, whose *l'Abbé Constantin* had appeared only the year before and bears a marked resemblance to much of Hardy's novel.[2] But the real reason for the novel's foreignness is theoretical and esthetic. Early in the novel several characters consider the relation between the romantic and the scientific and then move on to the universal and the particular. Hardy is interested in examining the implications of all parts of the analogy, and hence he need not concern himself unduly with detail. As he has his most sympathetic character, Roger Lande, say, "these accessories, of time, and place, and manners, they are only the frame of the picture; it is the vulgar eye that is attracted to them solely" (54).

What is presented in this novel to the "vulgar eye" is a setting of middle-class French conservative-to-monarchist society during the period of the effort to restore the monarchy to "Henri V" after the collapse of the Thiers ministry. What is universal is a love story between a man and two women, the man a young and intelligent doctor, the two women a contrast between innocent youth and sophisticated maturity. There is little suspense in the triangle—it is quite obvious even to nonreaders of romance that youth and innocence will be more attractive than maturity—but Hardy produces a neatly turned ending for the older woman, Stephanie, that carries some suspense to the final chapter. The story is really only a frame for the development of several themes which grow from the specific characters and situations of the novel. Most prominent is the theme of culture vs. nature, or reason vs. passion, or theology vs. science, all of which are interwoven contrapuntally through the action. The themes and motives are all sympathetically presented as food for thought for the characters (and the reader) by spokesmen for each who are certainly advocates, but are no less urbane for that. Among them are three remarkable ecclesiastics presenting what must be three different degrees of the Roman Catholic position. To the right is Soeur Ursule, who seems to exist primarily to prick the consciences of the good but worldly. In one scene, she compliments the novel's hero, Dr. Roger Lande, on his work in the wards of the Hôtel-Dieu St. Luc:

"Doctor," she said, entering quietly behind him, and closing the door, "you were very successful this morning."

Roger himself had been well satisfied. The two operations of the morning had passed off well, his thoughts had been clear, and his words at his command, as the applause of the students had testified.

"Yes, everything went off well," he said, sitting down at his table, and taking up the reports awaiting inspection.

"Moreover, you spoke well, doctor."

"Ah! you think so? I am glad of it"; and he began to open his papers.

"How much, in all this, did you think of the glory of God, doctor?" pursued Soeur Ursule, quietly.

"Pouf! so much only, I'm afraid, sister," he said, with a puff of imaginary smoke in the air.

"And that only will be left at the day of judgment," she replied calmly. (39)

At the other extreme is a somewhat mysterious priest named Father Roche, apparently a Jesuit, who bridges the political element of the plot with the love triangle, as he is a confidant of the older woman, Stephanie. Hardy describes his face as having a "marked intellectuality . . . at times so transfigured by a persuasive sweetness as to destroy any impression of coldness which might first have been made. So the soft lights of a crystal hide its angles without causing us to forget its hardness" (24). Father Roche engages Roger in a remarkably wide-ranging conversation as they wander in the gardens of the Alhambra in Granada. They move from history to botany to the sciences in general. "I love much the sciences," says the priest. "Then you do not fear them," Roger asks. "Those who fear science live in ruts so deep that they cannot see over them," the priest replies. Roger then embarks on a diatribe on the struggle between science and religion—part attack, part confession it seems, demanding part defense, part absolution from the priest—digging deeper and deeper into his own subconscious fears and desires, and ending with an existential uncertainty:

"Experience is not limited to sensation, and science herself raises the question which she cannot answer. But within her province, verification justifies induction and furnishes a unit of certainty. In that very tumult of opinion and change, with which men reproach her, goes on, as with the alembic of the chemist, a constant precipitation which increases her capital. Without, there is inference, but no verification; motion, but no progress. The questions remain, for the answers never emerge from the region of hypothesis. It is the wheel of Ixion."

Father Roche does not reply for five minutes, "though he did not have the air of one who was silenced." When he does reply, it is, inferentially, both defense and absolution for Roger: "You were speaking of religion. Philosophy is not religion." That this most subtle reminder of the centrality of love and faith to religion is not lost on Roger is made clear by the one-sentence paragraph following the priest's words: "Roger thought of Renée, at this reply" (271-273).

The third ecclesiastic is the fulcrum for the entire plot. Father LeBlanc manipulates the destinies of the lay characters of the novel as though he were himself some kind of minor deity. As friend and counselor to all three of the central figures of the novel, he uses his position to assure that everything will work out for the best for everyone. Thus, when Roger appears as though he might be shocked into some precipitate action when he discovers that young Renée has planned since her youth to enter a convent, Father LeBlanc counsels him very "delicately," as Hardy says, using the first person plural: "My son, this first voice that speaks to mademoiselle seems to her a voice from heaven. Let us wait a while patiently, lest, perchance, we strive against God" (67).

To advise Stephanie about how she should relate to the complicated problem of her dual relationship with Roger, whom she realizes she loves, and Renée, for whom she feels a deep sisterly affection, Father LeBlanc leaves a copy of Pliny dogeared to the story of Arria's suicide to encourage her husband's courage. The text is in Latin, which Stephanie cannot read but Renée can. The ensuing conversation, in which Renée engages in all innocence, but which has overtones to the more sophisticated Stephanie, allows her to contemplate all the aspects of her situation, to see it in all its complexity, and yet to drive her inescapably to the conclusion LeBlanc desired. When Stephanie asks her maid if it was Father LeBlanc who left the book there, Hardy gives the screw another turn. Lizette confesses to her mistress that the priest replied when she asked if she should say who sent it, "If she does not know, there is no need to tell her." Thus Hardy ties in one knot the relationship between innocence and experience in Renée's telling the story to Stephanie, and the relationship between worldly sophistication and morality in Stephanie's guessing correctly the purpose behind the event. Henry James is rarely so subtle or understated.

When the two women go for a holiday in Spain and Renée becomes ill, it is Father LeBlanc who sets up the machinery to test Roger's love for Renée and to bring the lovers together. When Roger is leaving, Father LeBlanc tells him to "say to Mademoiselle Renée that M. Michel [her father] sent you, and to Madame Milevski [Stephanie], that it was I," thus preparing correct expectations from each woman. LeBlanc is clearly a literary type—the wise French curate, like the abbé Constantin, who is primarily a friend to his spiritual advisees and a gifted psychologist, especially of women, with a talent for manipulation. He seems amoral, casuistic, in some of his machinations, but his ends are always unexceptionable. Hardy makes him believable by adding details that support this central and traditional character. He puts down de Merzac in a discussion of Sartain's fiction; he reveals his passion and his discrimination as a collector, since "the novel and the bizarre never blinded his keen eye for the beautiful, and he did not tarry long before objects whose claims to consideration rested only on their being old, or from over-seas." He is thus an abbé Constantin with several other dimensions and a further refined subtlety and invention.

Subtlety and invention mark Hardy's style throughout the novel, both in original wit and in allusion. Individual epigrams stay in one's memory for their innate value, and are equally appropriate to the character of the speaker. It is Father LeBlanc who remarks that "the young look into women's eyes to see their own reflections; the old, to see the woman" (44). Later he comments, "Nature is like a woman. In the morning she is fresh from her bath, at noon she is in her working dress, and at night she wears her jewels. As for me, I like them both best in the morning" (101). Eminently quotable, both of those, and perfectly appropriate to their speaker, who presses duty upon the mature Stephanie and delight upon Renée. In conversations between Stephanie and Roger, the *bons mots* trip from Stephanie's greater maturity, while Roger plays straight man:

[Roger] The power to take in rapidly ought not to prevent us from enjoying.
[Stephanie] Well, it does; if only because possession always diminishes enjoyment.

*   *   *

[Roger] "Madame, it is impossible for you to deceive me!"
She misunderstood him willfully.
"I think you could be deceived very easily, M. Lande."
"Not by you. You are incapable of it."

"On the contrary, I am deceiving you this instant."
She laughed nervously, and he regretted the directness of his compliment.
(91-92)

Allusion and reference are used no less well, as in the story from Pliny already discussed, and a stunning casual quotation from *Ecclesiasticus* of the *Apocrypha* which carries with it far-ranging overtones and echoes. Hardy is constantly surprising the reader with evidence of his artistic genius.

All of which makes the lapses from excellence the more striking. One can forgive the occasional stylistic eccentricities which make the novel sound like a poor translation from French—*assist* at a lecture for *attend, piece* for *play* at the theater—these are perhaps even intentional efforts at a Gallic rhythm in speech. But Hardy's ease in the French milieu he chose for the main action of the novel contrasts curiously with his shakiness in description of the tour made by the two women in Spain. In Paris, Hardy is at home; in Granada, he is only a tourist, and a very uncertain one at that, gingerly tasting the food and sipping the water, and making racial reflections on the Mediterranean type. Similarly, the urbanity and sophistication of the plot in Paris is most strikingly upset by the intrusion of violent melodrama from Spain. The villain, de Merzac, is a believable seducer in Parisian society; he stretches our credulity too far when he appears in Spain, guidebook in hand, tupping every available wench in a peasant blouse. Hardy should have stayed in Paris—or perhaps had his two women visit Berlin or London, where their creator was probably more at home.

These are minor flaws in a strikingly well-written novel. However, they are symptoms of unease which runs deeper in Hardy's later works. In The *Wind of Destiny* (1886) and its sequel, *His Daughter First* (1903), Hardy resists less successfully his tendency toward melodrama.[3] The *Wind of Destiny* actually has a scene in which the heroine, Gladys Temple, goes to the studio of the man she has always loved, and falls unconscious, overcome by passion, at his doorstep in a pelting rainstorm. Shades of Mrs. Southworth! Hardy then shows his true ability as a writer by having the reluctant lover return the unconscious Gladys to her husband and deal with the messy aftereffects of her passion realistically:

"You don't think I came here to talk, do you? All I want to say is this: if what has happened doesn't kill her, the sight of you, or me either, will. When are you going away?"

"You might have spared yourself any anxiety on that score," replied Rowan.

"Well, I thought so; but some people are always standing on their rights, you know." (229)

Gladys' later suicide is also, on balance, believable, even without reference to the unlikeliness of the original scene of her shame. The sequel follows the later life of Gladys' widower and his daughter through her maturation and his courtship of a second wife. Lacking the passion of a Gladys, the novel is much more Howellsian—which is another way of saying that it is at once better written and less interesting.

Passe Rose (1889), Hardy's historical novel set in the time of Charlemagne, has its author's careful research as a justification for its melodramatic content. The title character's search for her lost love moves the action among various social milieus in Maestricht and Aix, chiefly, and Hardy conscientiously includes materials both sympathetic and unsympathetic, to provide historical balance. The sudden violence is there, the carelessness for human life, but so is the incredible piety and the power, always for good, of belief. *Helen* (1916) is in some ways a *Passe Rose* made contemporary.[4] Helen Lee is a thoroughly modern woman of mixed parentage and international experience who discovers first her passion for a young Frenchman, Jean de Trecour, then her more mature love for an older advisor, David Fearing. As with Hardy's other novels, the support, advice, and sympathy of the church are well represented.

Hardy was never more than an *amateur* at fiction, diverting only a small part of his incredible energy to what must have been for him a pleasant pastime for the gentleman. Like E. P. Roe and Josiah Holland, he is essentially a Christian apologist in his novels, but with oh! what a difference in subtlety, tone, and intelligence. Still he is not "modern"; his power comes from those qualities that made the Victorian novel great, his weaknesses from its flaws. He is best at drawing subtle, intelligent characters who, when forced to make primordial moral decisions, reveal their true selves in ways which the reader has already anticipated from their behavior to that point. Those who have made suspiciously supercilious comments about the eternal verities, reveal their animal atavisms; those who have seemed uncertain but loving return us to the Golden Age, and the plot works out for Hardy as it did for Mrs. Southworth. Thus the pleasure that the modern reader finds in Hardy's novels is more likely to be in the secondary characters and in the less central situations, and even there he must be ready to forgive a good deal of unconscious racism, elitism, and hidden provincialism. With most of Hardy's novels— certainly in *But Yet a Woman*—the pleasure is worth the effort, but we are always aware that he is not of our time.

Hardy is thus largely independent of the influence of Henry James, rather drawing directly from some of the same antecedents as James. That is definitely not the case with Anne Douglas Sedgwick, in all of whose writings the influence of The Master may be clearly observed. Indeed, in her own life she seemed to follow either the Jamesian pattern, allowing for the difference in sex, or that of a typical James heroine. Although she spent but few of her earliest years in America, and those insulated from the ordinary democratic experiences by being privately tutored in the family home at Irvington-on-Hudson, in her maturity she romanticized this influence and thought of herself "in *temperament* and point of view . . . far more American than English."[5] She nevertheless concluded her education in England and then spent five years studying painting in Paris during one of art's most exciting periods, when Impressionism was gaining its audience. The experience was to be of great use in her writing; her comments on art and taste are always more detailed and specific than James's or Wharton's, they are usually more apt, and she is equally capable of playing theme and variation on the artist-writer metaphor. Finally, in 1908, when approaching the peak of her writing career, she married Basil de Selincourt, an eminently eligible bachelor three years her junior, and slipped into the comfortable role of an English landed gentlewoman. Except for two brief visits to the United States, she remained in England for the rest of her life. If the story of her life and career seems a happier version of *A Portrait of a Lady*, her first novel, *The Dull Miss Archinard* (1898) is very early Jamesian in the simplicity of its plot and the detail of the cultured Old World setting. Romantically enough, it is also reputed to have been written for the entertainment of her sisters and published only when her father showed it to a publisher in London. The novel's success spurred her to continue in the same vein, which she did with a series of novels, each more Jamesian than the last. *The Confounding of Camelia* (1899) is as slight as *The Dull Miss Archinard*, but *The Rescue* (1902) is interesting for both its characters and its style.[6] It is, like most of Sedgwick's best work, the study of the effect of a strong personality on those around it; and it is told from a center of consciousness slightly outside the main psychological action, for the first half of the novel at least.

The novels that followed this first group continued to show Sedgwick's apprenticeship to James, but finally led her to an expression of her own which is Jamesian in outline only. *Paths of Judgment* (1904) continues the experimental vein opened in *The Rescue* of the study of Continental personality in contrast to the more phlegmatic English. *The Shadow of Life* (1906) is more specifically Jamesian with its Basil Marcher hero, and *A Fountain Sealed* (1907) is very much like *The Europeans* in its contrasting of English and American climate and character. *Amabel Channice* (1908) is rather more daring than any novel Sedgwick had written to then. The story is all about illicit passion and its aftereffects, the "living down" a moment of passion, and English hypocrisy about money and morality. As is always true with Anne Sedgwick's fiction, the novel is conservative in its morality, but it is sympathetic to Amabel Channice's departure from the straight and narrow and her moral superiority over those who take advantage of her lapse. Daring in a different way is *Franklin Winslow Kane* (1910), an ironic comedy quite unlike anything of James's (except, superficially, *The Europeans*) in which two Americans are diddled in a romantic confidence game by an English couple.[7]

None of these is really an adequate preparation for the brilliance of Sedgwick's next novel, *Tante* (1911),[8] one of the finest and certainly most modern studies of the egotism of genius and its effect upon social relations. The plot is simple. Madame Mercedes Okraska von Marwitz, who is called Tante by her intimates, especially her adopted child, Karen Woodruff, is a concert pianist of international fame, with a distinctly grand manner. An English younger son of a good family, Gregory Jardine, falls in love with Karen, marries her, and almost loses her to the machinations of his wife's guardian (his guardian-in-law?), who cannot tolerate even such a minor diminishment of her ego. The novel has been praised primarily for the sheer size of the title character, and Mercedes von Marwitz is indeed a considerable creation, perhaps even an overwhelming one. But the novel is no less remarkable for several other qualities well worth examination: its balance in characterization, its use of minor characters, and its use of symbols. In all three areas the novel excels in a peculiarly modern way.

Mme von Marwitz threatens at every moment of the novel to become a monster; she never does. Gregory Jardine threatens at every moment to become the well-tubbed English hero of romance; he never does. It is here, in the balance and the realism of her central antagonists, that Sedgwick has achieved her greatest success. Our discovery of the depths of Tante's behavior—her annulment of her first marriage, her driving her second husband and her lover to suicide—comes from her old nurse, Mrs. Talcott, who is quick to forgive her, and who puzzles over the riddle of her behavior simplistically but sympathetically:

> Mercedes has got a powerful sight of will-power; but look at all she's got to use up in her piano-playing. There she is working up to the last notch all the time, taking it out of herself, getting all wrought up. Well, to live so as you won't be spoiling things for other people needs about as much will-power as piano-playing, I guess, when you're as big a person as Mercedes and want as many things. And if you ain't got any will-power left you just do the easiest thing; you just take what you've a mind to; you just let yourself go in every other way to make up for the one way you held yourself in. That's how it is perhaps. (312)

For all its down-home aura of folk wisdom, her explanation of the selfishness of genius is profound. Again, at the conclusion of the novel, when Tante has been defeated utterly and her cruelty toward Karen turned totally against her, it is Mrs. Talcott who sticks with her and offers her such solace as is available to her. Mrs. Talcott is a "touchstone" character; the reader is aware that her analyses of motivation, simple and innocent as they seem, are intended to represent the reality of things. Her staying with Tante is the best testimony of her real feelings.

Gregory Jardine is developed even more subtly. He seems at first simply naive about art and incapable, as he discovers during his first conversation with Mme von Marwitz, of rising "*à la hauteur*" of his interlocutor (38). We sympathize with him as his love for Karen grows and he becomes critical of the conventionality of the society of which he has been a satisfied member to that point. As he explains to Karen,

"They haven't been trained to see differences," said Gregory, and he summed up the Lavingtons in the aphorism to himself as well as to Karen; "only to accept samenesses." (99)

Later he summarizes society as a series of little boxes and its denizens as people who worry only about the plates things are served on, incapable of noticing the difference between an exquisite charlotte russe and a stewed rhubarb, as long as the plates are correct. He retains some sympathy through the novel; he is always capable of seeing through *some* of his class's hypocrisy. But it is nevertheless true that he reveals himself to be quite limited as a human being (and therefore, much more real as a character in fiction).

The scene in which he proposes to Karen is a fine example. She confesses her love, they revel in their happiness for some time, then Karen says, "I hope we may be married." Gregory is somewhat taken aback when she tells him that she must have Tante's permission before she will marry him. In the discussion that follows, "all his happiness was blurred. He felt as if a great injury had been done him." Finally, he bursts out in a most unlawyerly (and unloverly) fashion,

"If you loved me I should certainly expect you to say that you would marry me whether your mother consented or not. You are of age. There is nothing against me. Those aren't English ideas at all, Karen."

To which Karen applies the *coup de grace:*

"But I am not English. . . . My guardian is not English. They are our ideas." (113)

Convicted of a narrow provinciality, Gregory then goes on to prove his childish pettishness.

"If she [Mme von Marwitz] did refuse, what reason could she give for refusing? As I say, there's absolutely nothing against me."
Karen had kept her troubled eyes on his downcast face. "There might be things she did not like; things she would not believe for my happiness in married life," she replied.

"And you would take her word against mine?"

"You forget, I think," he had lifted his eyes to hers, and she looked back at him, steadily, with no entreaty, but with all the perplexity of her deep pain. "She has known me for eleven years. I have only known you for three months."

He could not now control the bitterness of the dismay; for, coldly, cuttingly, he knew it, it was quite possible that Madame von Marwitz would not "like things" in him. Their one encounter had not been of a nature to endear him to her. "It simply means," he said, looking into her eyes, "that you haven't any conception of what love is. It means that you don't love me."

They looked at each other for a moment and then Karen said, "that is hard." (114)

Did ever a marriage begin so inauspiciously? Gregory's "love" clearly includes a large sense of ownership, and jealousy of Karen's guardian. He caps this utter foolishness with his crudest mistake of all. When Karen mentions that Tante had mentioned a prospective husband for her, and that she had said she did not love him, and ended the matter there, Gregory pursues the matter:

"Who was the young man," he asked. Not that he really cared to know.

"His name is Herr Franz Lippheim" said Karen gravely. "He is a young musician."

"Herr Franz Lippheim," Gregory repeated, with an irritation glad to wreak itself on this object presented opportunely. "How could you have been imagined as marrying someone called Lippheim?"

"Why not, pray?"

"Is he a German Jew?" Gregory inquired after a moment.

"He is, indeed, of Joachim's nationality," Karen answered, in a voice from which the tears were gone. (115)

His faux pas and the justness of her retort are borne out by the appearance of Franz later in the novel. He is also a "touchstone" character, like Mrs. Talcott, and his personal goodness is necessary to make the ending work.

As the plot wears on, just as the reader is about to forget this evidence of Gregory's possessiveness under the weight of the misery his wife's guardian inflicts upon him (all sons-in-law must empathize with him more than the critical modicum!), he destroys the reader's sympathy with new evidences of his conventionality. Tante behaves outrageously at a dinner party, and he quarrels with Karen when she tells him, simply, that their "best was not good enough for her," even though the statement is patently true. Tante plays off his sister against the two of them; Gregory sees through the stratagem, grants Karen all her guardian had asked of her, and then cannot resist two very foolish and Victorian actions: he tells Karen that he sees through her guardian's motives, and he sends her off to bed instead of discussing the matter, treating her like a child instead of his wife. He later compounds the sin by imagining that she has gone off to sleep when she is lying sleepless, waiting for him to take her in his arms.

And so the novel goes, with Gregory's stiff conventionality intruding again and again upon the couple's happiness and the reader's sympathy with his suffering. When the final climax arrives, one expects him to act the perfect boor that he does, sending Karen off with a sneer about the possibility of her committing adultery and an underhanded reference to her illegitimate birth. There can be no doubt that *Tante* owes something to James's *The Bostonians*, but in Gregory Jardine, Sedgwick has created a character with ten times the vexing and vexed humanity of Basil Ransom.[9]

If the major characters are balanced and realistic in their humanity, the minor ones are brilliantly presented for whatever purposes they may have, from the slenderest of *ficelles* to the broadest of bases for comparison. Franz Lippheim provides a fine example. He is the merest *ficelle* in terms of the plot, serving as a "rejected alternative" to Gregory first, then as a supposititious adulterous companion for Karen at the novel's conclusion. He appears in only two settings, playing chamber music to the annoyance of Gregory and rescuing Karen from her sickness and despair. His Jewishness is remarked only twice, but it is always present, balancing out his goodness somehow, restraining the Victorian reader from granting full sympathy to him. Opposed to it is his position in a musical metaphor. When he looks at Karen he *thinks* Schubert and Mozart, exactly the right touch for his position as contrast to Tante. As she is the egotistical performing artist, so he is the self-effacing member of a string quartet, satisfied to love music and identify all joy with elements of it. When at the end of the novel he is being manipulated by Tante as a means of continuing her control over Karen, the modern reader undoubtedly responds rather differently to the situation than the reader of 1911.

The other minor characters of Madame von Marwitz's entourage all serve multiple purposes too. Most of them are opportunities for satire of the hangers-on around a great performing artist. Miss Scrotton is a marvelous example of the type who willingly accepts crumbs from the banquet and jealously guards the most meaningless and trivial prerogatives. Claude Drew is utterly obnoxious and completely believable as the young-man-on-the-make contemptuously seducing a middle-aged lady for whatever advancement it can bring him, and so stupidly overconfident of his powers that he misreads the situation with Karen completely. Mrs. Forrester is important as the character who bridges conventional society and the milieu of von Marwitz brilliance and egotism. Blessed with an infinity of wealth and an equally infinite respect and tolerance for genius, she provides comfort and security for the *artiste*, insulating her from bores and conventionality. She is also a figure who compares with Gregory, since it is Gregory's failure to provide an ambiance as pleasant as Mrs. Forrester's when Mercedes descends on him that produces the rupture. The scene between Gregory and Mrs. Forrester after the break then explores the obligations of both sides—conventionality and genius—most meaningfully. And Talcott, as the old servant who knows where all the bodies are buried and who nevertheless remains faithful and, as far as possible, serves as a conscience to Mercedes, is simply perfect. It was wise of Sedgwick to make her American; her plain-spokenness succeeds where, for example, James's Mrs. Bread is ambiguous. There is, in short, not a dull character in this novel, not one who does not draw the reader more deeply into his or her own complexity and its effect upon the larger questions of the novel.

And these larger questions are, of course, terribly important. *Tante* raises the central question of the relationship between art and society, between conventionality and genius, and explores the ramifications of the conflict with as balanced a perspective as one gets in the novel before Joyce Cary's Gully Jimson novels. The problem is so important that it is no surprise that Sedgwick hedges her bets somewhat in her opening (and only) description of Madame Okraska's playing:

Only a rare listener, here and there among her worldwide audiences, was aware of deeper deficiencies and of the slow changes that time had wrought in her art. For it was inspiration no longer; it was the memory of inspiration.

The Nemesis of the artist who expresses, not what he feels, but what he is expected to feel, what he has undertaken to feel, had fallen upon the great woman. (15)

But balanced against this criticism are the many references to the demands of art—the practicing, the pressure of performance, and, yes, the adulation that inevitably goes with it, with its negative effect upon character. Tante is doubtless a completely selfish bitch, utterly destructive to Karen and her husband, and completely deserving the total defeat she suffers. And yet—the real center of the novel is not in what happens but how it happens, and for that most interesting part, Sedgwick established a whole series of symbols which tell a story not always identical to the plot.

The most striking symbol of the novel is the Buddha in a shrine which Tante sends as her wedding gift to the young couple. It is a grotesque present and an even more grotesque symbol, yet, with remarkable simplicity, Sedgwick carries it off. As a gift it is completely in character—grandiose yet beautiful, a criticism of Gregory's "smallness" and a shout of Mercedes' bravado, a white elephant and a constant reminder of the painfulness and ambiguity of art. Both Gregory and Karen are aware of its symbolic content, of course, so there are a number of references to it which adumbrate its central ambiguity. When Mercedes arrives to stay with them in Gregory's flat, she "overflows the flat the way the Bouddha overflows the study" (197); when the two lovers quarrel, the Buddha smiles down on them ambiguously; when Gregory contemplates Mercedes, he thinks of her as the Buddha made flesh:

Seated on his chintz sofa in the bright, burnished room, all in white, with a white lace headdress, half veil, half turban, binding her hair and falling on her shoulders, she made him think, in her inappropriateness and splendour, of her own Bouddha, who, in his glimmering shrine, lifted his hand as if in a gesture of bland exorcism before which the mirage of a vulgar and trivial age must presently fade away. The Bouddha looked permanent and the room looked transient; the only thing in it that could stand up against him, as it were, was Karen. To her husband's eye, newly aware of esthetic discriminations, Karen seemed to interpret and justify her surroundings, to show their commonplace as part of their charm and to make the Bouddha and Madame von Marwitz herself, in all their portentous distinction, look like incidental ornaments. (166–167)

Thus the Buddha teaches as well as symbolizes—but, alas, the lesson is lost on Gregory later, as he allows Karen to leave him but keeps the Buddha. It should be noticed that the Buddha is also ludicrous, as the situation of the mother-in-law joke is ludicrous too. Ludicrous, yet apt and, indeed, profound, it is an incredibly successful symbol.

The Buddha is only the most important of a whole series of symbols or images of the implications of taste and genius in art. Tante is wickedly exact in describing Gregory's library before she sets foot in it.

"Has it red wall-paper, sealing wax red; with racing prints on the walls and a very large photograph over the mantelpiece of a rowing crew at Oxford?" Madame von Marwitz questioned with a mixture of roguishness and resignation. (180)

She is surprised to discover some teacups in good taste, and pointedly compliments Karen in her choice of husband's great-grandmother, from whom she assumes, correctly, they descended as heirlooms. Then there is the often ironically contrapuntal imagery of music. At the end of the novel, when the passionate climax is inevitable, it is to Bach that Madame Okraska retreats in her practicing, and Karen plays a Bach prelude, all innocently, for the insidious delectation of Claude Drew; but Tante's playing of the "Appassionata" of Beethoven is described in detail at the beginning of the novel, and clearly the romantic is her forte.

Sedgwick's inventiveness in imagery is climaxed at the end of the novel with an effort at the sublime which will fail for some readers, but will not appear ridiculous to those who read her intelligently. One must not lose sight of Mercedes' love for Karen in the details of her egotism, bitchiness, and selfishness, else the breakdown she undergoes at the end of the novel when Karen is lost and then found again will appear staged. Karen is her surrogate for the child she never had, and manipulative as her behavior toward her is, it is the behavior of a mother. Thus, when Sedgwick has Talcott pinion Mercedes' legs to the sofa she is lying on so that Gregory can be free to talk to Karen in the room upstairs, the symbol of parturition is quite deliberate, however much it shocks the reader at first. When it is followed by the conversation between Talcott and Mercedes, as midwife to patient, resuming the old ties and returning the action to the original status quo, the perceptive reader is stunned by its aptness. Life does go on in precisely this way, and the Jardines' marriage and Madame Okraska's performances, public and private, will persist.

Tante is a fine novel indeed, perhaps the finest to be discussed in this work. It was followed by others only less successful. *The Encounter* (1914) is closely related to *Tante* in its subject, a philosopher with a dominating personality named Ludwig Wehlitz who attracts about himself a circle of disciples not unlike the campfollowers of Madame Okraska. The rocky love affair he undergoes with a young American girl, Persis Fennamy, provides a less successful plot center for contrasting effects than the love affair in *Tante*. *The Third Window* (1920) is really little more than a *nouvelle*, but it is interesting as Sedgwick's parallel to *The Turn of the Screw*.[10] The story tells of an ambiguous appearance of the ghost of Antonia Wellwood's ex-husband, who died in the war; the intent of the apparition is to end the engagement of Antonia with Bevis Saltonhall, and it seems to be a real ghost because the woman who sees it, Cicely, the dead man's cousin, describes details which she could not know about his fatal wound. Sedgwick's alternative explanation for the supernatural appearance of the ghost is to tie it with the paranormal rather than, as James did, with the obsessional. Cicely can describe the details of the wound because she read Bevis's mind! To many readers that will seem a distinction without a difference, but to Bevis Saltonhall it offers some cold comfort—which grows colder when Antonia dies anyway.

The Third Window would not be worth discussing except for the fact that it immediately preceded the novel that is generally considered Sedgwick's best, *Adrienne Toner* (1922).[11] Whether or not it was her best, that novel was certainly her most popular, and for good reasons. The title character has a touch of the paranormal about her—she cures headaches with a laying on of hands. She is an American, fabulously wealthy, an Emersonian transcendentalist by persuasion, and a hater of the conventional, like Tante. She manages to ruin a number of English lives among the family she marries into, and then redeems herself by martyring herself personally and nationally by building and serving in hospitals for "our boys" on the Continent. Several of her behavior patterns, especially toward the end of the novel when she is deeply occupied with self-sacrifice, hint uncomfortably of jingoistic allegory—Columbia fumblingly repairing her failure to act earlier through a deeper redemption, etc. All that is too mawkish to examine in detail, but was undoubtedly a popular position to hold right after the war, and perhaps is the key to the novel's success.

Certainly the manner with which it was written offers no explanation for its popularity. Its style could best be described as deepest, darkest James—not so much in sentence structure, although one finds, if one pursues, the odd example like this one:

> With an irony, kindly enough, yet big, he knew, with unfavourable inferences, he even recognized, reconstructing the moment in the light of those that followed, that in rising to meet him as he was named to her, it had been, rather than in shyness or girlishness, in the wish to welcome him and draw him the more happily into a group she had already made her own. (24)

—which is as impenetrable unintentionally as this parodic effort has been by design. No, the novel is Jamesian primarily in its structure. The center of consciousness is in Roger Oldmeadow. Roger has Strether's sensibilities and the Assinghams' driving curiosity in an unholy alliance. He is peripheral to most of the plot, until the final pages of the novel, and spends most of his time discussing events after the fact with other nonparticipants, as the Assinghams do in *The Golden Bowl*.[12] Like Strether, he has a certain moral weight, and even, from time to time, opportunity to use it. On these occasions he falls painfully short. There is the time, for example, when he is accompanying Adrienne at the piano when she sings a Schubert song. She sings it well—drily, with no great voice, but a respect for the music—and he compliments her afterwards:

> "Thank you. That was a pleasure," he said.
>
> It was a pleasure. It was almost a link. He had found a ground to meet her on. He saw himself in the future accompanying Barney's wife. He need, then, so seldom talk to her. But alas! she stepped at once from the safe frame of art.
>
> "If we can rise from loss to feel like that, if we can lift our sorrows like that, we need never turn to palliatives, need we, Mr. Oldmeadow?" she said.
>
> Stupidity, complacency, or power, whatever it was, it completely disenchanted him. It left him also bereft of repartee. What he fell back upon, as he looked up at her and then down at the keys again, was a mere schoolboy mutter of "come now!"
>
> After all a schoolboy mutter best expressed what he felt. She was not

accustomed to having her ministrations met with such mutters and she did not like it. That was apparent to him as she turned away and went back to the sofa and Barney. She had again tried him and again found him wanting. (95)

The problem is that Adrienne holds all the cards. She appears— and is—monstrous in her willingness to live up to her ideals and to encourage others to do the same, at all costs. One by one they fail and turn against her, until only Palgrave is left, her Paladin, as she calls him. His unconventionality takes the form of pacifism, and he dies, for unexplained reasons, in a prison, following his principles. Even though Adrienne no longer agrees with him, she supports his right to act according to principle. Her atonement binge in France follows directly upon his death. Thus the novel reflects that most uncomfortable of cliché situations: the moral absolutist who causes discomfort among her inferiors—relativists all—and must atone for her sins by becoming even more saintly. That is, of course, the ultimate Jamesian subject, and one can sense Maggie Verver and Millie Theale in the character and effects of Adrienne Toner. The novel might even have succeeded, had Adrienne been allowed to proceed by her example to force her fierce morality upon the others in the normal run of things. But the war upset that possibility for Sedgwick, and she could not resist the beatification of Adrienne as a manifestation of the "American principle" in Old World affairs. Because of that, Adrienne's rejection of Oldmeadow's offer of love at the very end of the novel seems an inevitable conclusion from the *force majeure* of the war's influence.

These criticisms are of the novel as a whole; individual parts of it are as fine as anything Sedgwick ever wrote, truly the touches of genius. Oldmeadow's dreams of Adrienne are well woven into the action in a way that is far superior to the use of the paranormal in *The Third Window*. His perceptions are either intellectually rigorous, and hence a suitable counter for Adrienne's force of personality, or they are couched in images that the reader comes to see are perfect for the situation. A good example is Oldmeadow's perception of Eric Hayward, a minor character who is glimpsed only once in the entire novel. Eric is a married man who is Meg Chadwick's lover (Meg is Adrienne's sister-in-law). After the two of them begin a surreptitious affair, Adrienne advises them to live together openly, in defiance of convention. The one time Oldmeadow sees Eric, he is seated in a brougham with Adrienne and Meg, and is turning his face away from Meg at that moment, just, Oldmeadow thinks, as his old retriever, John, would turn his face away when presented with a new kitten. Oldmeadow recollects the image several times in the novel, but never so effectively as when he is told of Eric's death in France, when "There passed through his mind the memory of the embarrassed, empty, handsome young face in the brougham and, again, the memory of his dog John. He had seen John die and his eyes of wistful appeal. So Eric Hayward's eyes might have looked as he lay in the barn dying." T. S. Eliot's "objective correlative" is not usually so effectively in evidence.

The novel is ahead of its time in introducing several social issues which are typical of the twentieth century. The "generation gap" is a frequent topic to Oldmeadow, who is constantly surprised when he discovers that one or another of the more level-headed (he believes) of the younger people are turned by Adrienne's influence. Sexism is also a frequent topic. This novel is the earliest I have read in which extensive criticism is raised about the treating of women as chattels. In the two situations in which adultery, once real, once imagined, serve as cause for divorce, Sedgwick has made considerable progress since *Tante* in her sophisticated acceptance of the necessity for broader legal grounds for divorce. And, finally, in the central conflict of the novel between a self-reliant, Emersonian, American girl and an English family who accept her because of her money and because of their misunderstanding of the force of her convictions and their own capability to live with them, Sedgwick extends the "international theme" of James into a new dimension. One of the minor images she uses for the purpose is worth considering. Adrienne is always curiously clumsy when pouring tea. The detail is minor but appropriate to her character. She has little gift for the conventional or the traditional, it suggests. But at the end of the novel Oldmeadow recalls her clumsiness at pouring tea and the act ripens into new significance:

"You've the gift of leadership. The gift for big things generally."
She nodded. "I'm only fit for big things."
"Only? How do you mean?"
"Little ones are more difficult, aren't they? My feet get tangled in them. To be fit for daily life and all the tangles; that's the real test, isn't it? That's just the kind of thing you see so clearly, Mr. Oldmeadow. Big things and the people who do them are just the kind of things you see through."

"Oh, but you misunderstood me—or misunderstand," said Oldmeadow. "Big things are the condition of life; the little things can only be built up on them. One must fight wars and save the world before one can set up tea-tables." He remembered having thought of something like this at Lydia's tea-table. "Tea-tables are important, I know, and the things that happen round them. But if one can nurse a ward of typhus patients single-handed one must be forgiven for letting the tea-pot slip."

Had Sedgwick left the matter there, it would have been a telling image. But she carries it too far, by letting Adrienne go on to say, self-deprecatingly, "I wasn't . . . capable of being truthful in drawing-rooms when other women made me angry. But I can go on battlefields and found hospitals and tend the sick and dying. Shells and pestilences . . . if people knew how trivial they are—compared to seeing your husband look at you with hatred" (319-320). The reader is simply embarrassed by such a speech; Sedgwick has given up *showing* us the American character and is now telling us.

Sedgwick's last four novels, *The Little French Girl* (1924), *The Old Countess* (1927), *Dark Hester* (1929), and *Philippa* (1930), carry her well into the modern period and are at once more "modern" and less successful than either *Tante* or *Adrienne Toner*.[13] They deal more specifically with sexual matters, are more international in character, and concentrate, as an older woman novelist's last novels well might, on the relations between the older and younger generations. They are powerful novels, all of them, but they seem somehow old-fashioned—the delicacy of Jamesian style out of place in the New Freedom of expression. They are, nevertheless, considerable achievements, and deserve with Sedgwick's earlier and better works to be remembered. One wonders, if Anne Douglas Sedgwick had been more firmly fixed in one country or another, America or England, and in one period or another, Victorian or modern, would she not be better remembered today?

II *In the Wake of Norris, Dreiser, and Sinclair:*
The New Subject Matter

Serious writers who happen to be born in an age of transition should carefully choose the subject matter of their writings if they want to be remembered. An old-fashioned style may be forgiven, but old-fashioned concerns are the direct route to the remainder tables. The writers who are considered in the rest of this chapter either took up subject matter for which the world was not yet ready or dealt with it in a manner that contemporary and later critics felt was insufficiently *engagé*. As will be seen, some of these critical appraisals ought to be revised.

Anna Katherine Green (1846–1935) was certainly ahead of her time in her decision to devote herself to the writing of detective fiction. Her background gives no hint as to why she would make such a choice. An 1866 graduate of Ripley Female College of Poultney, Vermont, her first intentions were to write poetry, a vocation encouraged by Ralph Waldo Emerson, who knew her as a schoolgirl and corresponded with her later in life. *The Leavenworth Case,* her first novel and in some ways her best, was published in 1878.[14] In the next fifty years she was to produce some thirty-five more, all with similar virtues and flaws. Thus a consideration of this one novel provides a fair critical summary of all her work.

The most prominent difficulty in Anna Green's writing is her style. In dialogue particularly her Victorian limitations are clearest. Here, for example, is a crucial inquiry between the coroner and one of the characters:

"Mr. Harwell," the coroner began, "we are told of the existence of a pistol belonging to Mr. Leavenworth, and upon searching, we discover it in his room. Did you know of his possessing such an instrument?"

"I did."

"Was it a fact generally known in the house?"

"So it would seem."

"How was that? Was he in the habit of leaving it around where anyone could see it?"

"I cannot say, I can only acquaint you with the manner in which I myself became cognizant of its existence." (53)

Caught up in the quasilegal terminology of the coroner, she forgets and lets it carry over to Trueman Harwell's speech. She is also fond of the melodramatic protestation, both of innocence and guilt. Here is Eleanore Leavenworth proving her innocence to the narrator:

"You have said that if I declared my innocence you would believe me," exclaimed she, lifting her head as I entered. "See here," and laying her cheek against the pallid brow of her dead benefactor, she kissed the claycold lips softly, wildly, agonizedly [!], then leaping to her feet, cried in a subdued, but thrilling tone, "Could I do that if I were guilty? Would not the breath freeze on my lips, the blood congeal in my veins, the life faint away at my heart? Son of a father loved and reverenced, can you believe me to be a woman stained with crime when I can do this?" (128)

We are obviously closer to the world of E. D. E. N. Southworth than that of Dashiell Hammett. So we are when the murderer whom in the best tradition of detective fiction, I shall not name—confesses:

A silence ensued which like the darkness of Egypt could be felt, then a great and terrible cry rang through the room, and a man's form rushing from I knew not where, shot by me and fell at Mr. Gryce's feet, shrieking out,

"It is a lie! a Lie! Mary Leavenworth is innocent as a babe unborn. I am the murderer of Mr. Leavenworth, I! I! I!" (434)

Green is somewhat more fortunate in her dealings with another Victorian phenomenon, the concept of the gentleman, in that it allows her to split her protagonist into a commoner-detective and gentleman-narrator, a device which seems more natural than Conan Doyle's unexplained division between Holmes and Watson. The scene in which her detective, Ebenezer Gryce, invokes the aid of the narrator reads like a petroglyph of another epoch:

"Now you, I dare say, have no trouble—" [Gryce] exclaimed, "was born one, perhaps [a gentleman]. Can even ask a lady to dance without blushing, eh?"

"Well," I commenced—

"Just so," he replied, "now I can't. I can enter a house, bow to the mistress of it, let her be as elegant as she will, so long as I have a writ of arrest in my hand or some such professional matter upon my mind, but when it comes to visiting in kid gloves, raising a glass of champagne in response to a toast— and such like, I am absolutely good for nothing." (149)

To a modern reader the comedy of the detective who "knows his place" is curiously distasteful. But Green uses this division to add depth to the characters of both detective and narrator. Gryce's habit of seeming to stare in inappropriate places while questioning people is at once endearing and effective as a technique to ascertain truth.

And their different ways of evaluating the same evidence comes finally to imply that the difference between the gentleman and the *roturier* is only superficial.

Green's chief virtue as a writer of detective fiction is a superficial verisimilitude in matters of law; her chief flaw is insufficient awareness of psychological factors. The most salient fact of *The Leavenworth Case*, for example, is that Mr. Leavenworth left all his money to one niece, nothing to the other one, yet that matter is passed over by everyone as curious but not essential until the denouement. Any modern writer would supply the reader with some explanation, however incorrect, until the conclusion, if only to conceal the importance of the fact. Green miscalculates human nature—both her characters' and her readers'.

A different kind of subject matter engaged the early literary efforts of Henry Harland (1861-1905). Harland's first four novels, published under the pseudonym of Sidney Luska, explore the day-to-day life and emotional crises of the Jews of New York city, a milieu which Harland knew in youth and escaped by converting to Christianity just before he began writing novels. His writing reflects that love-hate relationship about Jewish culture one has come to expect in novelists like Herbert Gold and Philip Roth, but which sounds strange in the idiom of the *fin-de-siècle* romance. That duality is compounded by an even more striking division between Harland's treatment of daily life in the Jewish community with an almost Flemish realism and extraordinarily bizarre plots, all of which turn on strange psychological aberrations based on sexual taboos. Indeed, one might say that every one of these four novels exhibits in microcosm the grappling in the soul of Henry Harland between the forces of idealism and realism typified by the transition from the Victorian to the modern age—and if one did, one would be parodying the hypertense style that Harland affected in the worst moments of these novels!

A brief consideration of the best two of these novels will illustrate the point. *As It Was Written: a Jewish Musician's Story* (1885) has all the crudeness one might expect of a first novel, along with evidence of considerable force. It is a Jekyl-Hyde story of a musician named Ernest Neuman who murders his fiancée, Veronika Pathzuol, while under the influence of the submerged half of his split personality. He is not convicted of the crime because no motive can be found. Later the truth is revealed to him in a most striking way. A letter from his dead father suggesting that his proposed marriage would be incestuous causes him to write an inspired piece of music which then concludes in a prose confession of his guilt for the murder. Improbable as this sounds in summary, Harland made it convincing, chiefly by judiciously setting these events in a meticulously realistic milieu of the Jewish community and by allowing the reader to make all the connections himself about the relationship between art and violence, conventionality and repression—although the implications are not always obvious. In fact, it is likely that the modern reader, better versed in psychology than Harland's contemporaries, will notice elements in the novel which, had they been observed when it was written, might have made it as unpublishable as Stephen Crane's *Maggie, Girl of the Streets.*[15]

The Yoke of the Thorah (1887), which followed the somewhat less successful *Mrs. Peixada* (1886), is an even more brilliant study of pathological behavior in an everyday setting.[16] Elias Bacharach falls in love with a beautiful Christian girl named Christine Redwood. Their marriage is thwarted by Elias's uncle Felix, who, knowing that Elias is subject to epileptic seizures, brings one on for Elias on his wedding day and then convinces him that what had happened was the direct intervention of Jehovah, angered by Elias's effort to debase His Chosen People. Uncle Felix then shrewdly manipulates Elias to marry a nice Jewish girl, Matilda Morganthau, and take his rightful place in the community. But Elias, who never twigs to the "scientific" explanation of the jilting of his first fiancée, becomes convinced that he is the personal battleground for the forces of light and darkness, writes an impassioned letter to Christine which he does not mail, and then an incoherent one which he does have delivered upon hearing that she is about to marry a Christian. He then goes to wait for her in Central Park and dies of exposure after another seizure.

Now then, is it agreed that anyone who could make a believable novel out of that hash must be a genius? Harland does it by use of his blend of archetypes and realism, characters who are deeply conventional and constantly surprising, as people are in real life. Thus we first see Elias as a thoroughly modern young man, a bohemian, a painter, a lover of the poetry of the Rossettis, fond of avant-garde music, and tolerant of his uncle, whom he finds neither "patriarchal nor picturesque" when describing him to Christine. This character is undercut by two brief scenes between Elias and Felix, both of which suggest the anathema upon mixed marriage derivable from Deuteronomy—Torah and Targum. One of the central acts of his courtship of Christine is to take her to a performance of Berlioz's *The Damnation of Faust*, and the two lovers discuss the opera and its differences with Goethe's *Faust* at length. The parallels the reader draws between the opera and Elias's situation are then subtly reinforced by Harland. Elias undergoes one crisis of conscience in darkness after his uncle reminds him of his cultural heritage; he relapses into love for Christine in light. He submerges his feelings about his violation of Jewish culture and tradition, the indication of which is that he does not even tell his uncle of his wedding until the night before it is to take place, and then only because of his fiancée's insistence. Felix's manipulation of him from that point on is "explained" by his epilepsy, but makes more sense in terms of the triangle Faust-Marguerite-Mephistopheles, which Harland never mentions but the reader senses.

Harland's "second act" is a retreat into the real world of the Jewish business community of New York with Uncle Felix playing "Fiddler on the Roof" instead of Mephistopheles. His role culminates in one magnificent aria of rabbinical casuistry. Felix argues,

"Well and good. Then what I want you to consider is this. In the first place, here is a young lady, whom you like very much, ready and willing to become your wife. You've got to take her or leave her. Unless you profit by your chances, and secure her now, you'll have to give her up altogether, and lose her for good. In the second place—whether intentionally or unintentionally doesn't matter—you have, by your assiduous devotion, contrived to win her love, and to cause her and her family to expect that you were going to ask her for her hand in marriage. Consequently in the event of your now abruptly breaking off with her, discontinuing your visits, you will occasion the young lady herself much unmerited grief and humiliation, you'll set busybodies far and wide to gossiping, and you'll bring no end of odium down upon yourself. Consider these things, and you'll see that you've got yourself into a very unpleasant situation, a very tight fix. There's only one way out of it! but that way is strewn with roses. Matrimony! Marry her! Why, if I were in your place, I shouldn't hesitate an instant." (241–242)

Q.E.D. How could Elias resist? (Unless Uncle Felix, as Zero Mostel might play the role, argued the other side and convinced him equally of that!)

Readers of Harland's day were simply not prepared to accept the kind of mixture this novel presents, the "black farce" of the insidious limitations Jewish culture can have upon the young who rebel against it. Elias Bacharach is not that different from Portnoy—or better, Portnoy's friend who hanged himself and left a note to his mother that her Mah-Jongg group was postponed. Harland returns the novel to its tragic side by having Elias write a long and tortured letter to Christine which thematically reveals the conflict that drives him to a kind of suicide, but that is, in a larger sense, the tragedy of the transitional character caught between his dream of the ideal and the stultifying reality of his day-to-day existence. In his derangement, Elias brings together the disparate elements that are the symbols of his impending tragedy, without, of course, ever seeing their thematic purpose. Thus he compares "the past and the present! What I had given up, and what I had got in place of it! After my glimpse of you, the reality—Tillie!" (273) just before going on to a long revery of his seeing *The Damnation of Faust* with Christine at his side. It is all very subtle and intriguing to the modern reader, but must have seemed simply in bad taste to Harland's contemporaries. In any event, the modern Jewish novel begins with Henry Harland, and may be seen almost completely developed in his four earliest works.

Harland's achievement in these four novels is the more extraordinary when one considers his later career as editor of *The Yellow Book*. From pioneer of the Jewish novel to quintessential decadent of the *fin de siècle,* from prototype of Portnoy to chief *épateur des bourgeois*—a truly incredible career. It is so incredible and archetypally *modern*, that we shall pass quickly over his later novels, which are anything but modern. The truth is, however, that shortly after Harland gave the world his delightfully ascerbic criticism as "The Yellow Dwarf" of *The Yellow Book*, he turned away from the kind of writing he had been doing in his Jewish novels to a much more refined and Victorian style in the manner of Arthur Sherburne Hardy, culminating in his most successful novel, *The Cardinal's Snuff-Box* (1900). This novel and the others he wrote in the same style, *The Lady Paramount* (1902), *My Friend Prospero* (1904), and *The Royal End* (1909), are charming, eminently readable, with here and there a striking reminder of the author's American background (never a hint of his Jewishness).[17] They are, in short, attractive Victorian or romantic novels and a far cry from his cruder but more modern early work. If

Harland is forgotten today, it is undoubtedly his own fault. In turning deliberately away from the modern to a fictional analogue of the well-made play, he was denying his birthright only less tragically than Elias Bacharach brought himself to deny his.

John Luther Long (1861–1927) has come to be associated with quite a different ethnic specialty, the exotic Japan of his best-known work, *Madame Butterfly* (1898). Long did not fetter his imaginative view of the country that was to be the setting for almost all of his work with any firsthand knowledge; he was content with the Japan of books and of the reminiscences of his sister, who had been a resident of Japan for many years. While Long is remembered only for the one work—and, at that, only for the play he made from it with David Belasco, or perhaps more properly and even more attenuated, for the opera by Puccini derived from the play—several other of his works in Japanese settings are hardly less good. *Miss Cherry Blossom of Tokyo* (1895) is somewhat melodramatic and sentimental, but in the character of Sakura-san, the Japanese heroine who was educated at Bryn Mawr, Long had a charming and complex creation. She has little in common with Cho-Cho-san of *Madame Butterfly* except her charm, since she safely straddles the two ways of life while Cho-Cho-san is truly a tragic victim of cultural difference. *The Fox Woman* (1900) is a *Madame Butterfly* with the sexual roles reversed.[18] The cruel Western woman becomes the title character (in Japanese, a woman with no soul is a "fox woman") by using the love she inspires by her beauty to deform and destroy a trusting Japanese artist. The novel lacks the classic simplicity of *Madame Butterfly*, but is powerful in a grotesque and exotic way. Both novels, of course, are modern in their suggestion of sexual exploitation, but Long is tentative, and ultimately quite Victorian, in the plotting of rewards and punishments for sexual transgression.

The earliest example of a relatively non-Victorian attitude toward sex and retribution for it is an enigmatic novel by James P. Story—perhaps a pseudonym—*Choisy,* published in Boston by James R. Osgood in 1872.[19] *Choisy* tells of how young Charley Wales, son of Edward Wales, banker, gambled, lost, and then stole to make up for his losses. He is sent to Europe to weather the scandal, leaving the field clear for Dick Huntley, who engineered his disgrace, to win the heart of his fair cousin Emma. Scapegrace Charley, surely not the average hero of a Victorian novel, arrives in Paris with a letter of introduction to Huntley's pal Somers, who proceeds to show him the seamier and more interesting aspects of the city. They gamble at Longchamps, they take in the can-can at Mabille, which Somers observes is worth looking at once, "*en touriste*," but is small potatoes compared to the illicit pleasures he has in mind. Those pleasures turn out to be two. The more public one is absinthe, which Somers calls the "best abused blessing of the age," and which produces a monumental hangover for Charley, in which his sleep "was a sequence of painful interviews with [his] whole line of ancestors." His (slightly) more private pleasure is Nina Choisy, a gray-eyed courtesan of intelligent conversation and voluptuous sensuality. After winning his mind and heart, she takes his body as well, leaving little to the imagination:

> She kept her swimming eyes on his, drew his hand to her heart, and her lips murmured softly, "Bébé!"
> And he leaned down and kissed her silently. (88)

There is no thunder or lightning, no instant retribution; there is rather an *affaire* in which Charley grows up and finally away from Nina, returns eventually to New York and "Lombard Street" to succeed in business, to win Emma away from the evil Dick Huntley, and, presumably, to live happily ever after, his wild oats suitably sown. Our last view of Nina Choisy is equally devoid of just deserts. She is at a gaming table:

> She was playing—playing with a listless, contemptuous hand—that tossed thousands upon the cloth with an air of utter indifference.

And the author's last comment on her is really directed to the reader: "Stone her if you will, ye righteous." (142)

If, as many critics believe, the best indicator of the difference between almost exact contemporaries in the matter of their "modernity" by comparing their treatment of sexual matters. To conclude seems, it was published exactly fifty years before *Ulysses*. And, of course, it is not alone. As with all "dividing lines" and "cleavage points" and such dividers of one age from another, the concept of a subject so taboo that writers could only broach it realistically if they are "modern" must be seen more as metaphor than as fact. But it remains at least metaphorically true that one can discern differences between almost exact contemporaries in the matter of their "modernity" by comparing their treatment of sexual matters. To conclude this chapter, no better comparison could be found than the careers and writings of two women who were exact contemporaries: Gertrude Atherton (1857–1948), a hard-core Victorian in spite of her efforts to the contrary, and Margaret Deland (1857–1945), as thoroughly modern about sex as Atherton is old-fashioned. There are paradoxes involved in this comparison which, once examined and perhaps explained, go a long way toward defining "modern" as applied to the novel.

Gertrude Atherton was a native Californian, born and raised in San Francisco, a city with which she closely identified and used prominently in her fiction. California, it would seem, is the archetypally "modern" state, whether it is seen as the Promised Land of the Joads or the earthly hell of Nathanael West, but it also has a longer and more incredibly romantic history than any other Western state, mingling Russian statesmen with Spanish grandees and hard-driving Americans. That romantic California was Atherton's first attachment, and her first writings were historical fiction about the California of missions, diplomacy with Mexico, and Russian princesses. These are exotic romances with a vengeance, perhaps the more so because they were well researched and, from the first, unusually outspoken about human passion, especially female. These early novels were popular and carried with them a certain notoriety. Atherton found herself considered one of the "erotic school" of fiction, along with Amelie Rives Troubetzkoy and Edgar Saltus, among others, and responded with a certain pride in the title and perhaps a further spur to annoy Mrs. Grundy.

Of these early novels *The Doomswoman*[20] is first, typical, and probably best. The plot is early-California Romeo and Juliet. The Estenega and the Iturbi y Moncada families are feuding, and Diego Estenega and Chonita Iturbi y Moncada are star-cross'd lovers caught in the feud with the usual results. But there is much more even to the plot. To begin with, Chonita is a Doomswoman, marked with a caul, as it were, for important things. Diego is also something special—he has such an eye for "fixing" people that he could have studied at the knees of the Ancient Mariner. He has the sexual magnetism of a Valentino. And he is ambitious for power for the greater glory of California through development by the Americans (who are, blessedly, not called "gringos" in this book, though a later novel bears the title *Before the Gringo Came* [1915]). Diego and Chonita meet as god-parents for a child of Alvaredo, the governor of the province, and Diego is a frequent visitor at the Iturbi y Moncada ranch, where the laws of hospitality protect him in his efforts to seduce Chonita. Thus, the feud does not seem too great a bar to the uniting of the lovers. But there are other problems. Chonita takes a holy vow against Diego, and the weight of the church holds her back from him for a while. His politics also stand in the way until he overcomes her prejudices. Her brother, Reinaldo, becomes his sworn enemy and must be dealt with. Then, just when everything seems ripe, Chonita finds him kissing Valencia in the garden. Diego enlists Chonita's duena, Estaquaria,[21] to explain the "double standard" to the poor misguided girl, and events proceed to what looks like a favorable denouement until Reinaldo interrupts what would technically be a rape by stabbing Diego—not to protect his sister's virginity but to avenge himself for having been fooled by Diego. It is Mrs. E. D. E. N. Southworth in a sombrero, a throwback to an earlier romantic eroticism, not an advance toward realism.

But the novel has redeeming qualities. To begin with, there is the well-researched detail of everyday life and, even better, *feria* days in the hacienda. Atherton's description of a bull-bear fight is horrendous and effective, especially when she touches on the feelings the struggle arouses:

[The bull] made a savage onset. The bear, with the dexterity of a vaquero, leaped aside and sprang upon the assailant's neck, his teeth meeting argumentatively in the rope-like tendons. The bull roared with pain and rage and attempted to shake him off, but he hung on; both lost their footing and rolled over and over amidst clouds of dust, a mighty noise, and enough blood to satisfy the early thirst of the beholders. Then the bull wrenched himself free; before the mountain visitor could scramble to his feet, he fixed him with his horns and tossed him on high. As the bear came down on his back with a thud and a snap which would have satisfied a bull less anxious to show what a bull could do, the victor rushed upon the corpse, kicked and stamped and bit until the blood spouted into his eyes, and pulp and dust were indistinguishable. Then how the delighted spectators clapped their hands and cried "Brava!" to the bull, who pranced about the plaza, dragging the carcass of the bear after him, his head high, his big eyes red and rolling! The women tore off their rebosos and waved them like banners, smashed their fans, and stamped their little feet; the men whirled their sombreros with supple wrists. (33)

The violence of scenes like that one is appropriate within the generally idyllic setting of California under Spanish rule. The image of Arcadia is evoked several times, and with it, through the voice of Diego Estenega, the equally pastoral convention of the death's-head motto, *et in Arcadia ego*. The secret of Diego's power is that he alone is experienced amid a land of innocents. In individual instances, it makes him sound like a know-it-all and an unconvincing character, but the total effect is striking. He horrifies one group of senoritas by doubting that "a freckled Virgin would have commanded the admiration of the centuries, or even of the Holy Ghost" (44). He converses philosophically with Chonita about his ambition with a *fin-de-siècle* assumption that its pointlessness is justification enough. He seems humanly inconsistent in two passages quite near each other, in one of which he assails monogamy and in the other defines love:

Tell her—explain to her—what men are. Tell her that the present woman is omnipotently present—no, don't tell her that. Tell her that history is full of instances of men who have given one woman the devoted love of a lifetime and been unfaithful to her every week of the year. Explain to her that a man to love one woman must love all women. (204)

*   *   *

Love is not passion, for one may feel that for many women; not affection, for friendship demands that. Not even sympathy and comradeship; one can find either with men. Nor all, for I have felt all, yet something was lacking. Love is the mysterious turning of one heart to another with the promise of a magnetic harmony, a strange original delight, a deep satisfaction, a surety of permanence, which did either heart roam the world it never would find again. (214)

Diego's character would be even closer to Lovelace's than to that of a modern hero were it not for a number of humanizing scenes. In the most striking, he is out riding with Chonita when they encounter a band of robbers despoiling a mission church. Diego and Chonita ride through the band, surprising them momentarily, but are vulnerable to their numbers. Diego rises to the occasion:

Estenega rose in his stirrups, his fine bold face looking down impassively upon the demoniacal gang who could have rent him apart, but who stood silent and startled, gazing from him to the beautiful woman, whose white gown looked part of the white horse she rode. Estenega raised his hand and pointed to Chonita.

"The Virgin," he said, in a hollow impressive voice. "The Mother of God. She has come to defend her church. Go." (72)

It works. When Estenega speaks again—"Go! lest she weep. With every tear a heart will cease to beat," the thieves run away, terrified. Chonita berates him for his blasphemy, then for risking their lives and her virtue. He replies matter-of-factly that had his ruse failed, he would have killed her rather than have her dishonored, but that he had no doubt the scheme would work. This Tom Sawyerish quality strikes the modern reader as more believable than his decadent posturing about willing to "dare all" for his ambition or his love, like Byron's heroes. It is only a touch, but it seems the most modern part of the book.

The materials were simply too intractable. Perhaps no writer could make modern fiction out of pre-Alamo California, or of the other historical topics and settings that Atherton chose to write about. Her particular blend of extensive but uncritical research (for *The Conqueror*, 1902, her best-seller biography of Alexander Hamilton, she said she read over 200 books), black versus white characters in conflict, and panting, breathless passion do not age well. Other subjects for her fiction were as intractable as history. Her one effort at a political novel, *Senator North* (1900), is puerile in comparison with Burnett's *Through One Administration*.[22] The title character is sixty years old, but is supposed to be attractive to the heroine because he has not lost his "sensuality." Compare the fatuousness of that motivation with Mrs. Burnett's characterization of Blunden and the difference between fiction and magazine fiction suddenly becomes clear.

But Gertrude Atherton attempted one topic that was ideal for creating a modern novel. Moreover, she wrote it during that *annis mirabilis* of modern writing, 1922, and attempted to gather in it most of the patently modern themes of current literature to fashion a masterpiece on a subject very dear to her heart. *Black Oxen* (1923) takes its title from William Butler Yeats' lines, "The years like great black oxen tread the world/And God the herdsman goads them from behind."[23] It was written as a result of rather more personal research than is common to fiction. Mrs. Atherton, feeling herself beginning to age at 66, had gone to the Austrian physician, Eugen Steinach, for a rejuvenation treatment and had had her gonads irradiated with X-rays. Whatever *Black Oxen* is as a novel, it was a million dollars worth of free publicity for Steinach.

The story is as simple as it is incredible. Mary Ogden was a belle of New York in the nineties when she married Prince Zattiany and moved into European high society. Then, after the war, a mysterious supposed "niece" of Madame Zattiany attracts the attention of a drama critic named Clavering for her beauty and for her incredible resemblance to the Mary Ogden of forty years before. He falls in love with her and still wants to marry her after she tells him that she is Mary Ogden, that she is fifty-eight years old, and that before she discovered the Roentgen-Steinach road to youth she had a parade of lovers that would make a nymphomaniac blush. He is not even importunate to discover if the rejuvenation of her face was achieved at the expense of her private parts, although she tells him that sterility was one side effect. Contented, they await the wedding day, surviving easily a few trials—young girls' catty remarks to her and a most unladylike attempt at his virtue by a young lady who has become a *folle de passion* over him. Just before the day, her European past catches up to her in the form of Count Hohenhauer, who convinces her that she should return to Austria with him to participate in the rebuilding of the country. She discovers that although her body has been rejuvenated, her mind recognizes the primacy of the drive for power over mere sexual passion.

Interwoven with this plot—it would be wrong to say integrated—is a series of thematic observations, subplots, and commentary. These range widely, but they are all very modern. There is much discussion of geopolitics, generally quite conservative, about what to concede to the masses to avoid their corruption by bolshevism. There is some literary criticism in which *Jurgen* figures prominently and both unnecessary censorship and undue realism are criticized. There is much talk of "flaming youth" and how the younger generation lacks seriousness, of liberated women and what asses they are, of the larger male atavism—war—and its female counterpart, cattiness. And underlying it all is sex, sex, sex. One of Mary Ogden's meditative moments might stand for all of the weltschmerz in the book:

Civilization had heaped its fictions over the bare fact of nature's original purpose, imagination lashing generic sexual impulse to impossible demands for the consummate union of mind and soul and body. Mutuality! When man was essentially polygamous and woman essentially the vehicle of the race. When the individual soul had been decreed by the embittered gods eternally to dwell alone and never yet had been tricked beyond the moment of nervous exaltation into the belief that it had fused into its mate. Life itself was futile enough, but that dream of the perfect love between two beings immemorially paired was the most futile and ravaging of all the dreams civilization had imposed upon mankind. (56-57)

If that seems a bit much to claim for civilization's overvaluing of the mutual orgasm, whether as metaphor or fact, its application to individuals is even more horrendous. The most striking example is Agnes Trevor, who enters the novel for only one scene. She is a forty-two-year-old spinster who comes to know Mary because she does a lot of volunteer work in the East side and takes on Mary's cause for the children of Vienna. Her only appearance in the novel is to burst out with a confession of the effect of sexual repression upon her:

Oh, Mary! You don't know! You don't know! You who've had all the men you ever wanted. Who, they say, have a young man now. The nights of horror I've passed. I've never slept a wink the nights our girls married. I could have killed them. I could have killed every man I've met for asking nothing of *me*. It seems to me that I've thought of nothing else for twenty years. When I've been teaching, counseling good thoughts, virtue, good conduct to those girls down there, it's been in the background of my mind every minute like a terrible obsession. I wonder I haven't gone mad. Some of us old maids do go mad. And no one knew until they raved what was the matter with them. When Hannah de Lacey lost her mind three years ago I heard one of the doctors telling Peter Vane that her talk was the most libidinous he had ever listened to. And she was the most forbidding old maid in New York. I know if I lose my mind, it will be the same, and that alone is enough to drive any decent woman mad. . . . I thought I'd get over it in time—I used to pray—and fight with my will—but when the time came when I should have been released I was afraid I would, and then I deliberately did everything I could to keep it alive. I couldn't lose my right—It was *my* right. I couldn't tell you all the things I've—Oh, I tell you that unless I can be young again and have some man—any man—I don't care whether he'll marry me or not—I'll go mad—mad! (262-263)

Mary's immediate solution for her is a dose of sal volatile; the longer-range plan is for a trip to Dr. Steinach. Both are, realistically considered, band-aids rather than cures for her malaise.

Even if we could see the Steinach solution as a metaphor for the treatment by the greater Viennese, Atherton's "modern" answer to the dislocation of the self through sexual repression is not satisfactory. The fault, dear Brutus, remains the same no matter what means is provided to relive that life we have so badly abused. By dealing honestly with her sexual appetites, Atherton manages to avoid making Mary Ogden appear only a ludicrous and grotesque old lady who is trying to be young again, but she cannot escape the essential futility of the proceeding, and Mary's eleventh hour escape to political seriousness in Vienna with Hohenhauer is, finally, an admission of that futility. Thus the apparent modernity of the novel in its complete absorption with sex is illusory; rather than being a totally modern novel, it is something like the apotheosis of the Victorian novel, since the implications of sexual dysfunction are sidestepped with the suggestion that seriousness of purpose is somehow a "higher" use of self. And that with the pathetic fate of Agnes Trevor still ringing in our ears. It is Agnes who will be the ludicrous and grotesque old lady upon her return from Steinach's clinic, with a "solution" which will only be a metaphor for a face-lift and a squad of discreet gigolos.

None of Atherton's other novels which essay modern themes succeeds any better than *Black Oxen. Tower of Ivory* (1910) was her own favorite of her almost sixty works, for reasons which would baffle the reader. Set in Munich, it is a study of a philosophic genius and the effect of passion upon him. Directly comparable with Sedgwick's *The Encounter*, it suffers immeasurably by the comparison. *Perch of the Devil* (1914) was Atherton's effort at a socially aware novel, set in Butte, Montana, during a period of economic and social violence. It has none of the realism of even Mary Hallock Foote's *Led Horse Claim. Mrs. Balfame* (1916), a murder mystery, is pale in comparison with any of Anna Green's mystery novels. Atherton's most successful novel, *The Conqueror*, is lurid and romantic even in comparison with such other examples of the historical novel as Winston Churchill's *The Crisis* or Lloyd Douglas's *The Robe*.[24] In short, in spite of her persistent efforts at taking on the latest modern theme or using the newest modern technique, her writing consistently fails to live up to the promises made for it. In spite of her efforts to be cosmopolitan and sophisticated, it remains provincial; in spite of her efforts to shock, it remains tame; in spite of her effort to be literary, it remains popular fiction and never anything more. Popular fiction could be literary in the days of Dickens and Thackeray; not so in the twentieth century.

Margaret Deland presents a complete and total contrast with Gertrude Atherton. With her childhood spent in western Pennsylvania, her young adult years in New York City, where she taught mechanical drawing at the Girls' Normal College of New York (now Hunter College), her early marriage and setting up housekeeping in Boston, she had nothing of the esoteric and romantic about her to compare with Atherton's stormy youth and marriage. She was a "Westerner" only by Boston standards—like Howells. Everything about her would seem to suggest Victorian gentility, an antithesis to Atherton. That she came to literature via writing verses for the earliest greeting cards, and that her first published volume of verse, *The Old Garden* (1886), was bound in flowered cretonne is to complete the picture of genteel Victorian prettiness outliving its usefulness.[25] Nevertheless, somehow or other, Margaret Deland managed to strike the modern tone in three novels and, only less successfully, in a long series of short stories in ways that are far beyond the capacity of Gertrude Atherton.

The topic and theme of her first novel, *John Ward, Preacher* (1888), came out of her family background and early married experience. Her family in Maple Grove, Pennsylvania, near Pittsburgh, was Presbyterian and rock-hard in doctrine. In her delightful autobiography, *Golden Yesterdays* (1941), Deland describes two separate examples of the extent of local orthodoxy.[26] One anecdote is about a poor plowman who is anathematized before the whole congregation for swearing at his horse; the other, more striking, tells how the minister at the funeral services for Deland's cousin took the opportunity to criticize her father for his failure to attend church regularly and blamed his lapse of attendance for his daughter's death. Margaret married a Unitarian and became friendly with and a communicant of the great Boston liberal Episcopalian, Phillips Brooks, so she knew both ecclesiastical worlds. *John Ward, Preacher* has as its central conflict the struggle between the orthodoxy of John Ward, a puritan in the mold of Jonathan Edwards, and Helen Jeffrey, his wife, who was raised by an Episcopal rector without much thought of dogma, but who comes to have a positive distaste for and disbelief in hell. The main plot too much resembles a theoretical construct—the immovable object and the irresistible force; resolution is impossible until Ward's death. But the reader's sympathy is perfectly balanced between the two characters, so carefully has Deland drawn Ward particularly, giving full expression to his loving human qualities and the honesty of his belief, that although the reader knows the novel is at heart an attack on unfeeling orthodoxy, his sympathies are invoked for all who have been driven by the iron law of belief to inhumanity to their fellowman.

That, however, is the effect upon the modern reader. For many of Deland's contemporaries the novel was a scandalous attack upon orthodox Christian belief. The fact that, purely by chance, the novel was published only six weeks after Mrs. Humphrey Ward's *Robert Elsmere* had drawn fire for its heretical implications from no less a literary critic than Gladstone only added to the furor.[27] Mrs. Grundy was alive and well in the Anglo-Saxon world, and when two transatlantic apostles of George Eliot seemed to be violating the first commandment of hypocrisy, they were to be told of their sins. Neighbors whispered about the Deland family, petty slights occurred, but the year was 1886, after all; the ideas of Darwin, Spencer, and Huxley were everywhere, and the *succès de scandale* ensured a distribution of the work that was bound to win readers to Deland's well-stated cause. Moreover, she had the public support not only of Brooks, which was perhaps to be expected, but also of William Campbell, the recently retired president of Rutgers University and a force in the Dutch Reformed Church, whose orthodoxy could not be questioned even if he was Margaret Campbell Deland's uncle.

The novel has aged extremely well, chiefly because of the balanced portraits of what are, after all, now just two opposed orthodoxies. It is particularly effective in the extensive subplot surrounding the lawyer, Denner, and the easy-going rector of Ashurst, Dr. Howe, and their conformity to the hypocritic gentility of their social circle, so much at odds with the force of their belief, let alone John Ward's. The most striking part of the novel is undoubtedly the deathbed scene of Denner, when his unspoken appeals for assurance of an afterlife are parried, sidestepped, and finally directly refused by the liberal Dr. Howe. Even with the direct refusal the charade of politeness continues:

He held up his little thin hand, peering at the light between the transparent fingers. "To think," he said slowly, with a puzzled smile, "to think that this is going to be still! It has never been any power in the world; I don't know that it has ever done any harm, yet it has certainly never done any good; but soon it will be still. How strange, how strange! And where shall I be? Knowing—or perhaps fallen on an eternal sleep. How does it seem to you, doctor? That was what I wanted to ask you; do you feel sure of anything—afterwards?"

The rector could not escape the penetrating gaze of those strangely bright brown eyes. He looked into them and then wavered and turned away.

"Do you?" said the lawyer.

The other put his hands up to his face a moment.

"Ah!" he answered sharply, "I don't know—I can't tell. I—I don't know, Denner!"

"No," replied Mr. Denner, with tranquil satisfaction, "I supposed not,—I supposed not. But when a man gets where I am, it seems the one thing in the world worth being sure of." (237-238)

Deland's next two novels, *Sidney* (1890) and *Philip and His Wife* (1894), are both rather unsubstantial examinations of the force of love—in *Sidney* of a father for his daughter, in *Philip and His Wife* of a husband for his wife and another woman. They—and a lengthy series of short stories Deland was writing during these same years— are interesting primarily as evidence of her increasing subtlety in the examination of moral problems and her settling upon a realized locale for her writings and a central consciousness as a touchstone for all her moral examinations. The setting is Old Chester, a composite western Pennsylvania village which Deland herself said "made her think of Manchester," a village near Maple Grove, her childhood home. It has nothing of the dimensions of Yoknapatawpha County, nor, for that matter, of Trollope's Barset, but she did use it to examine problems of race, country, tradition, and generations in the Faulknerian style, and not simply as a convenient never-never land like Crane's Whilomville. Chiefly, though, Old Chester exists as the village served by Dr. Edward Lavendar, parson *extraordinaire* and moral conscience supreme. Deland wrote later that Lavendar was a composite figure, "Looking like" the priest of an Anglican church in Pittsburgh, with some traits of her uncle, William Campbell, and some resemblance to Phillips Brooks, but she gave the game away when she admitted, "occasionally I borrowed a little of [her husband] Lorin's salt-and-pepper wit to put into his mouth" (315). If the husband she described in *Golden Yesterdays* is not a complete fictionalization, he is *the* pattern for Dr. Lavendar, who has merely aged a little and been put in ecclesiastical cloth.

Both the fictional curate and the real husband shared an ability to cut through moral hairsplitting to the center of an issue. In *Golden Yesterdays* Deland tells of how she received a check for $1000 from a publisher in England who had pirated *John Ward, Preacher*, quite legally, of course, since Longmans could hold no copyright on a work first published in America. Her husband then took her step by step through an examination of the situation until she concluded with him that even "common, garden-variety morality" required that she send the check and a letter to Longmans, with a copy to the pirate. The situation was strikingly similar to the basic plot of "The Note," collected in *Dr. Lavendar's People* (1903).[28] In that story Dr. Lavendar destroys a promissory note quite illegally and then writes checks for the amount himself, all to avoid a larger immorality. In the real event, Deland recorded that Longmans sued the pirate and lost; Dr. Lavendar is saved that turn of the screw.

Old Chester and Dr. Lavendar are important to the development of Deland's most important novel, *The Awakening of Helena Richie* (1906).[29] Helena Richie is married to a drunkard whom she despises, since he was responsible for the death of their child. Unable to divorce him, she takes a lover, Lloyd Pryor, and deceives the people of Old Chester by receiving him as her brother. She does this without the slightest qualm, since she dismisses ordinary conventionality as useless. But her deception leads young Sam Wright to fall in love with her, and when she is "unmasked" he commits suicide. Dr. Lavendar serves as prosecutor for her moral examination. She cannot see her own selfishness at work in the tragedy, and, indeed, Deland has balanced the situation so perfectly that the reader has almost equal sympathy with her. But Dr. Lavendar forces her to look from her individual behavior to its social implications and plants the seed that will lead eventually to a universal—in fact, to the categorical imperative. Helena argues her case with him:

"I never did any harm," then she quailed; "at least, I never meant to do any harm. So you can't say it was at anybody's expense."

"It was at everybody's expense. Marriage is what makes us civilized. If anybody injures marriage we all pay."

She was silent.

"If every dissatisfied wife should do what you did, could decent life go on? Wouldn't we all drop down nearer the animals?"

"Perhaps so," she said vaguely. But she was not following him. (329)

What is needed is a vehicle for her reward and/or punishment. That role is taken by a young orphan boy named David who is taken in by Helena as a surrogate for her dead child. Deland develops their relationship in part like Hester Prynne's relationship to Pearl in Hawthorne's *The Scarlet Letter.* The child says in perfect innocence things that are equivocal to the woman. She draws him out about Lloyd Pryor:

David meditated. "Is that gentleman my enemy?"

"Of course not! He isn't anybody's enemy," she told him reprovingly. David turned silently to his rabbits.

"Why did you think he was your enemy?" she persisted.

"I only just hoped he wasn't; I don't want to love him."

"What!"

"If he was my enemy I'd have to love him, you know," David explained patiently.

Helena in her confused astonishment knew not what to reply. She stammered something about that being wrong; of course David must love Mr. Pryor!

"They ought to have fresh water," David interrupted thoughtfully; and Helena had to reach into the hutch for a battered tin pan. (78)

David's innocent sensibility, like Pearl's, acts as a catalyst upon the moral awareness of Helena. After the suicide, she becomes acquainted with loss when David is taken away from her. Once she leaves Old Chester and resolves her moral confusion, Dr. Lavendar restores David to her.

Helena Richie is no Hester Prynne. She has no intellectual equipment to match Hester's "vain imagination" that she might be the "destined prophetess" who would "establish the whole relation between man and woman on a surer ground of mutual happiness." She is, rather, a shallow egotist who must be brought to Dr. Lavendar's social revisionism of Kant, that no person may do what, if done by all, would destroy society. Once she has been brought that far, the conventions may be upset again. Thus David, like Pearl, is the moral fulcrum for all the novel's action. When he is returned to her, a stasis has been achieved. Her situation has not been resolved, however, and Deland wrote a sequel to the novel to clarify it. *The Iron Woman* (1911) follows Helena and David Richie to Mercer, an iron manufacturing city, where David grows up to become a physician in the society of both the owner and the manager of the iron works. In the climax of this novel, Helena is forced to see her own earlier misstep in glaring light, and to confess it fully, when she sees David about to commit an almost identical repetition of it. The scene is melodramatic, but the logic of the relationship between Helena and David virtually requires it.

> "A man once talked to me just as you are talking to Elizabeth; he said he would marry me when I got my divorce. I think he meant it—just as you mean it now. At any rate, I believed him. Just as Elizabeth believes you."
> David Richie stepped back violently; his whole face shuddered. "You?" he said, "my mother? No!—no!—no!!"
> And his mother, gathering up her strength, cringing like some faithful dog struck across the face, pointed at him with one shaking hand.
> "Elizabeth, did you see how he looked at me? Some day your son will look that way at you." (275)

That "gathering up her strength" gives the game away: Helena is "playing" the melodrama for effect, just as Roxy plays her scene of revelation to her son in Twain's *Pudd'nhead Wilson*.[30] Outraging or outraged motherhood requires that the crime not be repeated.

Like Gertrude Atherton, Margaret Deland went to France during World War I and did relief work, receiving the cross of the Legion of Honor for her work. She also continued to write after the war, but her postwar novels and stories are pale in comparison with her earlier work. One cries for comparison with Gertrude Atherton's *Black Oxen*; *The Vehement Flame* (1922) is about a love affair between a boy of eighteen and a forty-year-old woman, but the subject seemed to have embarrassed Deland as much as the reader—and anyway, she had handled it better in the relationship between Sam Wright and Helena in *The Awakening of Helena Ritchie*. For the rest, Deland was content to write more Old Chester stories and a few novels in which, as with the earlier works, some kind of epiphany of moral growth is achieved. Her attitude is always objective; she is always mistrustful of whatever codification or dogma or social pressure or fad may be invoked to solve moral problems. Her characters are always tempted by these ready solutions, and always come, late or soon, to the dark night of the soul of searching their own hearts. In her work as a whole, nothing is sacred or profane. She believes in the sanctity of marriage, but no less in the necessity for divorce; all her characters busily pursue happiness, but all come finally to accept responsibility. Perhaps the overall feeling one has after reading a lot of Margaret Deland is that she has seen the world, the sordid no less than the ideal, the ugly with the beautiful, and would opt for the best where she could, but accept the worst where she must.

Notes and References

Because of the great number of works referred to in this study, the citations provided below supply full publication information, and thus can be used as a significant primary bibliography of authors and works. As a result, the "Selected Bibliography" which follows it does not repeat this information, but concentrates instead on surveys and critical studies of the novel and the identification of significant items about specific novelists.

All works cited in the notes are first-published editions. Where another edition has been used for quotations in the body of the text, the edition quoted is identified after the first entry.

Preface

1. Henry James, *The Ambassadors* (New York, Harper and Brothers, 1903). Eleanor H. Porter, *Pollyanna* (Boston L. C. Page and Company, 1913). Fanny Burnett, *Little Lord Fauntleroy* (New York, Charles Scribner's Sons, 1886).

2. Henry James, *Princess Casamassima* (London and New York, Macmillan and Company, 1886).

Chapter One

1. Quoted in Ralph P. Gardner, *Horatio Alger, or the American Hero Era* (Mendota, Ill., Wayside Press, 1964), p. 323.

2. Harriet Beecher Stowe, *Uncle Tom's Cabin* (Boston, John P. Jewett and Company, 1852). Horatio Alger, *Ragged Dick* (Boston, Loring, 1868).

3. Horatio Alger: *Luck and Pluck* (Boston, Loring, 1869); *Ragged Dick* (Boston, Loring, 1868); Collier, 1962 cited; *Ben the Luggage Boy, or Among the Wharves* (Boston, Loring, 1870); *Strong and Steady* (Boston, Loring, 1871); *Shifting for Himself* (Boston, Loring, 1876); *Bound to Rise* (Boston, Loring, 1873); *From Canal Boy to President* (New York, John R. Anderson Company, 1881); *From Farm Boy to Senator* (New York, J.S. Ogilvie and Company, 1882); *The Odds Against Him* (Philadelphia, Penn. Pub. Co., 1890); *Struggling Upward* (Philadelphia, Porter, Coates and Company, 1890); *Rough and Ready* (Boston, Loring, 1869); *Slow and Sure* (Boston, Loring, 1872).

4. Relating Alger's experience to his work is complicated by a biographi-

cal scandal. In 1928, Herbert R. Mayes, annoyed by the then-current fad of biographies which debunked well-known men by the application of Freudian claptrap without the scantiest awareness of the laws of evidence or the application of common sense, set out to parody the genre with an outrageously imaginative biography, *Alger: A Biography Without a Hero* (New York, Macy-Masius, 1928). Although he permitted no let or hindrance to his imagination, filling his text with utter nonsense (including a sex-filled episode in Paris while Alger was demonstrably a student at Harvard Divinity School), he builded better than he knew. Subsequent "scholars" and critics of Alger accepted Mayes' absurdities at face value, until more recently Frank Gruber and Ralph D. Gardner have set the record straight. The fictional and parodic Alger is on view, a snare and a delusion, in such authoritative works as *The Dictionary of American Biography* (shame, shame!) and in such recent "critical" works as John Tebbel's *From Rags to Riches* (New York, MacMillan, 1963). For an accurate version, see Gary Scharnhorst, *Horatio Alger* (Twayne, 1980).

5. It is tempting to imagine that Alger read Melville; his pre-Harvard reading included Dana's *Two Years Before the Mast* and Hawthorne's *Twice Told Tales* (Gardner, p. 97). The temptation arises especially from the similarity between Ragged Dick's flippancy and the similar characteristics of the boy described in Chapter 45 of *The Confidence-Man*. In the absence of direct evidence that Alger read the novel, one would have to note that the statistical likelihood is infinitesimal.

6. Josiah Gilbert Holland: *Timothy Titcomb's Letters to Young People, Single and Married* (New York, C. Scribner, 1858); *Bitter Sweet* (New York, C. Scribner, 1858); *Gold Foil Hammered from Popular Proverbs* (New York, C. Scribner, 1859); *Life of Abraham Lincoln* (Springfield, Mass., G. Bill, 1866); *Arthur Bonnicastle* (New York, Scribner, Armstrong and Company, 1873); *Sevenoaks* (New York, Scribner, Armstrong and Company, 1875); *Nicholas Minturn* (New York, Scribner, Armstrong, and Company, 1877).

7. Curiously, although the action of the novel takes place just after the Civil War and includes constant reference to the period of the War and immediately before it, the novel is singularly free of all references to the war of a specific nature.

8. Holland's choice of the name Belcher was surely made with the denouement in mind. The fact that Holland was born in Belchertown and spent most of his life in Springfield, Massachusetts, which is famous for its production of rifles, suggests a roman à clef. But Belchertown was named for the colonial governor, and the geography of the novel would place Sevenoaks far north of Springfield, somewhere in upstate New York not far from the Canadian border. The name Belcher is felicitous in other ways, of course—as the name for the rifle and as a reminder of the villain's less intellectual sins.

The true "key" to the novel is in the identification of the villain with James Fisk, Jr., as described in the text.

9. James Fenimore Cooper, *The Pioneers* (New York, Charles Wiley, 1823).

10. Nathaniel Hawthorne, *The House of the Seven Gables* (Boston, Ticknor, Reed and Fields, 1851).

11. William Dean Howells, *A Hazard of New Fortunes* (New York, 1889).

12. "Topics of the Times," *Scribner's Monthly* III (1872), 619.

13. Horace Traubel, ed., *With Walt Whitman in Camden* (New York, 1912), p. 184.

14. Quoted in Joyce Kilmer, *Literature in the Making* (New York, 1912), p. 8.

15. H. M. Plunkett, *Josiah Gilbert Holland* (New York, C. Scribners, 1894).

16. Carl Van Doren, *The American Novel* (New York, Macmillan, 1940), p. 113. Edward P. Roe, *Barriers Burned Away* (New York, Dodd and Mead, 1872).

17. Edward P. Roe: *Opening a Chestnut Burr* (New York, Dodd and Mead, 1874); *Near to Nature's Heart* (New York, Dodd and Mead, 1876); *A Knight of the Nineteenth Century* (New York, Dodd and Mead, 1877); *Without a Home* (New York, Dodd and Mead, 1881); *A Young Girl's Wooing* (New York, Dodd and Mead, 1884); *An Original Belle* (New York, Dodd and Mead, 1885); *Driven Back to Eden* (New York, Dodd and Mead, 1885); *He Fell in Love with His Wife* (New York, Dodd and Mead, 1886); *The Earth Trembled* (New York, Dodd and Mead, 1887); *Play and Profit in My Garden* (New York, Dodd and Mead, 1873); *Nature's Serial Story* (New York, Dodd and Mead, 1884).

18. John William DeForest, *Miss Ravenal's Conversion* (New York, Harper and Brothers, 1867).

19. William Dean Howells, *The Rise of Silas Lapham* (Boston, Tichnor, 1885).

Chapter Two

1. Herbert Ross Brown, *The Sentimental Novel in America* (Durham, N.C., Duke University Press, 1940), p. 176.

2. Henry R. Evans, *Old Georgetown on the Potomac* (Washington, D.C., 1933), p. 47.

3. E. D. E. N. Southworth: *The Mother-in-Law* (New York, D. Appleton and Company, 1851); *The Curse of Clifton* (Philadelphia, T. B. Peterson and Brothers [1852]); *Brandon Coyle's Wife* (New York, R. Bonner's Sons, 1893), p. 133.

4. E. D. E. N. Southworth, *A Leap in the Dark* (New York, R. Bonner's Sons, 1890), pp. 130–131.

5. E. D. E. N. Southworth, *Self-Raised* (New York, G. W. Dillingham and Co., 1897), p. 360.

6. Ibid., p. 191.

7. Susan Warner: *Melbourne House* (Boston, De Wolfe, Fiske and Company [1864]); *Daisy* (Philadelphia, Lippincott and Company, 1868).

8. A. D. J. Whitney: *The Gayworthies* (Boston, Loring, 1865); *Real Folks* (Boston, J. R. Osgood and Company, 1872); *Sights and Insights* (Boston, J.R. Osgood and Company, 1876); *Bonnyborough* (Boston and New York, Houghton, Mifflin and Company, 1886).

9. Jane Woolsey Yardley: *Little Sister* (Boston, Roberts Brothers, 1882); *A Superior Woman* (Boston, Roberts Brothers, 1885).

William Dean Howells *The Rise of Silas Lapham* (Boston, Tichnor, 1885); *A Modern Instance* (Boston, J. R. Osgood and Company, 1882).

Ellen Warner Kirk: *The Story of Margaret Kent* (Boston, Tichnor and Company, 1886); *Through Winding Ways* (Philadelphia, J.B. Lippincott and Company, 1880); *A Lesson in Love* (Boston, J.R. Osgood and Company, 1881); *Sons and Daughters* (Boston, Ticknor and Company, 1887); *Queen Money* (Boston, Ticknor and Company, 1888).

10. Mrs. Albert Payson Terhune: *Jessamine* (New York, G. W. Carleton and Company, 1873); *A Gallant Fight* (New York, Dodd and Mead, 1888).

Julia Constance Fletcher: *Kismet* (Boston, Roberts Brothers, 1877); *Andromeda* (Boston, Roberts Brothers, 1885).

11. Letter in *The Critic*, July 24, 1886, p. 38.

12. John Townsend Trowbridge: *Lucy Arlyn* (Boston, Ticknor and Fields, 1866); *Farnell's Folly* (Boston, Lee and Shepard, 1885); *My Own Story* (Boston and New York, Houghton, Mifflin and Company, 1903).

13. Irving Bacheller: *Eden Holden* (Boston, Lothrop, 1900); *Vergilius* (New York, Harper and Brothers, 1904).

14. While it is technically beyond the purview of this study, I cannot resist noting that Melville's *Pierre* certainly draws upon several of Mrs. Southworth's novels, both in general tone and style (which he parodied) and in several details. And it is perhaps no coincidence that one of Mrs. Southworth's novels is entitled *Ishmael* (1863) and that her *Vivia* (1856) echoes the name of the hero Pierre created for his ill-starred novel. Though the evidence thus suggests a reciprocal influence, alas one can find no suggestion of it in Mrs. Southworth's style.

15. Mark Twain, *A Connecticut Yankee in King Arthur's Court* (New York, C.L. Webster and Company, 1889). William Dean Howells, *A Fearful Responsibility and Other Stories* (Boston, Osgood, 1881). Stephen Crane, *The Monster* (New York, Harper, 1898). Frank Norris, *McTeague* (New York, Doubleday and McClure, 1899).

16. Henry James: *Washington Square* (New York, Harper and Brothers, 1881); "The Altar of the Dead," *Terminations* (New York, Harper and Brothers, 1895); "The Beast in the Jungle," *The Novels and Tales of Henry James*, XVII (New York, Charles Scribner's Sons, 1909); *The Wings of the Dove* (New York, Charles Scribner's Sons, 1902).

E. D. E. N. Southworth, *The Discarded Daughter* (Philadelphia, A. Hart, 1852), p. 120.

Chapter Three

1. Arlo Bates: *The Pagans* (New York, Henry Holt and Company, 1884); *The Philistines* (Boston, Ticknor and Company, 1889); *The Puritans* (Boston and New York, Houghton, Mifflin and Company, 1898).

Henry James: *Roderick Hudson* (Boston, J. R. Osgood and Company, 1876); *The Princess Casamassima* (London and New York, Macmillan and Company, 1886).

2. I have strung together here several statements of Arthur's which are interrupted by other speakers without, I hope, distorting his meaning. Much of the dialogue of this novel *seems* as perverse and epigrammatical as the most outrageous stuff of Oscar Wilde, but when presented in this way is as programmatic as an Emersonian essay.

3. Robert Grant: *An Average Man* (Boston, J. R. Osgood and Company [1883]); *The Opinions of a Philosopher* (New York, C. Scribner's Sons, 1893); *Search-Light Letters* (New York, C. Scribner's Sons, 1899).

4. Robert Grant: *The Confessions of a Young Girl* (Boston, A. Williams and Company, 1880); *Face to Face* (New York, C. Scribner's Sons, 1886).

John Hay, *The Breadwinners* (New York, Harper and Brothers, 1884).

Henry Adams, *Democracy* (New York, Henry Holt and Company, 1880).

5. Robert Grant, *Unleavened Bread* (New York, C. Scribner's Sons, 1900).

6. Grant's style is superb, showing as prominently in his triteness as in his originality. With each of Selma's submissions to her three husbands, she "nestles in the hollow of his shoulder," a thrice-repeated motif that serves multiple purposes.

7. Robert Grant: *The Undercurrent* (New York, C. Scribner's Sons, 1904); *The Orchid* (New York, C. Scribner's Sons, 1905); *The Chippendales* (New York, C. Scribner's Sons, 1909).

8. Robert Grant: *The High Priestess* (New York, C. Scribner's Sons, 1915); *The Bishop's Granddaughter* (New York, C. Scribner's Sons, 1925); *The Dark Horse* (Boston and New York, Houghton, Mifflin and Company, 1931).

John Phillips Marquand, *The Late George Apley* (Boston, Little, Brown and Company, 1937).

William Dean Howells, *A Modern Instance* (Boston, J. R. Osgood and Company, 1882).

Theodore Dreiser, *Sister Carrie* (New York, Doubleday, Page and Company, 1900).

9. Howard Overing Sturgis, *Belchamber* (New York, G. P. Putnam's Sons, 1905); Oxford University Press, 1935, cited.

10. Henry James, *The Wings of the Dove* (New York, C. Scribner's Sons, 1902).

11. George Santayana, *The Last Puritan* (New York, C. Scribner's Sons, 1936).

12. See Gerard Hopkins, "Introduction" to the World's Classics edition of *Belchamber* (London, Oxford University Press, 1935), p. x. Besides this novel's influence on Santayana's *The Last Puritan*, discussed in the text, it bears a most curious resemblance to Robert Graves's *I, Claudius*. A cynical reader of the two novels might even imagine Graves composing his novel with a copy of Suetonius on one side and *Belchamber* on the other.

13. Henry Adams, *The Education of Henry Adams* (Boston and New York, Houghton Mifflin Company, 1918).

14. Walt Whitman, "Song of Myself," *Leaves of Grass* (New York, W. R. Scott, 1855), section 32.

15. Sylvester Judd, *Margaret: A Tale of the Real and Ideal* (Boston, Jordan and Wiley, 1845).

16. Julian Hawthorne, *A Fool of Nature* (New York, C. Scribner's Sons, 1896). Louisa May Alcott, *Little Women* (Boston, Roberts Brothers, 1868). Henrietta Hardy Hammond, *A Fair Philosopher* (New York, George W. Harlan and Company, 1882).

17. Donald Grant Mitchell, *Doctor Johns* (New York, C. Scribner and Company, 1866). Nathan Henry Chamberlain, *The Autobiography of a New England Farmhouse* (New York, Carleton, 1865). G.H. Devereux, *Sam Shirk: A Tale of the Woods of Maine* (New York, Hurd and Houghton, 1871).

18. Bliss Perry, *The Broughton House* (New York, C. Scribner's Sons, 1890).

19. Kate Carrington, *Aschenbroedel* (Boston, Roberts Brothers, 1882). Jane G. Austin, *Standish of Standish* (Boston, Houghton, Mifflin, 1890); *Mrs. Beauchamp Brown* (Boston, Roberts Brothers, 1880).

Caroline G. Curtis, *The Love of a Lifetime* (Boston, J. R. Osgood and Company, 1884).

Caroline Chesebro, *The Foe in the Household* (Boston, J. R. Osgood and Company, 1871).

20. Elinor H. Porter, *Pollyanna* (Boston, L. C. Page and Company, 1913).

Chapter Four

1. Robert Underwood Johnson, *Remembered Yesterdays* (Boston, 1923), p. 123.

2. George Washington Cable, *Old Creole Days* (New York, C. Scribner's Sons, 1879).

3. Herbert F. Smith, *Richard Watson Gilder* (Twayne, 1969), p. 56.

4. John Saunders Holt, *The Life of Abraham Page, Esq* (Philadelphia, J. B. Lippincott and Company, 1868); *What I Know About Ben Eccles* (Philadelphia, J. B. Lippincott and Company, 1869).

5. Francis Christine Tiernan, *A Daughter of Bohemia* (New York, D. Appleton and Company, 1874). William Falkner, *The Little Brick Church* (Philadelphia, J. B. Lippincott and Company, 1882). Harriet Beecher Stowe, *Uncle Tom's Cabin* (Boston and Cleveland, John P. Jewett and Company, 1852).

6. Thomas Dixon, *The Leopard's Spots* (New York, Doubleday, Page and Company, 1902); *The Clansman* (New York, Doubleday, Page and Company, 1905).

7. *The Battle-Pieces of Herman Melville*, Hennig Cohen, ed. (New York, 1963), p. 197.

8. John William DeForest, *Miss Ravenal's Conversion from Secession to Loyalty* (New York, Harper and Brothers, 1867). Margaret Mitchell, *Gone With the Wind* (New York, Macmillan, 1936).

9. William Mumford Baker, *Colonel Dunwoddie, Millionaire* (New York, Harper and Brothers, 1878). Edmund Pendleton, *A Virginia Inheritance* (New York, D. Appleton and Company, 1888). Katherine Sherwood Bonner McDowell, *Like Unto Like* (New York, Harper and Brothers, 1878).

10. Mary Greenway McClelland, *Jean Monteith* (New York, H. Holt and Company, 1887).

11. John Fox, Jr., *A Mountain Europa* (New York and London, Harper and Brothers, 1899); *A Cumberland Vendetta* (New York and London, Harper and Brothers, 1900); *The Little Shepherd of Kingdom Come* (New York, C. Scribner's Sons, 1903); *The Trail of the Lonesome Pine* (New York, C. Scribner's Sons, 1908).

12. F. Hopkinson Smith, *The Tides of Barnegat* (New York, C. Scribner's and Sons, 1906).

13. Marion C. Legaré Reeves, *Ingemisco* (New York, Blelock and Company, 1867); *Randolph Honor* (New York, Richardson and Company, 1868); *The Little Maid of Acadie* (New York, D. Appleton and Company, 1888).

14. Julia Magruder, *Across the Chasm* (New York, C. Scribner's Sons, 1885).

15. Julia Magruder, *A Sunny Southerner* (Boston, L. C. Page and Company, 1901).

16. John Fiske, *Old Virginia and Her Neighbors* (Boston and New York, Houghton Mifflin and Company, 1897).

17. Henry George, *Progress and Poverty* (New York, J. W. Lovell Company [1879]). Benjamin Kidd, *Social Evolution* (New York and London, Macmillan and Company, 1894).

18. Lydia Maria Child, *The Romance of the Republic* (Boston, Ticknor and Fields, 1867).

Elizabeth Whitfield Croom Bellamy, *The Little Joanna* (New York, D. Appleton and Company, 1876).

Christine Brush, *The Colonel's Opera Cloak* (Boston, Roberts Brothers, 1879).

M. Jaqueline Thornton, *Di Cary* (New York, D. Appleton and Company, 1879).

James Maurice Thompson, *His Second Campaign* (Boston, J. R. Osgood and Company, 1883); *Alice of Old Vincennes* (Indianapolis, The Bowen-Merrill Company [1900]).

Amanda Minnie Douglas, *Osborne of Arrochar* (Boston, Lee and Shepard, 1890).

William Perry Brown, *A Sea-Island Romance* (New York, J. R. Alden, 1888).

19. This chapter was written before the appearance of Arthur Haley's *Roots* and especially the enormously influential television series drawn from it. Although that work has unquestionably changed popular attitudes toward the history of the South, I am not at all sure that it is not rather the substituting of one myth for another rather than the substituting of true history for myth.

Chapter Five

1. Henry James, *The Bostonians* (New York and London, Macmillan and Company, 1886).

William Dean Howells, *A Hazard of New Fortunes* (New York, Boni and Liveright, 1889).

2. Mark Twain and Charles Dudley Warner, *The Gilded Age* (Hartford, American Publishing Company, 1873).

Charles Dudley Warner: *Saunterings* (Boston, J. R. Osgood and Company, 1872); *My Winter on the Nile* (Hartford, American Publishing Company, 1876); *In the Levant* (Boston, J. R. Osgood and Company, 1877); *Our Italy* (New York, Harper and Brothers, 1891); *Their Pilgrimage* (New York, Harper and Brothers, 1887).

William Dean Howells, *Their Wedding Journey* (Boston, Houghton, Mifflin, and Company, 1871).

3. Charles Dudley Warner: *A Little Journey in the World* (New York, Harper and Brothers, 1889); American Publishing Co., Hartford, 1904,

cited; *The Golden House* (New York, Harper and Brothers, 1895); *That Fortune* (New York and London, Harper and Brothers, 1899).

4. The impregnable moral position of Evelyn Mavick in *That Fortune* might also serve the lesser purpose of publicizing *The Library of the World's Best Literature*, which Warner helped to edit in 1896 and 1897. But that would be too cynical.

5. Nathaniel Hawthorne, *The House of the Seven Gables* (Boston, Ticknor, Reed and Fields, 1851).

6. John Dos Passos, *USA* (New York, Harcourt, Brace and Company, 1937).

7. The flaw is most noticeable in *The Golden House* because Warner was deeply involved in the same reforms described in the novel, both in Hartford and in New York.

8. Henry James, *The Princess Casamassima* (London and New York, Macmillan and Company, 1886).

9. William Starbuck Mayo: *Kaloolah* (New York, G. P. Putnam, 1849); *The Berber* (New York, G. P. Putnam, 1850); *Never Again* (New York, G. P. Putnam, 1873).

Edwin Lasseter Bynner, *Tritons* (Boston, Lockwood, Brooks and Company, 1878).

10. Of all the sitting ducks of conspicuous consumption, taste in decoration was the one most often potted by the satirists at all levels of talent. James's description of Waterbath in *The Spoils of Poynton* proves that the abuse was not limited to New York, while Howells's comments on the "gimcrackeries" of New York in *A Hazard of New Fortunes* is definitely understated when compared with the works of lesser writers. Probably the high-water mark of the genre occurs in Warner's *A Little Journey in the World*, when Margaret Henderson allows no limitation of wealth or vulgarity to define or refine her intentions for her New York mansion:

"Don't you think, dear," she said puzzling over the drawings, "that it would look better to be all sandalwood? I hate mosaics. It looks so cheap to have little bits of precious wood stuck about."

"I should think so. But what do you do with the ebony?"

"Oh, the ebony and gold? That is the adjoining sitting-room—such a pretty contrast."

"And the teak?"

"It has such a beautiful polish. That is another room. Carmen says that will be our sober room, where we go when we want to repent of things."

"Well, if you have any sandalwood left over, you can work it into our Boys Lodging-house, you know."

"Don't be foolish! And then the ball-room, ninety feet long—it looks small on the paper. And do you think we'd better have those life-size figures all round, medieval statues, with the incandescents? Carmen says she would prefer a row of monks—

something piquant about that in a ball-room. I don't know that I like the figures, after all; they are too crushing and heavy."

"It would make a good room for the Common Council," Henderson suggested.

"Wouldn't it be prettier hung with silken arras figured with a chain of dancing-girls? Dear me, I don't know what to do. Rodney, you must put your mind to it."

"Might line it with gold plate. I'll make arrangements so that you can draw upon the Bank of England."

Margaret looked hurt. (319-320)

11. Constance Cary Harrison: *Golden Rod: An Idyll of Mount Desert* (New York, Harper and Brothers, 1880); *The Story of Helen Troy* (New York, Harper and Brothers, 1881); *The Anglomaniacs* (New York, Cassell Publishing Company, 1890).

12. Mary Elizabeth Wilson Sherwood, *A Transplanted Rose* (New York, Harper and Brothers, 1882).

13. William Henry Bishop: *Detmold* (Boston, Houghton, Osgood and Company, 1879); *Old Mexico and Her Lost Provinces* (New York, Harper and Brothers, 1883); *The Golden Justice* (Boston and New York, Houghton, Mifflin and Company, 1887); *The House of the Merchant Prince* (Boston and New York, Houghton, Mifflin and Company, 1882).

William Dean Howells, *The Rise of Silas Lapham* (Boston, Ticknor, 1885).

14. Elizabeth Whitfield Bellamy, *Four Oaks* (New York, Carleton and Company, 1867).

15. Harriet McClellan, *A Carpet Knight* (Boston and New York, Houghton, Mifflin, and Company, 1885). Marie Healy Bigot, *Lakeville* (New York, D. Appleton and Company, 1873).

16. W. H. Rideing, *A Little Upstart* (Boston, Cupples, Upham and Company, 1885). W. Fraser Rae, *Miss Bayle's Romance* (New York, H. Holt and Company, 1887).

18. Lucy H. Hooper, *Under the Tricolor* (Philadelphia, J. B. Lippincott and Company, 1880). Ada M. Trotter, *Bledisloe* (Boston, Cupples and Hurd, 1887).

Chapter Six

1. Leaf 3, unpublished ms. in possession of Mrs. George E. Cantrell, Haddonfield, N.J.; quoted in Martin I. J. Griffin, *Frank R. Stockton, A Critical Biography* (Philadelphia, 1939), p. 14.

2. Frank R. Stockton: *Rudder Grange* (New York, C. Scribner's Sons, 1879); *The Rudder Grangers Abroad* (New York, C. Scribner's Sons, 1891); *Pomona's Travels* (New York, C. Scribner's Sons, 1894); *The Casting Away of Mrs. Lecks and Mrs. Aleshine* (New York, The Century Company, 1886), Appleton-Century, N.Y., 1933, cited.

3. Frank R. Stockton, *The Hundredth Man* (New York, The Century Company, 1887), Charles Scribner's Sons, New York, 1899, cited.

4. Frank R. Stockton: *The Great War Syndicate* (New York, Collier, 1889); *The Great Stone of Sardis* (New York and London, Harper and Brothers, 1889).

5. S. V. "Frank Stockton," *Dictionary of American Biography*. For a more modern reevaluation see also Henry Golemba, *Frank R. Stockton* (Twayne, 1981).

6. John Ames Mitchell, *The Last American* (New York, F. A. Stokes and Brothers, 1889).

7. John Ames Mitchell, *Doctor Thorne's Idea*, first published as *Gloria Victus* (New York, C. Scribner's Sons, 1897). Frank Norris, *McTeague* (New York, Doubleday, McClure Company, 1899). John Ames Mitchell, *The Silent War* (New York, Life Publishing Company, 1906).

8. Ira Wolfert, *Tucker's People* (New York, L. B. Fischer, 1943).

9. John Ames Mitchell, *Drowsy* (New York, F. A. Stokes [1917]).

10. Edward Bellamy, *Looking Backward* (Boston, Ticknor and Company, 1885). Albert Chavannes, *The Future Commonwealth* (New York, True Nationalist Publishing Company, 1892). Solomon Schindler, *Young West* (Boston, Arena Publishing Company, 1894). Henry Olerich, *A Cityless and Countryless World* (Holstein, Ia., Gilmore and Olerich [1893]). Castello N. Holford, *Aristopia* (Boston, Arena Publishing Company, 1895).

11. Luis P. Senarens: *Lost in a Comet's Tale* (New York, F. Tousey, 1895); *Frank Reade, Jr., and His Airship* (New York, F. Tousey, 1884); *Frank Reade and His Steam Man* (New York, J. Tousey, 1883).

Chauncey Thomas, *The Crystal Button* (Boston and New York, Houghton, Mifflin and Company, 1891).

12. Ignatius Loyola Donnelly, *Caesar's Column, a Story of the Twentieth Century* (Chicago, F. J. Schulte and Company [1890]). Mark Twain, *A Connecticut Yankee in King Arthur's Court* (New York, C. L. Webster and Company, 1889). Albert Chavannes, *In Brighter Climes* (Knoxville, Tennessee, Chavannes and Company, 1895). William Dean Howells, *A Traveller From Altruria* (New York, Harper and Brothers, 1894).

William Dean Howells, *A Traveller From Altruria* (New York, Harper and Brothers, 1894).

13. Thomas A. Janvier: *The Aztec Treasure House* (New York, Harper and Brothers, 1890); *Color Studies* (New York, C. Scribner's Sons, 1885).

14. H. Rider Haggard: *King Solomon's Mines* (London and New York, Cassell, 1885); *She* (New York, Harper and Brothers, 1887).

15. Willa Sibert Cather, *Death Comes to the Archbishop* (New York, A. A. Knopf, 1927).

16. Mary Hallock Foote, *The Led Horse Claim* (Boston, J. R. Osgood and Company, 1883).

17. Rodman W. Paul, ed., *A Victorian Gentlewoman in the Far West; the Reminiscences of Mary Hallock Foote* (San Marino, Cal., 1972), p. 17.

18. Owen Wister, *The Virginian* (New York and London, Macmillan and Company, 1902).

19. James Fenimore Cooper, *The Prairie* (Philadelphia, Carey, Lea, and Carey, 1827). Washington Irving, *Adventures of Captain Bonneville* (Philadelphia, Carey, Lea and Blanchard, 1837).

20. Emerson Hough, *The Story of the Cowboy* (New York, D. Appleton and Company, 1897), New York, Appleton, 1922, cited.

21. Emerson Hough, *The Covered Wagon* (New York and London, D. Appleton and Company, 1922).

22. Andy Adams, *The Log of a Cowboy* (Boston and New York, Houghton, Mifflin and Company, 1927).

23. James K. Folson, *The American Western Novel* (New Haven, 1966), p. 25, notes the impersonal quality of Adams's creation, but concludes that his purpose was "a historical one . . . a report of the facts of a way of life which has vanished." J. Frank Dobie, on the other hand, in a comment which in context praises Adams's historical accuracy, cites the parallel of Melville: "If all literature on whales and whalers were destroyed with the exception of *Moby-Dick*, we could still get from that novel a just conception of whaling." (In "A Salute to Gene Rhodes," p. xiii, *The Best Novels and Stories of Eugene Manlove Rhodes* [Boston, 1949]).

24. Joe Bertram Frantz and Julian Ernest Choate, *The American Cowboy: The Myth and the Reality* (Norman, University of Oklahoma Press, 1955).

25. William Faulkner, *"The Bear,"* in *Go Down Moses* (Random House, 1942).
Herman Melville, *Moby-Dick* (New York, Harper and Brothers, 1851).

26. Frank H. Spearman, *Whispering Smith* (New York, C. Scribner's Sons, 1906).

27. Stewart Edward White: *The Westerners* (New York, McClure, Phillips and Company, 1901); *The Claim Jumpers* (New York, D. Appleton and Company, 1901); *The Blazed Trail* (New York, McClure, Phillips and Company, 1902); *Gold* (New York, Doubleday, Page and Company, 1913); *The Grey Dawn* (New York, Doubleday, Page and Company [1915]); *The Rose Dawn* (New York, Doubleday, Page and Company, 1920).

28. Charles C. Park, *A Plaything of the Gods* (Boston, Sherman, French and Company, 1912).

29. Roger Pocock, *Curly* (Boston, Little, Brown and Company, 1905).

Chapter Seven

1. Mark Twain and Charles Dudley Warner, *The Gilded Age* (Hartford, The American Publishing Company, 1873).

2. Henry Adams, *Democracy* (New York, Henry Holt and Company, 1880). Henry James, *Pandora* (Boston, J. R. Osgood and Company, 1885).

3. *The New Yorker*, December 19, 1977, p. 141.

4. Robert Grant, *Unleavened Bread* (New York, C. Scribner's Sons, 1900).

5. Frances Hodgson Burnett, *Through One Administration* (New York, C. Scribner's Sons, 1881).

6. Josiah Gilbert Holland, *Sevenoaks* (New York, Scribner, Armstrong and Company, 1875).

7. R. O. Beard, "A Certain Dangerous Tendency in Novels," *The Dial* III (October, 1882), 110-112, attacked the appearance "in the pages of our best monthly periodicals [the] dangerous tendencies" of *Through One Administration*, along with Constance Fenimore Woolson's *Anne*, George Parson Lathrop's *An Echo of Passion*, and Thomas Hardy's *Two on a Tower*. All of these novels, according to Beard, betrayed "a disposition, which may well be called alarming, to trifle with the marriage relation."

8. Just before writing *Through One Administration*, Burnett had been impressed by both *The Europeans* and *Daisy Miller*. She wrote Gilder her admiration for the "neatness" of James's imagination, how "he leaves . . . no ends straggling—no gaps—no thin places." Quoted in Ann Thwaite, *Waiting for the Party: The Life of Frances Hodgson Burnett, 1849-1924* (London, 1974), p. 70.

9. Frances Hodgson Burnett, *Little Lord Fauntleroy* (New York, C. Scribner's Sons, 1886).

10. Herbert F. Smith, *Richard Watson Gilder* (Twayne, 1970), p. 29.

11. Frances Hodgson Burnett, *The Secret Garden* (New York, Grosset and Dunlap, 1911).

12. Paul Leicester Ford, *The Honorable Peter Stirling and What People Thought of Him* (New York, H. Holt and Company, 1894).

13. Alfred Henry Lewis, *The Boss, And How He Came to Rule New York* (New York, A. L. Burt Co., 1903).

14. Isaac Kahn Friedman, *The Radical* (New York, D. Appleton and Company, 1907).

15. Friedman commented on his heroine, Inez, that her "idea of poverty had been gleaned from such polite books as 'The Princess Casamassima,' which is like learning what the pains of rheumatism are from the third cousin of the man who had it" (52).

Chapter Eight

1. Arthur Sherburne Hardy: *Francesca of Rimini* (Philadelphia, J. B. Lippincott and Company, 1878); *Things Remembered* (New York and Boston, Houghton, Mifflin and Company, 1923); *Passe Rose* (Boston and New York, Houghton, Mifflin and Company, 1889); *But Yet a Woman* (Boston and New York, Houghton, Mifflin and Company, 1883).

2. Ludovic Halévy, *L'Abbé Constantin* (Paris, C. Lévy, 1882).

3. Arthur Sherburne Hardy: *Wind of Destiny* (Boston and New York, Houghton, Mifflin and Company, 1886); *His Daughter First* (Boston and New York, Houghton, Mifflin and Company, 1903).

4. Arthur Sherburne Hardy, *Helen* (Boston and New York, Houghton, Mifflin and Company, 1916).

5. Letter to Jane Pittman, 15 June 1902; in *Anne Douglas Sedgwick: A Portrait in Letters* (Boston, Houghton Mifflin and Co., 1936), p. 39.

6. Henry James, *A Portrait of a Lady* (Boston, Houghton, Mifflin and Company, 1882).

Anne Douglas Sedgwick: *The Dull Miss Archinard* (New York, C. Scribner's Sons, 1898); *The Confounding of Camelia* (New York, C. Scribner's Sons, 1899); *The Rescue* (New York, The Century Company, 1902).

7. Anne Douglas Sedgwick: *Paths of Judgement* (New York, The Century Company, 1904); *The Shadow of Life* (New York, The Century Company, 1906); *A Fountain Sealed* (Boston and New York, Houghton, Mifflin and Company, 1907); *Amabel Channice* (New York, The Century Company, 1908); *Franklin Winslow Kane* (New York, The Century Company, 1910).

Henry James, *The Europeans* (Boston, Houghton, Osgood and Company, 1879).

8. Anne Douglas Sedgwick, *Tante* (New York, The Century Company, 1911).

9. Henry James, *The Bostonians* (New York and London, Macmillan, 1886).

10. Anne Douglas Sedgwick: *The Encounter* (New York, The Century Company, 1914); *The Third Window* (Boston and New York, Houghton, Mifflin and Company, 1920).

Henry James, *The Turn of the Screw* (London and New York, Macmillan and Company, 1898).

11. Anne Douglas Sedgwick, *Adrienne Toner* (Boston and New York, Houghton, Mifflin and Company, 1922).

12. Henry James, *The Golden Bowl* (New York, C. Scribner's Sons, 1904).

13. Anne Douglas Sedgwick: *The Little French Girl* (Boston and New York, Houghton, Mifflin and Company, 1924); *The Old Countess* (Boston

and New York, Houghton, Mifflin and Company, 1927); *Dark Hester* (Boston and New York, Houghton, Mifflin and Company, 1929); *Phillippa* (Boston and New York, Houghton, Mifflin and Company, 1930).

14. Anna Katherine Green Rohlfs, *The Leavenworth Case* (New York, Putnam, 1878).

15. Henry Harland, *As It Was Written: a Jewish Musician's Story* (New York, Cassell and Company, 1885). Stephen Crane, *Maggie, Girl of the Streets* (New York, D. Appleton, 1896).

16. Henry Harland: *The Yoke of Thorah* (New York, Cassell and Company, 1887); *Mrs. Peixada* (New York, Cassell and Company, 1886).

17. Henry Harland: *The Cardinal's Snuff-Box* (London and New York, J. Lane, 1900); *The Lady Paramount* (London and New York, J. Lane, 1902); *My Friend Prospero* (London and New York, J. Lane, 1904); *The Royal End* (New York, Dodd, Mead and Company, 1909).

18. John Luther Long: *Madame Butterfly* (New York, The Century Company, 1898); *Miss Cherry Blossom of Tokyo* (Philadelphia, J. B. Lippincott and Company, 1895); *The Fox Woman* (Philadelphia and London, J. B. Lippincott and Company, 1900).

19. James P. Story, *Choisy* (Boston, J. R. Osgood and Company, 1872).

20. Gertrude Atherton: *The Doomswoman* (New York, Continental Publishing Company, 1901); *Before the Gringo Came* (New York, F. A. Stokes and Company, 1915).

21. Atherton's use of Estaquaria in the novel is a good indicator of the amateurishness of her writing: Estaquaria is a pointless narrator and center of consciousness, since she cannot know at first hand about half of what she tells in the novel.

22. Gertrude Atherton: *The Conqueror* (New York, Macmillan, 1902); *Senator North* (New York and London, J. Lane, 1900).

23. Gertrude Atherton, *Black Oxen* (New York, Boni and Liveright [1923]).

24. Gertrude Atherton: *Tower of Ivory* (New York, Macmillan Company, 1910); *Perch of the Devil* (New York, F. A. Stokes and Company [1914]); *Mrs. Belfame* (New York, F. A. Stokes Company [1916]).

Mary Hallock Foote, *The Led Horse Claim* (Boston, J. R. Osgood and Company, 1883).

Winston Churchill, *The Crisis* (New York and London, Macmillan, 1901).

Lloyd Douglas, *The Robe* (Boston, Houghton, Mifflin and Company, 1942).

25. Margaret Deland, *The Old Garden* (Boston and New York, Houghton, Mifflin and Company, 1886).

26. Margaret Deland: *John Ward, Preacher* (Boston and New York,

Houghton, Mifflin and Company, 1888); *Golden Yesterdays* (New York and London, Harper and Brothers, 1941).

27. Mary Augusta Ward, *Robert Elsmere* (London and New York, Macmillan and Company, 1888).

28. Gertrude Deland: *Sidney* (Boston and New York, Houghton, Mifflin and Company, 1890); *Philip and His Wife* (Boston and New York, Houghton, Mifflin and Company, 1894); *Dr. Lavendar's People* (New York and London, Harper and Brothers, 1903).

29. Gertrude Deland, *The Awakening of Helena Richie* (New York and London, Harper and Brothers, 1906).

30. Gertrude Deland, *The Iron Woman* (New York and London, Harper and Brothers, 1911). Mark Twain, *Pudd'nhead Wilson* (Hartford, Connecticut, American Publishing Company, 1894).

Selected Bibliography

The special contents of this volume demand that this bibliography be even more "selected" than usual. None of the multitude of primary works discussed in the text are noted here; instead, full publication information about them is provided in the Notes and References section, which thus constitutes a primary bibliography. This section then identifies significant secondary material, though mostly without the customary annotation in order to conserve space. Part I includes general works on the novel that are most concerned with the minor writers of the period, and thematic works that deal to some extent with one or another type of fiction discussed. Part II includes books and articles—but not reviews or obituary articles—about specific writers, named in alphabetical order.

I. General Works

BARNETT, LOUISE. *The Ignoble Savage; American Literary Racism, 1790-1870.* Westport, Connecticut: Greenwood Press, 1975.

BEER, THOMAS. *The Mauve Decade.* New York: Knopf, 1926.

BERTHOFF, WARNER. *The Ferment of Realism: American Literature, 1884-1919.* New York: The Free Press, 1965.

BOATRIGHT, MODY C. "The Beginnings of Cowboy Fiction." *Southwest Review,* LI (Winter, 1966), 11-28.

———. "The Formula in Cowbow Fiction and Drama." *Western Folklore,* XXVIII (April, 1969), 136-45.

BRANCH, E. DOUGLAS. *The Cowboy and His Interpreters.* New York: D. Appleton and Company, 1926.

BROOKS, VAN WYCK. *New England: Indian Summer.* New York: E. P. Dutton, 1940.

———. *The Confident Years, 1885-1915.* New York: E. P. Dutton, 1952.

BROWN, HERBERT ROSS. *The Sentimental Novel in America, 1789-1860.* New York: Pageant Books, 1959. See Chapter 2.

BUCK, PAUL. *The Road to Reunion.* Boston: Little, Brown, 1937.

CANBY, HENRY SEIDEL. *The Age of Confidence.* New York: Farrar and Rinehart, 1934.

CARGILL, OSCAR. *The Social Revolt: American Literature from 1888 to 1914.* New York: Macmillan, 1933.

CAWELTI, JOHN G. *The Six-Gun Mystique*. Bowling Green: Bowling Green University Popular Press, 1971. Excellent Bibliography.

CHASE, RICHARD VOLNEY. *The American Novel and Its Tradition*. London: G. Bell, 1958. General background only; no discussion of minor writers.

DEBOUZY, MARIANNE. *La Genèse de l'Esprit de Révolte dans le Roman Américain, 1875-1915*. Minard: Lettres Modernes, 1968.

DIETRICHSON, JAN W. *The Image of Money in the American Novel of the Gilded Age*. Oslo: Universitetsforlaget, 1965.

DOBIE, J. FRANK. *Guide to Life and Literature of the Southwest*. Dallas: Southern Methodist University Press, 1943.

EAKIN, PAUL JOHN. *The New England Girl*. Athens: University of Georgia Press, 1976. General study of cultural ideals.

ETULAIN, RICHARD W. AND PAUL R. WILSON. *The Frontier and the American West*. Arlington Heights, Illinois: A. H. M. Publishing Corporation, 1977. Excellent bibliography.

FIEDLER, LESLIE. *Love and Death in the American Novel*. New York: World, 1960. Important for sentimental novel's background.

FISKE, HORACE SPENCER. *Provincial Types in American Fiction*. New York: Century, 1903.

FLORY, CLAUDE R. *Economic Criticism in American Fiction, 1792-1900*. Philadelphia: University of Pennsylvania Press, 1936.

FOLSOM, JAMES K. *The American Western Novel*. New Haven: College and University Press, 1966.

FRANTZ, JOE B. AND JULIAN E. CHOATE, JR. *The American Cowboy: The Myth and the Reality*. Norman: University of Oklahoma Press, 1955.

FREDERICK, JOHN T. *The Darkened Sky: Nineteenth Century American Novelists and Religion*. South Bend: University of Notre Dame Press, 1968.

FRENCH, WARREN. "The Cowboy in the Dime Novel." *Texas Studies in English*, XXX (1951), 219-234.

GAINES, FRANCIS P. *The Southern Plantation: A Study in the Development and Accuracy of the Tradition*. New York: Columbia University Press, 1924.

GILMORE, MICHAEL T. *The Middle Way: Puritanism and Ideology in American Romantic Fiction*. New Brunswick, New Jersey: Rutgers University Press, 1977. Precedes the period, but excellent background material.

GROSS, SEYMOUR L., and JOHN E. HARDY, eds. *Images of the Negro in American Literature*. Chicago: University of Chicago Press, 1966.

GUILDS, JOHN CALDWELL. *Nineteenth Century Southern Fiction.*
Columbus, Ohio: Merrill, 1970.

HALL, ERNEST JACKSON. *The Satirical Element in the American
Novel.* New York: Haskell House, 1966.

HALL, WADE. *The Smiling Phoenix: Southern Humor from 1865 to
1914.* Gainesville: University of Florida Press, 1965.

HERRON, IMA H. *The Small Town in American Literature.* Durham:
Duke University Press, 1939.

HOLLIDAY, CARL. *A History of Southern Literature.* New York:
Neale Publishing Company, 1906.

HOLMAN, C. HUGH. *The American Novel Through Henry James.*
New York: Appleton-Century-Crofts, 1966.

HUBBELL, JAY B. *The South in American Literature, 1607–1900.*
Durham: Duke University Press, 1954.

———. *Who Are the Major American Writers?* Durham: Duke
University Press, 1972.

JOHANNSEN, ALBERT. *The House of Beadle and Adams and Its Dime
and Nickel Novels.* Norman: University of Oklahoma Press,
1950.

KAUL, A. *The American Vision; Actual and Ideal Society in Nineteenth Century Fiction.* New Haven: Yale University Press, 1963.

KEISER, ALBERT. *The Indian in American Literature.* New York:
Oxford University Press, 1933.

KNIGHT, GRANT C. *The Critical Age in American Literature.*
Chapel Hill: University of North Carolina Press, 1951.

———. *The Strenuous Age in American Literature.* Chapel Hill:
University of North Carolina Press, 1954.

LEACH, JOSEPH. *The Typical Texan: Biography of an American
Myth.* Dallas: Southern Methodist University Press, 1952.

MARCHAND, ERNEST. "Emerson and the Frontier." *American Literature,* 111 (May, 1931), 149–74.

MARTIN, JAY. *Harvests of Change: American Literature, 1865–1914.*
Englewood Cliffs, New Jersey: Prentice-Hall, 1967.

MCILWAINE, SHIELDS. *The Southern Poor White from Lubberland
to Tobacco Road.* Norman: University of Oklahoma Press,
1939.

MEYER, ROY W. "Character Types in Literature about the American
West." *Opinion,* XIII (December, 1969), 21–29.

MILNE, GORDON. *The American Political Novel.* Norman: University
of Oklahoma Press, 1966.

———. *The Sense of Society: A History of the American Novel of
Manners.* Rutherford, New Jersey: Fairleigh Dickinson University Press, 1977.

MIMS, EDWIN. *History of Southern Fiction.* Vol. VIII of *The South in the Building of the Nation.* Richmond, Virginia: The Southern Historical Publication Society, 1909.

MOSES, MONTROSE J. *Literature of the South.* New York: Crowell, 1910.

MOTT, FRANK LUTHER. *Golden Multitudes.* New York: R. R. Bowker Company, 1947. Most important work for study of the popular novel.

———. *A History of American Magazines.* Cambridge, Mass., Harvard University Press, 1957.

———. *American Journalism.* New York, Macmillan, 1962.

NOBLE, DAVID. *The Eternal Adam and the New World Garden; The Central Myth in the American Novel Since 1830.* New York: George Brazillier, 1968.

NOEL, MARY. *Villains Galore . . . the Heyday of the Popular Story Weekly.* New York: Macmillan, 1954.

ORMOND, JOHN R. "Some Recent Products of the New School of Southern Fiction." *South Atlantic Quarterly,* III (1904), 285–89.

PAPASHVILY, HELEN. *All the Happy Endings.* New York: Harpers, 1956.

PATTEE, FRED L. *A History of American Literature Since 1870.* New York: Century, 1915.

———. *The Feminine Fifties.* New York: Century, 1940. Precedes the period but excellent on the sentimental novel.

PEARSON, EDMUND. *Dime Novels.* New York: Kennikat Press, 1929.

PELHAM, EDGAR. *The Art of the Novel from 1700 to the Present Time.* New York: Macmillan, 1933.

PHILLIPS, JAMES E. "Arcadia on the Range." *Themes and Directions in American Literature; Essays in Honor of Leon Howard,* eds. Ray B. Browne and Donald Pizer. Lafayette: Purdue University Press, 1969.

POLI, BERNARD. *Le Roman Américain, 1865–1917.* Paris: Librarie Colin, 1972.

QUINN, A. H. *American Fiction; an Historical and Critical Survey.* New York: Appleton-Century, 1936. Of all the general histories, considers most minor writers.

RIDEOUT, WALTER BATES. *The Radical Novel in the United States 1900–1954.* Cambridge, Massachusetts: Harvard University Press, 1956.

ROEMER, KENNETH M. *The Obsolete Necessity: America in Utopian Writing.* Kent: Kent State University Press, 1976.

ROSA, JOSEPH G. *The Gunfighter: Man or Myth.* Norman: University of Oklahoma Press, 1969.

RUSK, RALPH LESLIE. *The Literature of the Middle Western Frontier.* 2 vols. New York: Columbia University Press, 1925.

SCHNEIDER, ROBERT W. *Five Novelists of the Progressive Era.* New York: Columbia University Press, 1965. Howells, Crane, Norris, Dreiser, and Winston Churchill.

SHAUL, LAWANA J. "The West in Magazine Fiction, 1870-1900." *Studies in the Literature of the West.* Laramie: University of Wyoming, 1956.

SHURTER, ROBERT L. *The Utopian Novel in America, 1865-1900.* New York: AMS Press, 1973.

SPEARE, MORRIS EDMUND. *The Political Novel; Its Development in England and America.* New York: Oxford University Press, 1924.

SPENGEMANN, WILLIAM C. *The Adventurous Muse: The Poetics of American Fiction, 1789-1900.* New Haven: Yale University Press, 1977. On travel writers.

STECKMESSER, KENT L. *The Western Hero in History and Legend.* Norman: University of Oklahoma Press, 1965.

TAYLOR, WALTER FULLER. *The Economic Novel in America.* Chapel Hill: University of North Carolina Press, 1942.

TINKER, EDWARD L. *The Horsemen of the Americas and the Literature They Inspired.* Austin: University of Texas Press, 1967.

TUTTLETON, JAMES W. *The Novel of Manners in America.* Chapel Hill: University of North Carolina Press, 1972.

UNDERWOOD, JOHN. *Literature and Insurgency.* New York: M. Kennerley, 1914.

VAN DOREN, CARL. *The American Novel, 1789-1939.* New York: Macmillan, 1940.

————. *Contemporary American Novelists, 1900-1920.* New York: Macmillan, 1923.

WAGENKNECHT, EDWARD. *Cavalcade of the American Novel.* New York: Holt, 1952.

WALCUTT, CHARLES CHILD. *American Literary Naturalism, A Divided Stream.* Minneapolis: University of Minnesota Press, 1956.

WALKER, FRANKLIN. *A Literary History of Southern California.* Berkeley: University of California Press, 1950.

WASSERSTROM, WILLIAM. *Heiress of All the Ages; Sex and Sentiment in the Genteel Tradition.* Minneapolis: University of Minnesota Press, 1959.

WHITE, G. EDWARD. *The Eastern Establishment and the Western Experience*. New Haven: Yale University Press, 1968.

WILLSON, LAWRENCE. "The Transcendentalist View of the View." *Western Humanities Review*, XIV (1960), 183–91.

WOODWARD, C. VANN. *Origins of the New South, 1877–1913*. Baton Rouge: State University Press, 1951.

ZIFF, LARZER. *The American 1890's*. New York: Viking Press, 1966.

II. Works on Specific Writers

Andy Adams

BRUNVALD, J. H. "Sailors and Cowboys' Folklore in Two Popular Classics."*Southern Folklore Quarterly*, 29 (1965), 266–83.

DOBIE, FRANK. "Andy Adams, Cowboy Chronicler." *Southwest Review*, 11 (January, 1926), 92–101.

HUDSON, WILSON MATHIS. *Andy Adams, His Life and Writings*. Dallas: Southern Methodist University Press, 1964.

Horatio Alger, Jr.

FALK, ROBERT. "Notes on the 'Higher Criticism' of Horatio Alger Jr." *Arizona Quarterly*, 19 (Summer 1963), 151–67.

FIORE, J. D. "Horatio Alger Jr., as a Lincoln Biographer." *Journal of the Illinois State Historical Society*, 46 (August 1953), 247–53.

FISHWICK, MARSHALL. "The Rise and Fall of Horatio Alger." *Saturday Review*, 39 (November 17, 1956), 15–16, 42–43.

GARDNER, RALPH D. *Horatio Alger, or, The American Hero Era*. Mendota, Illinois: Wayside Press, 1964.

HOLLAND, N. N. "Hobbling with Horatio, or the Uses of Literature." *Hudson Review*, 12 (Winter 1959), 549–57.

HOYT, EDWIN PALMER. *Horatio's Boys: the Life and Works of Horatio Alger Jr*. Radnor, Pa.: Chilton Book Company, 1974.

MAYES, HERBERT RAYMOND. *Alger; A Biography Without a Hero*. New York: Macy-Masius, 1928.

SCHROEDER, FRED. "America's First Literary Realist: Horatio Alger, Junior." *Western Humanities Review*, 17 (Spring 1963), 129–37.

TEBBEL, JOHN. "Horatio Alger, Jr., and the American Dream." *Arts and Science*, 2 (Spring 1963), 17–22.

———. *From Rags to Riches; Horatio Alger and the American Dream*. New York: Macmillan, 1963. See notes to Chapter 1.

Gertrude Atherton

ANONYMOUS. "Gertrude Atherton Writes Her 56th Book." *Life*, 21 (November 11, 1946), 95–98.

CLEMENS, CYRIL. "Gertrude Atherton." *Overland Monthly*, 90 (October 1932), 239–59.

McCLURE, CHARLOTTE S. *Gertrude Atherton*. Boise: Boise State University Press, 1979.

McELDERRY, B. R. "Gertrude Atherton and Henry James." *Colby Library Quarterly*, 3 (November, 1954), 269–72.

STEVENSON, LIONEL. "Atherton versus Grundy: The Forty Years War." *Bookman*, 69 (July, 1929), 464–72.

VAN VECHTEN, CARL. "A Lady Who Defies Time." *Nation*, 126 (February 14, 1923), 194–96.

Irving Bacheller

HANNA, ALFRED JACKSON. *A Bibliography of the Writings of Irving Bacheller*. Winter Park, Fla.: Rollins College, 1939.

Frances Hodgson Burnett

BURNETT, VIVIAN. *The Romantick Lady, the Life Story of an Imagination*. New York: C. Scribner's Sons, 1927.

LASKI, MARGHANITA. *Mrs. Ewing, Mrs. Molesworth, and Mrs. Hodgson Burnett*. London: A. Barker, 1950.

THWAITE, ANN. *Waiting for the Party; the Life of Frances Hodgson Burnett*. London: Secker and Warburg, 1974.

Margaret Deland

FORD, M. K. "Margaret Deland." *Bookman*, 25 (July, 1907), 511–19.

GOULD, M. D. "Of Margaret Deland and *Old Chester*." *Colby Library Quarterly*, Series 2: number 10 (May, 1949), 167–71.

HUMPHRY, JAMES. "The Works of Margaret Deland." *Colby Library Quarterly*, Series 2: number 8 (November 1948), 134–40.

KANTOR, J. R. K. "*The Damnation of Theron Ware* and *John Ward, Preacher*." *Serif*, 3 (March, 1966), 16–21.

Thomas Dixon

BLOOMFIELD, MAXWELL. "Dixon's *The Leopard's Spots*: A Study in Modern Racism." *American Quarterly*, 16 (Fall, 1964), 387–401.

CARTER, EVERETT. "Cultural History Written with Lightning: The Significance of *The Birth of a Nation.*" *American Quarterly,* 12 (Fall 1960), 347–57.

COOK, R. A. "The Literary Principles of Thomas Dixon." *Georgia Review,* 13 (Spring, 1959), 97–102.

———. "The Man Behind *The Birth of a Nation.*" *North Carolina Historical Review,* 39 (October, 1962), 519–40.

———. "The Versatile Career of Thomas Dixon." *Emory University Quarterly,* 11 (June, 1955), 103–12.

OAKES, FRANCES. "Whitman and Dixon: A Strange Case of Borrowing." *Georgia Review,* 11 (Fall, 1957), 333–40.

Mary Hallock Foote

JOHNSON, LEE ANN. *Mary Hallock Foote.* Boston: Twayne Publishers, 1980.

PAUL, RODMAN W., ed. *A Victorian Gentlewoman in the Far West.* San Marino, Ca.: Huntington Library, 1972.

John Fox, Jr.

TITUS, WARREN IRVING. *John Fox, Jr.* New York: Twayne, 1971.

Robert Grant

GRANT, ROBERT. *Fourscore, an Autobiography.* Boston: Houghton and Mifflin Company, 1934.

HAMBLEN, A. A. "Judge Grant and the Forgotten Chippendales." *University of Kansas City Review,* 33 (1967), 175–79.

Henry Harland

O'BRIEN, JUSTIN. "Henry Harland, An American Forerunner of Proust." *Modern Language Notes,* 54 (June, 1939), 420–28.

Julian Hawthorne

DASSAN, MAURICE. *Hawthorne's Son: The Life and Literary Career of Julian Hawthorne.* Columbus: Ohio State University Press, 1970.

HAWTHORNE, JULIAN. *Shapes That Pass.* Boston: Houghton, Mifflin, 1928.

Josiah Gilbert Holland

BLOOM, MARGARET. "Emily Dickinson and Dr. Holland." *University of California Chronicle,* 35 (January, 1933), 96–103.

PLUNKETT, H. M. *Josiah Gilbert Holland.* New York: C. Scribner's Sons, 1894.

Emerson Hough
    GRAHAME, PAULINE. "A Novelist of the Unsung." *Palimpsest,*
        11 (1930), 67–77.
    HUTCHINSON, W. H. "Grassfire on the Great Plains." *Southwest
        Review,* 41 (1956), 181–85.
    WYLDER, D. E. "Emerson Hough's *Heart's Desire:* Revisit to
        Eden." *Western American Literature,* 1 (1966), 44–54.

Bliss Perry
    PERRY, BLISS. *And Gladly Teach.* Boston: Houghton, Mifflin and
        Company, 1935.

E. P. Roe
    MAURICE, A. B. "E. P. Roe's *Barriers Burned Away." Bookman,*
        33 (May, 1911), 247–53.

George Santayana
    ASHMORE, JEROME. *Santayana, Art and Aestheticism.* Cleveland:
        Western Reserve University Press, 1966.
    BALLOWE, J. C. "*The Last Puritan* and the Failure in American
        Culture." *American Quarterly,* 18 (Summer, 1966), 123–25.
    ——. "*The Last Puritan* and Its Philosophical Critics." *Dis-
        course,* 9 (1960), 245–53.
    BEATTY, LILLIAN. "The Natural Man versus the Puritan." *The
        Personalist,* 40 (1959), 22–30.
    CONNER, F. W. "*Lucifer* and *The Last Puritan." American Litera-
        ture,* 33 (March, 1961), 1–19.
    HAZEN, B. F. "*The Last Puritan." Cronos,* 1 (Summer, 1947), 1–5.
    LUBELL, A. J. "George Santayana and the New England Mind."
        South Atlantic Quarterly, 57 (1958), 295–310.
    MARSHALL, W. H. "An Expanding Theme in *The Last Puritan."
        The Personalist,* 45 (January, 1964), 27–40.
    PAPAJEWSKI, HELMUT. "Santayana's *The Last Puritan* und seine
        Kulturkritik des Amerikanismus." *Germanisch-Romanische
        Monatschrift,* 30 (January, 1942), 21–39.

Francis Hopkinson Smith
    HORNBERGER, THEODORE. "The Effect of Painting in the Fiction
        of Francis Hopkinson Smith." *University of Texas Studies
        in English,* 23 (1943), 162–92.
    ——. "Painters and Painting in the Writing of Francis Hopkin-
        son Smith." *American Literature,* 16 (March, 1944), 1–10.

H. O. Sturgis

JAMIESON, JOHN. "An Edwardian Satirist." *Chimera*, 4 (1946), 49–54.

Frank Stockton

CHISLETT, WILLIAM. *Moderns and Near-Moderns*. Freeport, NY: Books for Libraries Press, 1967.

FOX, R. C. "Before the Nautilus." *American Neptune*, 20 (July, 1960), 174–76.

GRIFFIN, MARTIN I. J. *Frank R. Stockton: A Critical Biography*. Philadelphia: University of Pennsylvania Press, 1939.

PFORZHEIMER, W. L. "The Lady, the Tiger, and the Author." *Colophon*, 1 (August, 1935), 261–70.

WERNER, W. "The Escapes of Frank Stockton." *Essays in Honor of A. Howry Espenshade*, (1937), 21–45.

Maurice Thompson

WHEELER, OTIS B. *The Literary Career of Maurice Thompson*. Baton Rouge: Louisiana State University Press, 1965.

John Townsend Trowbridge

COLEMAN, R. A. "Trowbridge and Clemens." *Modern Language Quarterly*, 9 (June, 1948), 216–23.

———. "Trowbridge and Shillaber." *New England Quarterly*, 20 (June, 1947), 232–44.

———. "Trowbridge and Whitman." *PMLA*, 63 (March, 1948), 262–73.

TROWBRIDGE, J. T. *My Own Story*. Boston: Houghton, Mifflin and Company, 1903.

Charles Dudley Warner

CAMERON, K. W. "Literary Manuscripts in the Trinity College Library." *Emerson Society Quarterly*, 14 (1959).

VAN WHY, J. S. "Nook Farm." *Stowe, Beecher, Hooker, Seymour, Day Foundation Bulletin*, 1 (1962), 1–34.

Susan Warner

FOSTER, EDWARD HALSEY. *Susan and Anna Warner*. Boston: Twayne, 1978.

LOCHHEAD, MARION. "Stars and Striplings: American Youth in the Nineteenth Century." *Quarterly Review*, 297 (April, 1959), 180–88.

OVERMYER, GRACE. "Hudson River Bluestockings—The Warner Sisters of Constitution Island." *New York History*, 40 (April, 1959), 137–58.

Index

Abbott, Lyman, 14
Adams, Andy, 93–94
Adams, Henry, 38, 45, 49, 96, 97
Addison, Joseph, 51
Alcott, Louisa May, 47
Alger, Horatio, Jr., 1–6, 13, 14, 17; *Ragged Dick* (1868), 2–6
Arendt, Hannah, 55
Atherton, Gertrude, 149–56; *Black Oxen* (1923), 152–55; *The Doomswoman* (1901), 149–52
Austen, Jane, 26
Austin, Jane G., 49

Bacheller, Irving, 28
Baker, William Mumford, 56
Balzac, Honore de, 1
Barth, John, 82
Bates, Arlo, 30–37, 41, 45, 70; *The Pagans* (1884), 31–37
Baudelaire, Charles, 67
Beard, R. O., 102
Bellamy, Edward, 86, 87
Bellamy, Elizabeth Whitfield Croom, 61, 74
Berger, Thomas, 95
Bigot, Mary Healy, 75
Bishop, William Henry, 73–74
Blackwell, Antoinette, 49
Bonner, Sherwood, 57
Borges, Jorge Luis, 82
Bowles, Samuel, 6
Bright, Matilda, 49
Brown, Herbert Ross; *The Sentimental Novel in America, 1789-1860*, (1940) 20
Brown, William Perry, 62
Brush, Christine, 61
Burnett, Frances Hodgson, 97–103, 105; *Through One Administration* (1881), 98–103, 106, 115, 117

Burns, Robert, 55
Bynner, Edwin Lasseter, 71–72

Cabell, James Branch, 153
Cable, George Washington, 52, 56
Campbell, William, 157
Carrington, Kate, 49
Carter, James, 69
Cary, Joyce, 133
Cather, Willa, 90
Chamberlain, Nathan H., 48
Chavannes, Albert, 82, 86
Chesebro, Caroline, 49
Child, Lydia Maria, 61
Churchill, Winston, 155
Clark, Walter Van Tilburg, 94
Cleveland, Grover, 103, 105
Cooper, James Fennimore, 8, 73
Crane, Stephen, 28, 36, 44
Crawford, F. Marion, 27
Curtis, Caroline, 6, 49

Dauge, Henri, 47
DeForest, John, 9, 15, 56
Deland, Margaret, 149, 156–62; *John Ward, Preacher* (1888), 156–58; *The Awakening of Helena Richie* (1906), 159–60
Devereux, G. H., 48
Dickens, Charles, 1, 7
Dixon, Thomas, Jr., 52, 53, 54–55, 61, 97
Donnelly, Ignatius, 84, 87
Dos Passos, John, 68
Douglas, Amanda Minnie, 62
Douglas, Lloyd, 155
Douglas, Norman, 74
Doyle, Arthur Conan, 142
Dreiser, Theodore, 42
Durkheim, Emile, 33

Ehrlichmann, John, 97
Eliot, George, 1
Eliot, T.S., 139
Emerson, Ralph Waldo, 1, 12, 32, 33, 34, 51
Evans, Augusta, 54

Fadette, 59
Falkner, William, 54
Faulkner, William, 52, 53, 54, 94
Fawcett, Edgar, 28
Fiedler, Leslie, 22
Fisk, James Jr., 12
Fitzgerald, F. Scott, 81
Flaubert, Gustave, 1, 25, 38, 121
Flemming, Harford, 74
Fletcher, Julia Constance, 27
Foote, Mary Hallock, 90-91, 55
Ford, Paul Leicester, *The Honorable Peter Stirling* (1894), 103-106, 107, 108, 111, 112, 113, 114, 115, 117
Fox, John, Jr., 57-58
Freeman, Mary E. Wilkins, 9, 26, 48, 49, 50
Freud, Sigmund, 155
Friedman, I.K., 113-18; *The Radical* (1907), 113-18

Garland, Hamlin, 15
George, Henry, 60
Gilder, Richard Watson, 53, 103
Glasgow, Ellen, 62
Goethe, Johan Wolfgang von, 32
Gold, Herbert, 143
Goncourt, Edmond and Jules, 121
Grant, Robert, 30, 37-42, 45, 70, 71, 120; *Unleavened Bread* (1500), 38-42, 97; *The Chippendales* (1905), 41-42
Green, Anna Katherine, 141-43, 155; *The Leavenworth Case* (1878), 141-43
Green, Martin, *The Problem with Boston* (1966), 30
Grey, Zane, 94

Haggard, H. Rider, 88
Halévy, Ludovic, 121
Hammett, Dashiel, 142
Hammond, Henrietta, H., 47

Hardy, Arthur Sherburne, 120-27, 146; *But Yet a Woman* (1883), 121-25
Hardy, Thomas, 1
Harland, Henry, 143-47; *As It Was Written* (1885), 143-44; *The Yoke of the Thorah* (1887), 144-46
Harrison, Constance Cary, 72
Hawthorne, Julian, 14, 47
Hawthorne, Nathaniel, 9, 19, 30, 36, 44, 49, 64, 67, 78, 160
Hay, John, 38
Hoffer, Eric, 53
Hogg, James, 55
Holford, Costello N., 86, 87
Holland, Josiah Gilbert, 1-2, 6-13, 14, 27, 26; *Sevenoaks* (1875), 7-13, 17, 100
Holt, John Saunders, 53-54
Hough, Emerson, 91-93, 94; *The Story of the Cowboy* (1897), 91-93
. Howells, William Dean, 9, 11, 13, 15, 17, 18, 19, 26, 28, 36, 38, 40, 42, 64, 65, 70, 73, 74, 78, 87, 119, 120

Irving, Washington, 91

James, Henry, 1, 18, 19, 24, 29, 31, 42, 43, 44, 49, 53, 64, 70, 76, 78, 96, 97, 101, 116, 120, 127, 128, 132, 133, 136, 137, 138
James, William, 45
Janvier, Thomas A., 87-90; *The Aztec Treasure House*, 88-90
Jewett, Sarah Orne, 26, 49
Johnson, Robert Underwood, 51
Judd, Sylvester, 47, 48

King, Edward, 75
King, Grace, 57
Kirk, Ellen Warner, 26
Knox, Adeline Trafton, 49

Lawrence, D.H., 25
Lewis, Alfred Henry, 106-13; *The Boss* (1903), 106-13, 114, 118
Lewis, C.S., 92
Long, John Luther, 147
Loring, A.K., 2
Lowell, A. Lawrence, 37

Lowell, James Russell, 51
Luska, Sidney, 143-46

Macauley, Thomas B., 51
McClellan, Harriet, 75
McClelland, Mary Greenway, 57
McDowell, Catherine Sherwood Bonner, 57
Magruder, Julia, 58-61
Marlowe, Christopher, 107
Marquand, John P., 42
Marvel, Ik, 47
Matthiessen, F.O., 19
Maugham, W. Somerset, 25
Mayo, William Starbuck, 71
Melville, Herman, 44, 55, 78, 93-94
Mencken, H.L., 119
Mitchell, Donald G., 47
Mitchell, John Ames, 82-86; *The Last American* (1889), 83; *The Silent War* (1906), 84-86
Mitchell, Margaret, 52, 56
Murfree, Mary N., 57
Murieta, Joaquin, 95

Nabokov, Vladimir, 82, 104
Norris, Frank, 28, 84

O'Connor, Charles, 3
Olerich, Henry, 86, 87

Page, Thomas Nelson, 52, 57, 58
Park, Charles C., 95
Peale, Norman Vincent, 6
Pendleton, Edmund, 56-57
Perry, Bliss, 48
Philips, Daniel Graham, 74
Plunkett, Mrs. H.; *Josiah Gilbert Holland* (1894), 13
Pocock, Roger, 95
Poe, Edgar Allan, 21
Poole, Ernest, 74
Porter, Elmer H., 50
Porter, William Sidney, 71

Rae, W. Fraser, 75-76
Reeves, Marion C. Legaré, 59
Reid, Christian, 54

Reinhart, G.S., 66
Rideing, W.H., 75
Rhodes, Eugene Manlove, 91, 94
Roe, Edward P., 21, 13-17, 126; *Barriers Barred Away* (1872), 13-17; *The Earth Trembled* (1887), 16-17
Roth, Philip, 143, 146
Royce, Josiah, 45

Sacco, Nicola, 37
Saltus, Edgar, 149
Santayana, George, 30, 43, 45-47; *The Last Puritan* (1935), 45-47
Sartre, Jean-Paul, 6
Schindler, Solomon, 86
Scott, Walter, 51-52, 55
Scudder, Moses L., 76
Sedgwick, Anne Douglas, 120, 127-40, 155; *Tante* (1911), 128-36, 139, 140; *Adrienne Toner* (1922), 136-40
Senarens, Luis, P., 86-87
Sherwood, Mary E. Wilson, 73
Simenon, Georges, 120
Smith, Francis Hopkinson, 58
Southworth, Mrs. E.D.E.N., 19-24, 25, 26, 27, 28, 29, 47, 49, 142, 150
Spearman, Frank H., 94
Steinach, Eugen, 153, 154, 155
Stockton, Frank R., 78-82, 86, 120; *The Casting Away of Mrs. Lecks and Mrs. Aleshine* (1886), 79-80, 81; *The Hundredth Man* (1887), 80-81
Story, James P., 147-48
Stowe, Harriet Beecher, 2, 54
Stratton, Samuel W., 37
Sturgis, Howard O., 30, 42-45, 120; *Belchamber* (1904), 43-45

Tennyson, Alfred, 4
Terhune, Mrs. Albert Payson, 27
Thacker, William, 1, 51, 99
Thomas, Chauncey, 87
Thompson, James Maurice, 61
Thoreau, Henry David, 1, 53
Thornton, M. Jacqueline, 61
Thorpe, Kamba, 61, 74
Tierney, Francis C., 54
Tolkien, J.R.R., 82

Tolstoi, Leo, 1
Tourgee, Albion W., 56
Trollope, Frances, 102
Trotter, Ada M., 76
Troubetzkoy, Amelie Rives, 149
Trowbridge, John Townsend, 27
Turgenev, Ivan, 1
Twain, Mark, 1, 3, 17, 19, 28, 65, 87, 95, 96, 97, 114

Van Doren, Carl; *The American Novel* (1940), 13
Vanzetti, Bartolomeo, 37
Vonnegut, Kurt, Jr., 87

Ward, Mrs. Humphrey, 157
Warner, Charles Dudley, 65-70, 96; *A*

Little Journey Into the World (1889), 66-70, 171
Warner, Susan, 24-25
Warren, Robert Penn, 62
Watergate, 40, 97-98
Weed, Ella, 75
West, Nathanael, 149
White, Stewart Edward, 94-95
White, T.H., 82
Whitman, Walt, 13, 27
Whitney, Mrs. A.D.T., 25-26
Wilde, Oscar, 33
Winchester, Carrol, 49
Wister, Owen, 91
Wolfe, Thomas, 52
Wolfert, Ira, 84

Yardley, Jane Woolsey, 26
Yeats, William Butler, 152